Further Techniques for Coaching and Mentoring

Further Techniques for Coaching and Mentoring

David Megginson and
David Clutterbuck

ELSEVIER

AMSTERDAM • BOSTON • HEIDELBERG • LONDON • NEW YORK • OXFORD
PARIS • SAN DIEGO • SAN FRANCISCO • SINGAPORE • SYDNEY • TOKYO
Butterworth-Heinemann is an imprint of Elsevier

Butterworth-Heinemann is an imprint of Elsevier
Linacre House, Jordan Hill, Oxford OX2 8DP, UK
30 Corporate Drive, Suite 400, Burlington, MA 01803, UK

First edition 2009

British Library Cataloguing in Publication Data
A catalogue record for this book is available from the British Library

Library of Congress Cataloguing in Publication Data
A catalogue record for this book is available from the Library of Congress

ISBN: 978-1-85617-499-2

For information on all Butterworth-Heinemann publications
visit our web site at books.elsevier.com

Composition by Macmillan Publishing Solutions
www.macmillansolutions.com

Printed and bound in Great Britain
09 10 11 12 13   10 9 8 7 6 5 4 3 2 1

Contents

Contributors

David Clutterbuck is visiting professor in coaching and mentoring at Sheffield Hallam University and Oxford Brookes Business School. A co-founder of the European Mentoring and Coaching Council, he is senior partner of Clutterbuck Associates, the world's leading provider of mentoring programme support. He has been listed as number two in the *Sunday Independent*'s top 10 UK coaches and at number 14 in *HR Magazine*'s 2008 survey of the most influential thinkers in HR.

Dr. Daniel Doherty returned to academic life at the University of Bristol Department of Management in 2004, after thirty or more years practising as a strategy and organization consultant, and as an executive coach. In addition to lecturing and researching into management learning and strategic change, he is director of the University of Bristol Critical Coaching Research Unit. Throughout his career he has had a passion for the use of writing – and of reflective practice – for the personal development of managers, and for the development of teams and of organizations. This interest in writing as inquiry has expressed itself most recently in innovative research focusing on the use of researcher as subject, and of writing the self into manager narratives, including the creation of coaching narratives.

Marion Gillie has a background in organization development and now works internationally as a coach and consultant. She is a Chartered Occupational Psychologist and Gestalt Psychotherapist, and is Programme Director of the Postgraduate Diploma in Advanced Executive Coaching and the Master Practitioner Programme at the Academy of Executive Coaching in the UK. She is also a coach supervisor for programmes at Oxford Brookes University Business School and is a 'Next Generation' Faculty member of the Gestalt International Study Centre in Cape Cod, Massachusetts.

John Groom was born in Nottingham. He now lives and works in Auckland, New Zealand as a psychologist/coach and director of Groom and Associates. He can be contacted via www.johngroom. co.nz

Gladeana McMahon is a leading personal development and transformational coach. She was instrumental in founding the Association for Coaching for which she now holds the positions of Fellow and Vice President. She is also a Fellow of the BACP, The Institute of

Management Studies and The Royal Society of Arts. Gladeana is widely published with some 16 popular and academic books on coaching and counselling. An innovator, Gladeana is one of the UK founders of Cognitive Behavioural Coaching and currently works as the Director, Professional Coaching Standards for Cedar Talent Management and Co-Director of the Centre for Coaching.

David Megginson is Professor of Human Resource Development at Sheffield Hallam University. He is co-Chair of the European Mentoring and Coaching Council, and Chairman of The idm Group, a strategic change consultancy.

Megan Reitz is a Client and Programme Director at Ashridge Business School, teaching and consulting in the areas of coaching, team effectiveness, leadership, personal development and leading change with clients spanning the public, private and voluntary sectors. She runs the Future Leaders Experience, an open programme aimed at high potentials and also teaches on the Ashridge MBA. Her research interests include 'empathic resonance', analysing the way in which a deep relationship can be formed between a coach and client, and the development of 'future leaders' through understanding the critical incidents that experienced leaders learn from throughout their careers. Megan is a graduate of Cambridge University and the University of Surrey, a practitioner in neuro-linguistic programming, and a certified executive coach with Ashridge and the School of Coaching.

Alan Sieler is the Director of Newfield Institute, an international executive coaching, consulting and coach-training company. Alan has been an executive coach for more than fourteen years and leads the Vocational Graduate Diploma of Ontological Coaching, which is the Asia-Pacific region's most substantive and in-depth coach training programme. Alan works throughout Australia and in Asia, and coaching diploma graduates work with him as a team of executive coaches in organizations. Alan has published Volumes I and II of *Coaching to the Human Soul: Ontological Coaching and Deep Change*, which is being used in coach-training, leadership and organizational behaviour courses in universities in the United States, South Africa and Australia, as well as in other coach-training programmes.

Vivien Whitaker assists people to access their creativity, resolve issues and achieve their potential. She has developed an original model for *Managing People* (Harper Collins: 1994) and has co-written the CIPD core text on *Continuing Professional Development* (with David Megginson: 2nd edition, 2007).

She has a masters degree in organization development, and over 20 years' consultancy experience of resolving individual and organizational issues. She specializes in facilitating creative mentoring relationships and creative team development. She is a Visiting Fellow in the Coaching & Mentoring Research Unit at Sheffield Hallam University.

As a fine art sculptor, Vivien exhibits nationally. She has a first class degree in fine art and is an elected Associate of the Royal Society of British Sculptors. She is currently undertaking doctoral research at Loughborough University. www.vivienwhitaker.co.uk

Preface

In the foreword to *Techniques for Coaching and Mentoring*, the companion volume to this book, we positioned ourselves as standing resolutely against adopting a particular school of coaching or mentoring as our way of working. We argued for the pragmatic benefit of being able to use the best out of a range of models and frameworks. We felt that the competitiveness, the esoteric special languages, and the demand that the coach takes centre stage in running the process, all stand against the emancipatory power of seeing coach/mentoring as a normal conversation. We still do.

However, times move on, and, in the intervening years since the companion volume was published in 2005 (Megginson and Clutterbuck, 2005), the field of coaching and mentoring has developed and matured. So, many of the frameworks or approaches that seemed to be at the fringe then are now more widely accepted and expected from practitioners. We have responded to the change by having a different structure to this book from its predecessor in two respects. First, we have eight chapters about different frameworks (this is the term we use for models, approaches or traditions) that seem to us to add something for all coaches and mentors to enrich their practice. Three of the chapters are embedded in a philosophical or psychological framework – Gladeana McMahon's cognitive behavioural coaching, Marion Gillie's Gestalt approach and Alan Sieler's ontological coaching. Each of these authors has succeeded in conveying the principles of their framework and also in offering to the newcomer to the framework practical things that they can do to enrich their own practice without having to go on a two year course first. The other framework chapters seek to offer a lens through which the practice of coaching and mentoring can be viewed. Megan Reitz describes her research into intuition, Dan Doherty encourages us to use writing as an important means of learning in coaching, John Groom meditates on mindfulness in our mentoring practice and Vivien Whitaker emphasizes the exciting value of creativity techniques. All these are not so much schools of coach/mentoring as perspectives on our practice. The final framework chapter is David Clutterbuck's on team coaching, which seeks to separate out what is unique in the practice of working with groups rather than individuals in coaching and mentoring.

The second structural innovation in this book is that the techniques that we as authors have contributed have been organized into three broad chapters, depending upon their focus. The first and longest chapter offers techniques for the client. These resemble the techniques in the companion volume. Then we have techniques that focus on the coach/mentor and finally we review some techniques for working on the process of the relationship between coach/mentor and client.

We hope that the structure of this book and the content we have included will minimize the repetition between the two volumes and will justify seeing this book as a second volume with new materials and a new way of looking at the practice of coaching/mentoring quite different from our earlier volume.

David Megginson
David Clutterbuck
Sheffield Hallam University
November 2008

Reference

Megginson, D. and Clutterbuck, D. (2005). *Techniques for Coaching and Mentoring*. Oxford: Butterworth-Heinemann.

Acknowledgements

Our particular gratitude is expressed to the authors of our seven contributed chapters. Gladeana McMahon, Marion Gillie, Daniel Doherty, Megan Reitz, Alan Sieler, John Groom and Vivien Whitaker were everything that authors could dream of from contributors. They kept in touch, responded to feedback, delivered according to specification, maintained agreed time boundaries and were patient when we broke through ours. They also took an interest in the whole project of the book and are truly partners in the enterprise rather than hired hands.

We are also grateful to Bob Garvey for his case study of the 'Three stage process' which is included in Chapter 12, and to Susan Abson for providing client case studies.

We would like to acknowledge with thanks all the clients, students, supervisees and colleagues who have contributed ideas, stimuli and challenges that have helped us to forge a better book than would otherwise have been the case.

As ever, and the impact of this gratitude must be wearing thin nowadays, we are grateful to our wives for their forbearance while this book has been in gestation. 'Are you going to take a break after this one?' has been a frequently heard question in one household at least, and the answer is, 'Good idea, but then, there is the book on goals, and the long considered volume on supervision/reflective practice, and what about that idea for a history of mentoring and coaching based on our autobiographies'. So the answer is, 'Just a short break, perhaps'.

Part 1

Contextualizing techniques

What are the arguments for and against the use of techniques? How do frameworks for coaching or mentoring serve to organize and focus these techniques? How does this book address the relationship between technique and framework? The introductory chapter that forms the first part of this book answers these questions and orients the reader to what follows.

Chapter 1

Introduction

David Clutterbuck and David Megginson

Approaches to techniques

When we wrote the companion volume, *Techniques for Coaching and Mentoring*, we struggled to find resources beyond those which we had created or used in our own practice and experimentation. It seemed that most coaches were reliant on a very narrow range of models and techniques. Most commonly, coaches based their practice on the GROW model – an approach both of the authors have found in our separate researches to become inadequate as coaches/mentors acquired experience. Among the dangers of this 'one model' approach was that coaching becomes mechanistic, critical clues to the client context are missed or ignored, and, whatever may be claimed to the contrary, the client can easily become manipulated to fit the coach's agenda. This is especially true with regard to goal setting, where we find that fixing upon specific goals at the start of a relationship is primarily for the benefit of the coach or the sponsor, rather than that of the coachee.

Some coaches had progressed beyond a simplistic model to a process, which, in theory at least, allows for greater flexibility. For example, solutions focused coaching and clean language both add some level of theoretical rigour and expect the coach to exercise creativity in the order and structure of their approach. In practice, however, it can be very easy to fall back into mechanistic routines. A recent demonstration of 'good practice' in solutions focus observed by one of the authors at a conference was so robotic that the session could have been conducted by a machine. (In fact, a machine would have introduced fewer body-language distractions!)

Other coaches again were developing their practice within a particular discipline or theoretical framework – for example, cognitive-behavioural therapy, Gestalt or NLP – which offered a range of techniques within a broad philosophy of helping and human development. The aficionados of these philosophies or disciplines are often highly enthusiastic, but this enthusiasm may at times hide a dangerous man-trap – the implicit assumption that this philosophy, powerful as it may be, is always the best approach for every client.

Let us emphasize here that we are not decrying any of these approaches. All are valid ways of approaching coaching and mentoring assignments and all have – in appropriate circumstances – a track record of assisting people with major changes in their life, work and context. Our concern is that all can (and in observed cases of less effective practitioners, demonstrably do) lead to a rigidity of thinking about the client and their issues; and about the role and responsibilities of the coach or mentor. The toolkit (model, process, or theoretical framework) drives the learning conversation, rather than the learning conversation driving the selection of tools and techniques.

In the recent past, we have seen an encouraging growth of innovation in models, frameworks and processes. We have also observed the rise in highly confident and competent coaches of a fourth approach, which we call managed eclecticism. By this, we mean an intelligent, sensitive ability to select a broad approach, and within that approach, appropriate tools and techniques, which meet the particular needs of a particular client at a particular time. Central to this concept is that:

- The initial learning conversations provide the clues as to what approaches and frameworks may be best suited to the client;
- Every learning conversation is an experiment for both the coach/ mentor and the client.

A cogent argument can be made that this scale from models to managed eclecticism is a measure of the relative maturity of a coach or mentor – of how they think and behave – similarly, for example, Kegan's (1992) scale of cognitive and socio-emotional development or Torbert's (Rooke and Torbert, 2005) scale of leadership development. This is perhaps a step too far, if only because we have no direct evidence other than from unstructured observation and the nodding of wise heads at gatherings of experienced coaches (and coaching and mentoring are already riddled with far too many unevidenced assumptions!)

It's important as well, we suggest, not to confuse managed eclecticism with the random gleanings of coaches, who collect techniques and processes in the way a jackdaw collects shiny objects. Decoupled from the philosophies from which they derive, techniques may become meaningless, or worse, harmful. In a presentation to the 2007 European Mentoring and Coaching Council (EMCC) conference in Stockholm, Helena Dolny of South Africa's Standard Bank referred to a subset of coaches, who went through the company's assessment centres. These people had a lot of techniques, which they had failed to integrate or fully understand. Such coaches have also been likened to a handyman, who clouts nails with a screwdriver and fixes screws with a hammer. No consistency of process may be worse than over-rigid models and processes. The true eclectics we have encountered share a number of characteristics:

- They do not share a common philosophy; rather, they have developed their own philosophy – one which continually expands and adapts, evolving as they absorb new knowledge and ideas.
- They place great importance on understanding a technique, model or process in terms of its foundations within an original philosophy.
- They use experimentation and reflexive learning to identify where and how a new technique, model or process fits into their philosophy and framework of helping.
- They judge new techniques, models and processes on the criterion of 'Will this enrich and improve the effectiveness of my potential responses to client needs?'
- They use peers and supervisors to challenge their coaching philosophy and as partners in experimenting with new approaches.

If there is a ladder of coaching maturity along the lines suggested here (see Figure 1.1), then it is highly likely that coaches and mentors need to journey through each stage, before they are able to understand and encompass the next. Does this mean, then, that the inexperienced coach should stick to a very narrow range of tools and techniques? Our

Coaching approach	Style	Critical questions
Models-based	Control	How do I take them where I think they need to go? How do I adapt my technique or model to this circumstance?
Process-based	Contain	How do I give enough control to the client and still retain a purposeful conversation? What's the best way to apply my process in this instance?
Philosophy-based	Facilitate	What can I do to help the client do this for themselves? How do I contextualize the client's issue within the perspective of my philosophy or discipline?
Managed eclectic	Enable	Are we both relaxed enough to allow the issue and the solution to emerge in whatever way they will? Do I need to apply any techniques or processes at all? If I do, what does the client context tell me about how to select from the wide choice available to me?

Figure 1.1 A comparison of the four levels of coaching maturity in coaching conversations.

experience and observation suggests that, while trying to jump straight to the eclectic stage is unlikely to be beneficial, acquiring new techniques in response to specific experiences with clients is an important part of the maturation process. If the habits of purposeful technique acquisition and integration can be learned early on in the coaching journey, then the transition to full-fledged managed eclecticism ought to be faster and smoother.

A kaleidoscope of perspectives

In supporting coaches and mentors in becoming mature eclectics, we have structured this book into parts which we describe briefly below.

Part 1: Contextualizing techniques

Chapter 1. Introduction

In our introduction, which is this chapter, we outline our developing argument for how coach/mentors can approach techniques.

Part 2: Perspectives on techniques

Here, we give a chapter each to different frameworks from particular psychological or philosophical stances and others from a generative lens or perspective. Our criterion for inclusion of chapters here has been that the authors can present material in such a way that it displays the underlying principles of their framework and at the same time offers specific help in the practice of coaching/mentoring for those aspiring to the managed eclectic stance in Figure 1.1. Each of these frameworks is introduced below.

Chapter 2: Cognitive behavioural coaching

Gladeana McMahon, Vice-President of the Association for Coaching, has contributed a chapter on cognitive behavioural coaching (CBC). Like the chapters on Gestalt coaching and ontological coaching which follow, the framework is based on established psychological theory. CBC, however, differs from these other approaches by not being psychodynamic. Instead it is grounded in the study of rational thinking and of behaviour. For this reason, it may be seen as accessible to readers who do not have a psychodynamic background. Having said that, it is worth pointing out that each of the authors of the psychodynamic chapters has cast their contribution in a form that makes it useful for non-psychologist coaches who are open to working in a 'psychological way' (Lee, 2003).

This chapter is full of clear, structured and usable techniques, and it has some case studies of the technique in practice, which will allow readers to see or feel how they might apply the approach. The chapter begins with some preliminary techniques for orienting to the cognitive model used, including the thought record form and how to deal with cognitive distortions. There is then a section on techniques including cost/benefit analysis, contingency planning, allocating responsibility and dealing with negative emotions. The chapter concludes with a comprehensive and illuminating case study.

Mentors and coaches wanting to use this approach will need to understand the underlying principles of the framework that was developed in a counselling context. This framework is spelled out in outline in the chapter. There is quite a heavy emphasis on righting distortions and dealing with negatives. For those practitioners who like to emphasize the positive and the possible, this orientation may not be to their taste, but we found in studying this chapter that it addresses many of the career and life issues our clients face, and provides a means of going forward in a positive way.

Chapter 3: Gestalt coaching

Marion Gillie differentiates Gestalt coaching from its progenitor of Gestalt psychotherapy, which itself was developed by Fritz Perls from Gestalt psychology. Gestalt therapy approaches have been widely used in individual and organization development, going right back to Hermann and Korenich in 1977. Marion Gillie differentiates Gestalt coaching from Gestalt therapy or counselling by focusing on current material rather than earlier relationships with parents and other authority figures.

The core of this chapter, and indeed of Perls' (1971) own approach to intervention, as we said in the companion volume to this book, is that Gestalt practitioners value spontaneity and aim to create unique responses to each situation. Marion captures the emergent nature of this approach by developing the chapter with a long, continuous case study that is woven through the accounts of approaches and principles. There is also enough formal exposition of these principles for newcomers to the approach to connect with its underlying rationale. Lee (2003) provides a useful plain coach's guide to the relevance of transference and countertransference, two concepts mentioned but not discussed in the text.

Chapter 4: Ontological coaching

Alan Sieler's chapter offering his own brand of ontological coaching is an interesting synthesis of a number of other approaches, with a strong and helpful focus on purpose – on challenging the coachee/mentee to consider what they are here for. In contrast to Marion Gillie's account of Gestalt coaching, ontological coaching includes going back to address parental material. This may be inevitable – as getting to a core purpose must involve going back to old scripts and re-evaluating them.

This chapter too has some case studies which illuminate the processes described.

Chapter 5: Intuitive coaching

Intuitive coaching is not so much a brand or a discipline underlying coaching and mentoring. Rather, it represents a way of being a helper that can contribute, whatever types of mentoring or coaching you are using. Megan Reitz manages the difficult tightrope walk of giving a clear-sighted account of intuition in coaching, including summaries of key scientific studies of the topic, with a passionate case for enhancing the faculty of intuition in order to develop depth and focus in the one-to-one encounter.

This chapter is less technique oriented than most of the others in this book. This is entirely appropriate as intuition largely rests beyond the boundaries wherein technique operates. What Megan Reitz does instead is to help coaches think about the techniques that they can practice on themselves so that when they come into contact with their client, they have optimized the possibility of coming up with an intuitive response to what the client says. As such, it chimes in with Chapter 11, our coach/mentor focused techniques. Necessary warnings are offered against confusing intuition with giving gratuitous and unconsidered advice based on patterns in the helper that have sunk below the horizon of their awareness.

Chapter 6: Writing as inquiry

Insights from this chapter, like those from the chapter on intuition, can be used with any approach to coaching or mentoring. Daniel Doherty, from the Critical Coaching Group at Bristol University, reports his research and teaching of a process of writing your story. He makes a case for this being useful to both coaches and clients. Many of the examples cited are from work in progress in examining coaching through writing, and this chapter has a sense of excitement about a process being uncovered and a raw, unfinished feel as well. Much of the material he describes has this same feel, and so the account is congruent with the approach he advocates.

Coaches and mentors constantly rail against the unreflective lives of our clients; often attributing this incapacity to the unbearable pressure they put themselves and others under (Casserley and Megginson, 2008). Dan Doherty offers one means of addressing the lack of reflective ability, and this is a useful and important contribution to any book on techniques and indeed to the whole field of coaching and mentoring.

Chapter 7: Mindful mentoring

John Groom is a psychologist, using that professional training as a launching pad for developing his practice as a mentor and coach. He made a powerful impact at the Global Convention on Coaching in Dublin in 2008, with his process sensitivity and his acute awareness of what was going on in the room. And this is the essence of his mindfulness approach. Again his techniques are embedded in his practice. So, you will not find in this chapter techniques for fixing this or addressing that. What you get – and it is an important gift – is an orientation that will enable us, as mindful mentors, to connect at a deep and generative level with our clients. He then explores mindful listening in the context of his coaching practice, encouraging us to get out of our clients' way in their exploration of their issues in their own terms.

He offers some guidance to mentors and coaches in caring for ourselves so that we can deliver the mindfulness that makes a difference, which represents another link to Chapter 11.

Chapter 8: Creativity coaching

Vivien Whitaker is a sculptor as well as a coach and mentor. She makes a case for the power and effectiveness of creativity approaches to coaching and mentoring. It is not solely that they will appeal more to some people than just talking: creative techniques are also time effective. She argues that they help clients to move forward on issues where they have been blocked and where talking has not been powerful enough to release the energy needed to resolve the issue.

This chapter offers a wide range of techniques for those with visual, auditory and kinaesthetic preferences. There are case examples of their use in practice. These techniques can be used within the various traditions outlined by our other contributors.

Chapter 9: Team coaching

This chapter continues the debate between the two authors of this volume as to whether team coaching exists as a separate discipline or whether it is an attempt by those with a vested interest in coaching to extend their reach into areas occupied by others. The chapter makes a considered case for their being a separate discipline called team coaching with practices that are distinct from both one-to-one coaching and facilitation. It is written by David Clutterbuck, who is the true believer in this debate. David Megginson, as the sceptic, is happy to leave it to the reader to decide whether what is described here and in David Clutterbuck's 2007 book *Coaching the Team at Work*, is substantially different from processes of organization development and team building, which have been developed over the years since the late 1960s.

Part 3: Techniques for coach, client and process

This part of the book introduces a range of techniques that we have garnered or generated from our own practice as coach/mentors and from developing the practice of our associates and colleagues. They also come in some instances from our work as developers of coaches and mentors within organizations and from our teaching of the Sheffield Business School MSc in Coaching and Mentoring in Sheffield and in Switzerland. We are grateful to our participants on these programmes who have shared the journey of honing some of these techniques.

Chapter 10: Client focused techniques

These techniques are clustered in the following categories, which proved the most useful in the companion volume to this book:

- goals – goal-setting, goal pursuit and goal achievement
- decision making
- understanding the environment
- understanding self
- exploring beliefs and values
- managing emotions
- and finally, 100 additions to our collection of Massively Difficult Questions.

Chapter 11: Coach focused techniques

This chapter picks up on the attention paid in Chapter 5 by Megan Reitz on intuitive coaching and Chapter 7, John Groom's piece on mindfulness mentoring. It pays attention to the work that coach/mentors have to do on ourselves to make sure that we are clear and ready, and that we are doing appropriate work for our clients. This chapter considers our motivation and mindset, how we achieve equilibrium, and it addresses the value of curiosity as an orientation for coach/mentors. The second half of the chapter considers some underlying questions that coaches and mentors can bring to supervision. We outline the seven conversations that go on before, during and after a coaching/mentoring conversation, we look at how systems' thinking can help us get a perspective on our work, and what to do when we seem to be faced with an insoluble issue. We ask coaches and mentors to consider who they can or should work with, and we conclude with 25 questions to prepare you for a supervision session.

Chapter 12: Process focused techniques

Here we start by exploring the phases of the coaching/mentoring relationship and then we go on to look at how to move relationships successfully through these phases. We start with a general set of questions for reviewing relationships, and then explore ways of preparing the coachee to be coached. We touch on using 360 degree feedback in coaching and mentoring, including some hard earned learning on how to avoid getting bogged down in detail or defensiveness. We offer guidelines for referring clients on to others, and then present a framework for exploring the balance of thinking and feeling in a relationship. Bob Garvey offers a summary of his 'three stage process', which is a strong mentoring model for a session during the relationship. We then examine 'relationship droop', which can occur anywhere in the relationship, and offer some thoughts about managing it actively, and we conclude by looking at the related issue of moments of disconnect and how to manage these actively and positively.

Chapter 13: Conclusion: what we have learned about the place of techniques

In this chapter we reflect back on the journey we have taken in writing this book and its predecessor, and seek to draw conclusions about what we have learned in the process about the place of techniques in coaching and mentoring. We look at the different places that coaching and mentoring have started from and their direction of travel over the years that we have been thinking and writing about techniques. We round off the chapter and the book with some checklists to help the reader think about whether to use a technique on a particular occasion, and if so which technique to use and how to use it.

References

Casserley, T. and Megginson, D. (2008). *Learning from Burnout: Developing Sustainable Leaders and Avoiding Career Derailment*. Oxford: Butterworth-Heinemann.

Clutterbuck, D. (2007). *Coaching the Team at Work*. London: Nicholas Brealey.

Hermann, S. M. and Korenich, M. (1977). *Authentic Management: A Gestalt Orientation to Organizations and their Development*. Reading, MA: Addison-Wesley.

Kegan, R. (1992). *The Evolving Self*. Boston: Harvard University Press.

Lee, G. (2003). *Leadership Coaching: From Personal Insight to Organizational Performance*. London: CIPD.

Perls, F. (1971). *Gestalt Therapy Verbatim*. New York: Bantam.

Rooke, D. and Torbert, W. (2005). Seven transformations of leadership. *Harvard Business Review*, **83**(4), April, 67–76.

Part 2

Frameworks

In this part we include chapters on specific topics that yield a fresh perspective either on interventions which can be used with clients (all of them) or interventions that offer challenges for the coach/mentor (especially Chapters 5, 6 and 7). The chapters include frameworks drawn from psychology (Chapters 2, 3, 4 and 7) but also frameworks that take a particular perspective (intuition – Chapter 5; writing – Chapter 6; mindfulness – Chapter 7; creativity – Chapter 8; and teams – Chapter 9).

Chapter 2

Cognitive behavioural coaching

Gladeana McMahon

Origins of CBT

In the 1960s, US psychiatrist Aaron Beck noticed that his patients tended to engage in 'internal dialogue' as if they were talking to themselves. He realized that there was a link between thoughts and feelings and he created the term 'automatic thoughts' to describe these emotion-filled thoughts. Beck found that people were not always fully aware of such thoughts, but could learn to identify and report them. If people were feeling upset, their thoughts were usually negative and self-defeating. Beck discovered that, with help, individuals could identify these thoughts and were able to understand and overcome their difficulties. And so cognitive behavioural therapy (CBT) was born, which would later spawn cognitive behavioural coaching (CBC).

Principles of CBT

Cognitive behavioural coaching owes it origins to CBT and is a non-directive form of coaching, which does not seek to give people the answers to their difficulties but rather, through a collaborative process, termed 'guided discovery', assists individuals to devise their own conclusions and solutions. Guided discovery is based on what is called Socratic questioning, in which the coach asks the person a series of questions that enable the individual to become aware of the way he or she is thinking. The term derives from the method of philo-sophical inquiry originally developed by the ancient Greek philosopher Socrates. The practice involves asking a series of questions surrounding a central issue, that seek to assist the individual identify his or her ideas on the subject being explored. Questions such as, 'what do you mean by your difficulties relating to others?', 'what would be an example of your being overlooked?' or 'how does your relationship with your peers relate to your anxiety', are all examples of questions aimed at helping the individual uncover his or her own thinking on a particu-lar issue. Socratic questioning promotes insight, thus allowing a more rational decision-making process to take place. For example, this type of questioning can move an individual from his or her limiting style of thinking to a more flexible system of identifying a number of problem-solving strategies (Curwen, Palmer and Ruddell, 2000).

CBC is time-limited, solution-focused and based in the present. Historical material is only sought when necessary in order to elicit infor-mation about the past that usefully highlights why and how past events have shaped the individual's way of thinking and behaving. Coaching aims to assist individuals achieve goals and devise action plans to improve performance. It does so by taking into account the need for self-awareness of moods and emotions and, in this sense, assists people to become more emotionally intelligent. It works on the principle that understanding one's own emotions, motivations and ways of being, as well as that of others, will assist in becoming more effective in all that one does.

CBC is 'psycho-educative' in nature, which means that the goal of this form of coaching is to help individuals develop the necessary skills so that they can become their own coach in the future. As the coach-ing client becomes aware of his or her own thinking style, its strengths and limitations, and of alternative ways of thinking and alternative ways of behaving, the individual becomes more adaptable and flex-ible. By using this newly acquired knowledge, the individual develops more effective and satisfying ways of dealing with challenges and goal attainment.

The CBC process

The number and length of sessions depends on the individual's circum-stances. For example, a programme of six 90-minute sessions could be delivered as one session a week or fortnight for three sessions and then one session a month for the remaining three. Alternatively, it may be more helpful to engage in one 3-hour session in order to break the back of a particular issue, following this session with shorter sessions on a less regular basis.

At the beginning of the coaching process a 'Behavioural Contract' (McMahon, 2006; Skiffington and Zeus, 2003) should be drawn up which takes into account the needs of the sponsoring organization and the changes required from a corporate perspective, the needs of the coaching client and the changes that he or she wishes to make and the thoughts of the coach who synthesizes this information into a series of 'objectives' and their associated 'outcomes'. For example, the organization may wish to see an individual 'improve their communication skills in order to become a more effective leader' and the individual may want to 'gain confidence when dealing with superiors'. Both of these statements are regarded as overall objectives. However, neither of these objectives specifies what would need to be different in order for there to be a positive outcome or some sort of measurable change, or how the organization or individual will measure the aforementioned change(s). A series of further questions are used to elicit measurable outcomes such as:

If you were more confident, what would you be doing differently?
If you were a more effective leader, what behaviour would you be engaging in that would be different?

In addition to the questioning process used to elicit outcomes, consideration is also given to the key performance indicators already in use within the organization and how these can be used to measure change.

The role of the coach is to ensure that the outcomes are clearly stated, that all parties are on-board in relation to what is expected and that the number of desired outcomes can be obtained in the specified allotted time. In addition, during the contracting period, agreement is also reached regarding the type and method of feedback to be provided to the organization, the parameters of confidentiality and the terms and conditions related to the coaching assignment. Once all these factors have been agreed, the contract can be signed-off by all parties and used to evaluate the success of the coaching sessions at the end of the programme. There are, of course, occasions when the contract may need to be amended during the coaching programme, if new information comes to light or if circumstances change. In effect, the Behavioural Contract sets the agenda for change (Leimon, Moscovici and McMahon, 2005).

Sessions start with the coach ascertaining the client's current mood as well as what has happened to the client since the previous meeting. The coach then moves the client on to referring back to the behavioural contract to enable the client to choose one of the items listed to work on in the session. The session then focuses on the chosen item using whatever skills and/or techniques seem appropriate, and the client is then assisted to design his or her own homework assignment to take place before the next session. Finally, the session ends with the coach eliciting specific feedback on how the client has experienced the session and what has been helpful. CBC is a collaborative process so it is important that the client takes control of his/her subject matter, and provides feedback to the coach on his or her approach to the client.

The coach also takes into account the learning style (Baker, Jensen and Kolb, 2002) of the individual. For example, some clients prefer more information about the concepts behind the coaching style being used and want to engage in what could be termed 'bibliocoaching', an adaptation on the term 'bibliotherapy' (Pardeck, 1998) where reading material is recommended to backup the programme. Other clients may want to engage in more experiential learning and may not be so bothered about the theoretical concepts being used. If the coach can work with the client's learning style this can lead to more successful goal attainment.

Understanding thinking style

The individual is assisted to identify and understand the impact of his or her thinking style in a given situation (Neenan and Dryden, 2006). Negative Automatic Thoughts or NATs (those thoughts we engage that are self-defeating) are based on the 'Life Rules' or 'Underlying Assumptions' we have devised to function in our environment and, these in turn, are based on the core beliefs we hold about ourselves, others and the world in general (Figure 2.1).

An individual has been asked to spearhead a new project alongside a number of other complicated projects he is responsible for. The organization would like the individual to take on the project but it is not essential that he does as there are other people in the organization who could be approached.

Core Belief	I am a hard worker and success comes to those who work hard
Underlying Assumption or Life Rule	*If I* am offered an opportunity *then* I should take it
NATs	I can't say no

The person holds a core belief that he is a hard worker and that success is dependent on hard work. This Core Belief leads the person to develop an Underlying Assumption that whenever he is offered an opportunity he should take it. This could be seen as a rule that has served him well during the early part of his career while he was becoming established. By accepting opportunity, he has raised his profile and created opportunities to expand his knowledge. However, now that he is of senior status with

A Cognitive Model

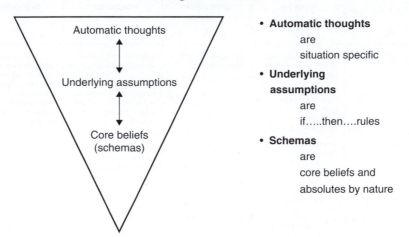

Figure 2.1   A cognitive model.

increasing level of demand being made of him, it is not practical or help-ful to accept every opportunity. Continuing to accept opportunity could potentially lead to the loss of the good opinion of others by not being able to deliver on time, by producing less satisfactory outcomes, or by simply leading to personal burnout (Casserley and Megginson, 2008) and the subsequent decline of performance in all areas.

In this case the individual was aware that he always took on too much and that he was now reaching his personal and professional lim-its. However, when he considered turning down opportunities he felt anxious and found himself saying yes and then worrying excessively about how to manage his workload.

Once the relationship between his Core Belief(s), his Underlying Assumption(s) and the ways his thoughts were triggered in such sit-uations were uncovered, he was able to stand back and see how such thoughts were unhelpful. It was now possible to develop an alternative Underlying Assumption of:

> If I am offered an opportunity then I need to evaluate it and consider whether it is useful to me and the organization to accept it.

Creating a new Underlying Assumption together with a practical framework for evaluating opportunity such as asking for 'thinking it over time' so that he could work out the pros and cons of taking on anything new and developing a matrix to assist with decision making meant that he was able to take control of his workload ensuring that he was able to deliver what was needed when it was needed.

Problem A	Self–defeating thinking B	Emotional/ behavioural reaction C	Healthy response D	New approach to problem E
Giving a public lecture	I must perform well or the outcome will be awful. **Logical:** *Just because I want to perform well, how does it logically follow that I must perform well?* **Empirical:** *Where is the evidence that my demand must be granted? Am I being realistic? If I don't perform well will the outcome be really awful?* **Pragmatic:** *Where is it getting me holding on to this belief?*	Anxious, inability to concentrate	**Logical:** *Although it is strongly preferable to do well, I don't have to.* **Empirical:** *There is no evidence that I will get what I demand even if it is preferable and desirable.* **Pragmatic:** *If I don't perform well, the outcome may be bad, but hardly devastating! If I continue holding on to this belief, I will remain anxious and be even more likely to perform badly.*	If I change my attitude I will feel concerned and *not* anxious, Also, I'll be able to concentrate and prepare for the lecture

Figure 2.2   Thoughts form.

Identifying thinking style

In CBC emphasis is put on identification of self-defeating thinking and thoughts are elicited by using tools such as a Thoughts Record Form where the individual is taught how to identify his or her thinking style (Figure 2.2).

In addition, the individual is also asked to begin to identify the types of cognitive distortions, as in Figure 2.3, he or she engages in which influences the way the person perceives situations (Neenan and Dryden, 2004).

Once the individual becomes aware of his or her ways of distorting reality they have the opportunity of putting in counter-measures. If an individual tends to see a mistake as something awful (*catastrophizing*), and the end of the world (*all or nothing thinking*), perceiving the situation as being all their fault (*personalization*) without taking into account others that may have contributed to the outcome, then this type of thinking rather than assisting the person do better next time, is more likely to make the individual feel stressed and anxious. However, if the person could stand back from the situation, thinking instead:

I am not happy about the error but it is not the end of the world and I was only responsible for part of what happened. What went wrong and what can I learn about this situation that will assist me the next time?

Distortion	Meaning
Discounting the positive	*'If I can do it, it doesn't count'*
All or nothing thinking	*'I pass or I fail', 'you win or you lose', 'it's right or it's wrong', 'I do it all now or do none at all'*
Labelling	*'I did something bad therefore I am bad', 'I said something silly therefore I am foolish'*
Mind reading	*'She didn't look at me therefore I have done something wrong'*
Fortune telling	*'I just know it will be awful'*
Catastrophizing	*'Oh my God this is SO terrible'*
Personalization	*'It's all my fault', 'I am the one to blame'*
Blame	*'It's all his/her/my fault'*
Generalization	*'All managers are the same', 'I never get what I want', 'it's always the same'*
Shoulds, Musts, Have tos and Oughts	*'I/you/she/he/they must..have to..ought to'*

Figure 2.3   Table of cognitive distortions.

It is likely that the individual will be better placed to correct the error, learn from it and devise systems and/or structures for the future.

In CBC there are three types of challenges that are used to help the client re-evaluate their thinking (Simos, 2002).

- *Empirical/evidence based* – 'Where is the evidence that if you make a mistake you are a failure?'
- *Logical* – 'Just because you would like never to make a mistake how does it logically follow that you must not make a mistake?'
- *Pragmatic* – 'Even if it were true that making a mistake means being a failure, do you feel better or worse for believing it, and does it help you stop making mistakes?'

The above aims to help the individual engage in realistic thinking which is more likely to assist him in reaching sensible, informed and sustainable decisions.

A CBC coach recognizes that the types of demands we make of ourselves, others and the world, are likely to generate either positive or negative outcomes (Dryden, 1999). For example, if I demand of myself that:

I must do well, if I do not then it is awful, or I must be approved of by others, if I am not then I have less worth

These thoughts are likely to result in stress, anxiety, depression, shame and guilt.

Demands of others such as:

> You must treat me justly, if you do not then it is not fair and you deserve to be punished

are likely to result in anger and passive-aggressive behaviour.

For those who believe that:

> Life must be as I want it to be and if it is not then that's awful

The outcomes are likely to be self-pity, addictive behaviour, depression and a tendency to procrastinate.

CBC can be used as a main approach to coaching an individual or as part of another approach. A number of coaches who do not identify themselves as being cognitive behavioural use many of the skills and techniques from this approach in their work with clients due to their tried and tested and effective nature.

There are of course those who do not subscribe to the CBC approach, believing that CBC is too focused and directive in nature. For these individuals coaching is totally reflective in nature. There is also a belief that this model only works in relation to a psychological coaching model and cannot be applied in a strictly business coaching arena. For those who support CBC it is seen as a 'life skills' approach that can be used alone or integrated into a range of other approaches. These individuals recognize that technical skills do not exist without a person to apply them and that, on many occasions; it is not the technical skills that an individual is lacking but the experience of struggling with some kind of faulty thinking or perception that makes the task more onerous than it need be.

CBC interventions

There are many different types of strategies, tools and techniques used in CBC, three of which have been listed above in Figures 2.1, 2.2 and 2.3. Interventions are aimed at either changing an individual's thoughts, feelings, behaviours and/or physiological reactions to situations. For example, a simple breathing exercise can be taught to a coaching client to help them manage the physiological fall-out of dealing with anxiety provoking situations. Alternatively, educating the client as to the cognitive model is in itself a strategy that can be used to provide the client with a model for understanding how he or she may have developed their thinking style.

Four more interventions are discussed below.

The cost–benefit analysis

This is an exercise that is used to assist coaching clients to consider the consequences of their actions (Neenan and Dryden, 2002).

The client writes down the problem he or she is experiencing and then on the right-hand side of the form, writes down all of the benefits of continuing with the status quo. On the left-hand side he or she writes down all the costs (emotional, practical, financial, etc.) of continuing with the same course of action (Figure 2.4). The cognitive behavioural coach helps the client evaluate what has been said while using his or her skill to assist the client identify self-defeating thinking, unhelpful beliefs and alternative ways of reframing such thinking into that which could be termed self-enhancing. This exercise can be used in its written form or undertaken as a discussion piece alone. There are no real pitfalls in using this exercise. However, as is the case with any exercise undertaken with a coaching client, the exercise has to be positioned so that the client needs to see the relevance of it and want to engage in the process.

Name: *Sue Jones*   Date: 9th September

Problem: *Don't seem to be able to make decisions*

Cost	Benefit
• Worry a lot • Other people make decisions that I don't like • Feel weak • Don't get what I want	• Can't be wrong • Don't have to stand up for myself • Can avoid difficult situations

Figure 2.4   Example of a cost–benefit analysis.

Contingency planning

The contingency planning exercise owes it origins to the work of Arnold Lazarus and his PR Plan (Lazarus, 1981). When an individual faces a difficult situation that he or she may find worrying, the individual tends to overestimate the dangers and underestimate the resources available (both internal and external) to deal with the situation. By doing this, the individual makes the situation worse rather than better

and hampers the chances of a positive outcome. Even if a positive outcome is achieved it may have cost the individual dearly in terms of the
stress and energy used to manage the situation.

Having identified the situation that is causing the individual concern,
the coach asks the client to list all the concerns that he or she may be
experiencing. The coach positively encourages the client to list as many
things that could go wrong as possible. This part of the exercise is only
complete when the client cannot think of anything else that could happen. The coach then encourages the client to come up with a series of
contingency plans against each of the items listed (Figure 2.5). By doing
this, the coach is assisting the client to recognize that all situations can
be dealt with, that nothing is the end of the world and that the coaching client can cope. In addition, from a cognitive perspective, by engaging the client in contingency planning it has the advantage of tricking
the brain into thinking that it has already dealt with this situation – in
a sense it is a kind or 'role rehearsal' and this too can have a calming
effect. This exercise does not have any real pitfalls providing the client
finds it of benefit.

Situation: Giving a board presentation

Situation = What could go wrong?	Action = What will I do if this does happen?
A Experience IT problems	A • Arrive early to check equipment • Arrange for an IT person to be present • Take data stick and spare laptop even though one will be available
B Forget my words	B • Take a deep breath • Acknowledge I have lost my place (it happens to everyone at some point) • Ensure I have my cue cards/PP slide printout close to check
C Asked a question I cannot answer	C • Simply state that I do not have the answer but that I can get it

Figure 2.5   **Example of contingency planning for managing difficult situations.**

Responsibility pie

The responsibility pie is a tool used to assist an individual to recognize
that he or she is only part of a much larger picture. Many people blame
themselves or others for things that are out of their control and this
exercise is a useful process for working out what part of the situation
belongs to whom (McMahon and Leimon, 2008).

In this exercise the coaching client is asked to describe the situation, all parties involved and the sequence of events. He or she is then asked to draw a circle to represent the whole of the situation. The individual is told that the circle or pie equates to 100% and is then asked to ascribe a percentage to all of the parties or circumstances.

For example, an individual was asked to submit a report by a certain deadline and then discovered that he had missed the deadline as the date had been brought forward. The individual concerned is a perfectionist and, as such, blames himself totally for the missed deadline. However, it soon became clear that an IT issue meant an email bringing forward the deadline date was never received and although his manager did think it was unusual not to receive an acknowledgement to his email he did not check to see that the client had received the new information. The individual did hear something through the office grapevine that had made him wonder if there could have been a change, but because he was busy he did not follow this up.

As a perfectionist, the client is unhelpfully engaging in punishing self-talk, ruminating over his error. He is defensive and irritable with those around him. The coach uses the responsibility pie to assist the client to engage in realistic thinking and by talking through each of the component parts encourages the client to consider the ways in which his current attitudes actually hamper rather than encourage good performance (Figure 2.6).

There are no real pitfalls in using this exercise.

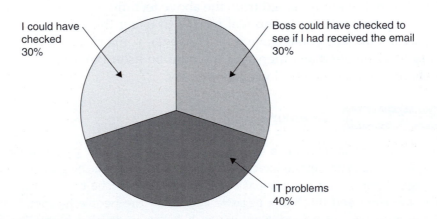

Figure 2.6   Sample responsibility pie to challenge faulty thinking.

Coping imagery to deal with negative emotions

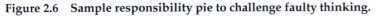

According to research visualizing a positive outcome means the individual is more likely to achieve one (Hodges et al., 1979). Coping imagery is used as a way of preparing for events.

The client is asked to write out a 'problem list' of all the people, places and situations he or she feels uncomfortable with or in. Then, using a 0–10 scale as a way of rating the degree of discomfort felt (0 = no discomfort and 10 = maximum discomfort) the client rates each of the aspects listed.

The client is encouraged to choose something that has a rating of no more than 5, as choosing a higher rating would be akin to attempting to tackle the most difficult situation first and choosing a lower rating would not be challenging enough and unlikely to provide enough learning for the individual.

The coach asks the client to close his or her eyes and imagine being at the beginning of the task. The coach asks the client to use all of their senses to imagine the sights, the sounds and the smells associated with the situation.

As the coaching client will have been given a range of coping strategies from breathing exercises to different ways of perceiving the situation prior to this exercise the client is asked to imagine using these as part of the coping imagery exercise.

The client is asked to visualize the situation two or three times, each time seeing him- or herself coping with the situation. By doing so the client will find that the difficulty rating he or she ascribed to the situation at the beginning reduces even though the individual is only using imagination. It is as if the brain is fooled into believing that the individual has already successfully managed the situation (McMahon, 2008).

Maximum benefit is gained from the above technique when you practise it frequently. There are no real pitfalls to using this exercise unless the client is unhappy to engage in it. However, some clients have more ability to visualize than others and it would be useful to ascertain from the client whether they find visualizing easy.

Case study   Communication

James, a senior director in an international financial services group responsible for structured finance execution, was referred for coaching by his line manager. Although he was seen as being technically able, he came across as cold and aloof and this had a negative impact on the people he met. One of the objectives of his coaching was to help James develop better interpersonal skills in order to make him a more effective marketer. A coaching contract of eight, one-and-a-half hour coaching sessions was agreed. His Behavioural Contract included the following two outcomes, 'to identify and develop relevant interpersonal skills associated with effective relationship building' and, 'to develop a framework for understanding my own thinking

(Continued)

processes and that of others to enable the recognition of the similarities and differences and associated possible outcomes'.

During his early sessions with his coach, James came to recognize that to progress further in the organization, he needed to develop his business organization skills. Psychometric profiling helped identify his personality type and James came to realize that his approach had a tendency to alienate individuals. By considering the impact he had on others, he was able to develop an awareness of his own 'natural' style of communicating and recognize that different people had their own preferences for communication.

The main hurdle James had to overcome was to appreciate that the organization of business was only partly to do with technical ability. He came to understand that a prospective client in the highly competitive banking market is going to rely on personal relationships in choosing the person and organization they wish to work with. The focus of his coaching sessions became the development of desired behaviours to improve personal relationships. A series of behavioural exercises was created in relation to networking and the social skills required for creating and maintaining effective relationships, in particular, the concept of using 'small talk' around non-technical subjects, such as finding out about the other person and looking for subjects of personal interest, were explored. To assist this process, James was helped to identify his thinking style. Two of his beliefs being 'I am at work to work and not to socialize' and that 'other people will think well of me if I am technically able and I must demonstrate this at all times'.

By the end of the coaching contract, James had managed to modify his behaviour and communication style to one that placed more emphasis on building individual relationships. The feedback received from his manager and from others in the organization demonstrated a positive change in the way James related to people. In addition, James found that his more open personal style was securing a more positive pay-off in terms of securing business.

References

Baker, A., Jensen, J., Kolb, D. (2002). *Conversational Learning: An Experiential Approach to Knowledge Creation*. Westport, CT: Quorum/Greenwood.

Casserley, T. and Megginson, D. (2008). *Learning from Burnout: Developing Sustainable Leaders and Avoiding Career Derailment*. Oxford: Butterworth-Heinemann.

Curwen, B., Palmer, S. and Ruddell, P. (2000). In: Palmer, S. and McMahon, G. (eds), *Brief Cognitive Behaviour Therapy*. London: Sage.

Dryden, W. (1999). *Rational Emotive Behavioural Counselling in Action*. London: Sage.

Hodges, W., McCaulay, M., Ryan, V. and Stroshal, K. (1979). Coping imagery, systematic desensitization, and self-concept change. *Cognitive Therapy and Research*, **3**(2), June, 181–92.

Lazarus, A. (1981). *The Practice of Multimodal Therapy: Systematic, Comprehensive, and Effective Psychotherapy*. New York: McGraw-Hill.

Leimon, A., Moscovici, F., McMahon, G. (2005). *Essential Business Coaching*. London: Brunner Routledge.

McMahon, G. (2006). *Behavioural Contracting: Coach the Coach*. London: Fenman.

McMahon, G. (2008). *No More Anger: Be your own Anger Management Coach*. London: Karnac.

McMahon, G. and Leimon, A. (2008). *Performance Coaching for Dummies*. London: John Wiley.

Neenan, M. and Dryden, W. (2002). *Life Coaching: A Cognitive-Behavioural Approach*. London: Brunner-Routledge.

Neenan, M. and Dryden, W. (2004). *Cognitive Therapy: 100 Key Points and Techniques*. London: Brunner-Routledge.

Neenan, M. and Dryden, W. (2006). *Cognitive Therapy in a Nutshell*. London: Sage.

Pardeck, J. (1998). *Using Books in Clinical Social Work Practice: A Guide to Bibliotherapy*. London: Haworth Press.

Simos, G. (2002). *Cognitive Behaviour Therapy*. London: Brunner-Routledge.

Skiffington, S. and Zeus, P. (2003). *Behavioural Coaching: How to Build and Sustain Personal and Organizational Strength*. Sydney, Australia: McGraw Hill.

Chapter 3

Coaching approaches derived from Gestalt

Marion Gillie

In 1973, Fritz Perls wrote: 'Any reasonable approach to psychology not hiding itself behind a professional jargon must be comprehensible to the intelligent layman, and must be grounded in the facts of human behavior' (p. 1). In this chapter I aim to offer a comprehensible account of the fundamentals of a Gestalt approach and show how they are grounded in research on human behaviour. Gestalt is essentially an optimistic approach, holding that people are trying to do the best that they can within a particular set of circumstances, and as such, even the most 'dysfunctional' behaviour is serving an important purpose for that person. This highly humanistic philosophy means that many coaches draw on Gestalt approaches in their work. As we know, coaching is not therapy, yet the roots of Gestalt lie firmly in therapy. In this chapter I give examples of how Gestalt approaches can be applied to coaching, and will clarify the boundary between coaching and therapy in the application of a Gestalt approach. Throughout I will give examples of client–coach dialogue, all of which have been taken from my own coaching practice.

A brief history

Fredrick 'Fritz' Perls, along with his wife Laura and Paul Goodman, are generally recognized as the originators of Gestalt therapy as we know it.

The influences on Perls were very varied, and it is fascinating to see how these 'show up' in the evolution of the practice of Gestalt. Perls, a Freudian psychoanalyst, became interested in the principles of Gestalt psychology as applied to learning and perception, which he felt could be applied to his own field of psychoanalysis. As well as this, Perls was fascinated by psychodrama and was influenced by Reich's body therapy. He developed a deep interest in phenomenology (a person's in the moment, here and now experience), existential philosophy and Eastern religion. From these influences he embraced a holistic perspective on the nature of existence, influenced in particular by Kurt Lewin's field theory – the notion that a person cannot be understood without reference to his or her 'context', which includes their immediate, current situation, their past experiences, their hopes, aspirations, anxieties, and both conscious and unconscious beliefs. The political forces at play in the world at that time also impacted him deeply, the rise of Fascism and anti-Semitism in Germany in the 1930s, and his subsequent flight to Holland and later South Africa as a refugee. Finally his move to America in 1946 ensured that Gestalt therapy grew up in the post-war climate of liberalism, and the individualistic, anti-establishment era of the 1950s and 1960s added more than a hint of egocentricity to the mix.

The principles and the practice

The holistic nature of experience

The term Gestalt is a German word which, though not easily translated, means 'shape', 'form' or 'pattern'. The concept was developed by a group of German psychologists who studied how people *create meaning*, i.e. how meaning takes shape in human perception. In 1926 Perls worked with Kurt Goldstein (a member of the Gestalt school of psychology) at The Institute for Brain Damaged Soldiers. Here the emphasis was on the holistic nature of human functioning, on the fact that brain injury affected not only the specific area of damage, but also the entire range of the person's behaviour. From this and other studies the Gestalt psychologists concluded that people don't perceive a single stimulus but strive to make meaning from the elements. Perls (1973) used the example of a man coming into a room of people, who doesn't perceive 'blobs of color and movement' but takes in a room of people. At a psycho-biological level, the familiar image of a face is not 'built' in the human brain by recognizing eyes, nose and mouth individually then putting them together and coming up with the composite face. People form an impression of the whole face, the whole picture, namely the *Gestalt*.

Furthermore, in Gestalt we talk about '*the figure of interest*', jargon that really means 'the thing we are interested in at this particular moment'. A second fundamental characteristic of perception, as found by the original Gestalt experiments, is that individuals will naturally move towards *closure* of each perceived figure, our perceptual process compels us to complete the figure or to 'fill the gaps'. For example, if you look at the diagram below, you will naturally see it as a complete figure (a face), although essentially there are only three straight lines and one curved line. Your brain automatically completes the picture.

The figure will be experienced as 'whole', bounded or *closed*. An individual will compensate for the perceptual gaps in the outline to make a complete figure, or complete Gestalt. Healthy psychological functioning will naturally move the person towards wholeness, stability and equilibrium. A closed or finished figure is more stable than an unfinished one and an individual will feel drawn to closure, whether the figure is perceptual, psychological, an action or an interaction between people. An incomplete figure, or '*unfinished business*', interferes with the formation of new figures, which results in the individual remaining preoccupied and less 'available' for something new.

Perls applied these principles to the emotional world. He proposed that we need sufficient closure in any interaction in order for it to be satisfying and/or complete. As a trivial example, how often, when someone turns the television or radio off mid-sentence or mid-song, do you find yourself completing the phrase in your head? Similarly when you have felt upset by something or someone, how often does the incident stay with you until you find a way of sorting it out? It is only at that point that the incident is genuinely finished and a complete Gestalt is formed.

This theme is an important one for the coach, who often has to deal with their clients' unfinished situations that appear to be blocking action, creativity and change. For example, your client arrives at a coaching session in an agitated state, complaining about a conversation that he'd had this morning with his boss. This piece of unfinished business is highly 'figural' for this client and likely to dominate (at least the early part of) the session until some kind of resolution is found.

Thus Gestalt is founded on the premise that human nature is organized into patterns and wholes, and that the whole is more than the sum of its parts. Another of the big implications of this for the Gestalt oriented coach lies in the fact that it is the client in front of us who is making the meaning, and as coaches we can only really begin to understand our client by exploring the meaning that he or she is making of the patterns in his or her world. For example:

> Client: When I think about my current situation, it feels like I'm on a bicycle, without my feet on the pedals, hurtling down a hill like a meteor.

How many of us would have been tempted, through an understandable desire to show empathy, to say something like:

> Coach: That sounds scary.

When I said this, the response from my client was:

> Client: No! No, not at all, it's exciting, exhilarating … real freedom at last!

A Gestalt coach would then explore the client's *lived experience* of their role, going beyond the usual 'What does that feel like?' They would pick up and develop the metaphor:

> Coach: Imagine you are on that bike right now, hurtling down hill … what is that like … (or what do you experience … or what happens in your body as you imagine this, or how about recounting it as though it is happening right now … 'I'm racing down hill …').

The rationale for this is that the more fully the client can *live* their real experience in the coaching session, the more likely it is that what matters most to them will be revealed. This is important, because it is often the case that when asked 'What is the most important thing for you to explore today?' many clients will not know or may censor their options and offer one that they think is 'appropriate' for coaching. However, their body knows, and will tell you if you know how to invite discovery … more of this later.

Figure and ground and the cycle of experience

Another Gestalt psychologist, Kurt Koffka (1935) described the process by which we organize our perceptions as that of *figure and ground*. When the man in Perls' example above walked into that room, he didn't perceive *all* of the people *and* the room at the same time. Instead he would have selected and focused on one thing (person or item in the room) at a time. The person or item focused on is *the figure*, whilst all else at that moment is *the ground*. Then attention moves on and that figure dissolves into the background and a new figure emerges. Perls developed this notion into the description of healthy human functioning as a continuous flow: a need arises, comes into awareness, becomes 'figural' is acted upon and recedes into the background.

You are in a coaching session with a client and are listening carefully to his story (the present figure). You begin to realize that you are uncomfortable in some way (sensation). As you listen, you shift about and gradually it dawns on you that you are uncomfortable because your chair is at the wrong height (awareness: a new figure form). Gradually, your concentration on your client is overtaken by the desire to alter the chair height (energy mobilization). You apologize to your client, get up (action) and fiddle with the chair (contact). You then sit down again, feel that the height is now right for you (resolution/closure) and begin to become absorbed in your client again (withdrawal of attention and formation of another figure).

This is the cycle of figure formation and destruction known as the Gestalt Cycle of Experience (see Figure 3.1). Furthermore, at the heart of Gestalt is the notion that no individual is self-sufficient, at any moment they are a part of a wider environment, and to satisfy their needs, they need to act upon the environment, e.g. find food, take a break, speak

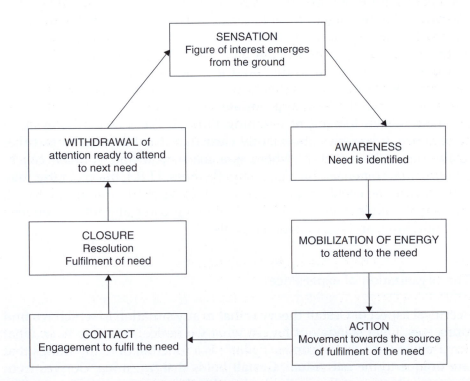

Figure 3.1   The Gestalt Cycle of Experience.

to someone. This is what Gestalt theory calls '*contact*'. This rhythm of contact/withdrawal is fundamental to Gestalt practice, and a measure of psychological health and well-being is how you move (or not) with grace through this never-ending flow. It is what Perls referred to as *self-regulation*.

The example of the coaching session above gives a simplified sequence of what happens all the time. In reality, there may be several figures jostling to emerge at one time. In this example, you could also be remembering that phone call you need to make, or you may be starting to notice the tone in which your client is talking.

It is easy to see how this works when looking at basic physical needs; emotional and psychological needs are more complicated. This is because individuals or organizations, groups or teams of people, often find it difficult to identify what those needs are or may not know how to satisfy them. If we revisit the example above of the client who is annoyed with his boss, in this example, there has been no resolution or closure, and the unfinished business remains very figural for that client. The job of the coach here is to facilitate a 'good enough' resolution, so that the client can move on, and key to this is gauging where in the cycle of experience the client is stuck. The Gestalt coach would spend time exploring what all of this means to the client. In the case above of the client who is agitated by his boss, clearly he is angry, but what is *the meaning* of his anger? It could mean many things, to start with, is he aware that the emotion concerned is anger? Has a value been violated? Is there a need that is not being met? Does he know why he is angry but doesn't know what to do about it? Does he know what to do but feels impotent to act? Until this is uncovered, it will be difficult for him to be clear about the most appropriate action to take.

Finally, when looking at coaching through the lens of the cycle of experience, it becomes abundantly clear that it is the *client's* need that is the one to be satisfied. When, as a coach, you find yourself coaching towards someone else's goal (e.g. the boss, H.R.), the coaching may fail because the client simply may not mobilize sufficient energy to act, unless, of course, you are able to facilitate greater alignment between the individual and organizational goals.

The organization of experience

A critical aspect of Gestalt theory is that in any situation in which we find ourselves, what stands out for us, what we notice, what we hear, what we assume (i.e. what becomes '*figural*') is a function of many things that are unique to the individual. Gestalt holds that 'meaning' derives from the *total situation* of *this* individual under *this* set of circumstances. The total situation includes past experiences, hopes and aspirations, anxieties, assumptions. For example, you are coaching several people in the same team. Their boss has given each of them a very challenging new task. One client is excited, ready for a stretch, another is highly anxious, and fears failure. Why? Because each person–situation event is unique. You are probably aware that you behave differently with different clients; each coach–client meeting is a unique event. This means there is no single way of working with a particular 'type' of client or 'type' of situation, every session that you go into presents you with a unique individual-situation. Even if this is your fifth session with the same client, the here and now individual-situation is new each time. You really do need to set aside your preconceived ideas of what it must be like in the client's shoes. Of course you need to show empathy, but you do it in a different way each time.

So back to our angry client: in order for the coach to facilitate a good enough closure of this unfinished Gestalt, the coach needs to 'get under the skin' of the client's experience. Our job is to help our client understand his own need in the situation, and facilitate his mobilization towards appropriate action that will satisfy the need, and the key to this is awareness, the cornerstone of Gestalt work.

Awareness: the key to working with 'what is'

The Gestalt approach is to respond to and deal with *what is* rather than *why it is* or what it *should be*. A big influence on Gestalt theory came from Arnold Beisser's Paradoxical Theory of Change, which holds that change occurs (paradoxically) when I fully become what *I am*, rather than trying to be what I am not, and that lasting change cannot be attained through coercion or persuasion (Beisser, 1970). The process of healthy self-regulation is the ability to be fully what *one is* and to meet one's genuine needs, as distinguished from external regulation (trying to be what I think I *should* be to meet some external demand, real or imagined). The route to healthy self-regulation is self-awareness and Perls maintained that awareness *per se* – by and of itself – can be curative.

Take the example above of the client who arrives agitated about his boss. Your coaching goal in this moment is to help your client become more fully aware of his need and/or appropriate action. We arrive at this awareness through interventions that bring your client as close as possible to his experience in the here and now. You do this by paying attention to what you see and hear your client saying and doing, and, in turn, asking your client to pay attention to *what is going on* for him in the here and now – his thoughts, behaviours and emotions. In our example, one starting point would be to invite him to re-live the situation with his boss. After contracting to do this you might say something like:

> Coach: OK, what I'd like you to do is to imagine that you are back there, in that meeting with your boss in front of you … (you could, if appropriate, even ask your client to close his eyes, I normally find that even the most senior executive is prepared to try this) … take a long look at your boss, what do you notice? Her tone of voice … what do you notice about your own reactions, feelings, sensations, thoughts …

Another starting point would be to invite your client to stay with their here and now experience in the immediate moment:

> Coach: As you are talking about your boss right now, what do you become aware of? (You could add the following prompts … in your body, what images come to mind, what thoughts, sounds, emotions?)

The underlying principle of this methodology (referred to in Gestalt circles as the use of the client's 'phenomenology') is to heighten awareness by staying with actual experience without interference or interpretation on the part of the coach.

Example: Using your own observations:

> Coach: As you are talking about your boss, I notice you clench your fist and you look as though you are tensing your arms (at this point, the coach would be very likely to mirror the movement as a way of focusing on the phenomenon rather than drawing too much attention to the verbal interpretation). How about you try staying with that movement and exaggerate it (again mirroring the movement). What comes up for you as you do that … (as before, image, thoughts, sound, emotion?)

With every move closer to the client's actual experience, the client becomes more and more aware of either the intensity of the feeling, which will lead to greater clarity about their own needs in the situation, or of what they would *really* like to say or do if no holds were barred. This is the use of active experimentation as a route to greater awareness in the service of exploring 'what is' (more on this later).

When the client is stuck somewhere in the cycle of experience (e.g. because they are not aware enough of the need or they are aware but unable to act) your task is to help the client explore how they are creating this blockage. This involves surfacing, listening to and experiencing *being stuck*. Paradoxically, if you and the client can *stay* with the block/stuckness/resistance, fully experience it (often by exaggerating it), we generally find that it will either dissolve or transform, thus freeing the client up to move forward (more on how to do this in the section below on active experimentation).

Presence as a route to awareness

Given that 'meaning' derives from the *total situation* of *this* individual under *this* set of circumstances and that satisfaction arises from acting appropriately with the environment, the coaching session itself is the here and now environment where meaning is unfolding, and you as coach are a critical aspect of the client experience. Your presence will inform (not necessarily consciously) what the client chooses to reveal. Perls went as far as saying that the 'self' only exists in the interaction between the person and their environment, between one person and another (Perls, 1978).

Presence is much more than how 'professional' you are as a coach. It includes how 'grounded' you are in yourself and your work, how able you are to 'reach' the client, even when they are difficult to reach. The Gestalt coach needs to be aware of what is going on within him or herself and between him/herself and the client *in the here and now*, and be prepared to articulate some of this to the client as one way of 'making contact'. This is the Gestalt notion of self-disclosure, paying close attention to your own reactions to your client, what he or she evokes in you, what images come to mind, what sensations are stimulated, and disclosing these to your client. You do this of course in the service of *their* awareness and part of the process is to find out what impact your disclosure has had on them:

> Coach: I am suddenly aware of a strong image as I hear you talk about that project ... I saw you rushing down a long tunnel which is almost black ...(*pause for reaction ... then if no or little reaction ...*) Does that image have any meaning for you in relation to your situation?

The coach's image is particularly vivid and it has arisen within the interaction between coach and client, so it is a fair bet that it has some relevance to the client's situation and is worth checking out. Here is a different kind of example:

> Coach: Joe, can I interrupt for a moment, I notice that I keep losing the thread of your story and find myself working over-hard to understand you (*pause to gauge reaction*).

> Client: (looks surprised) Well, I have had feedback from a few people that I sometimes over-explain things.
> Coach: You said it happens 'sometimes'. What might be at play here in our coaching that has 'hooked' you into over-explaining?

This second example is what Mary Beth O'Neill (2000) calls 'immediacy', (a) the capacity to scan for 'the parallel process', i.e. when what happens 'out there' starts to happen 'in here', (b) the ability to recognize your own reaction, and (c) the boldness to speak directly to the client about your reaction to them. O'Neill says, 'without immediacy, it is impossible to get at the heart of some issues' (p. 35). Some clients remain oblivious to their patterns until they are held up for scrutiny in the here and now contact between coach and client. These interventions clearly have roots in psychodynamic concepts such as transference and counter-transference.

Active experimentation as a route to awareness

Although Perls often said that full awareness in itself brings growth, he also acknowledged that awareness alone could be a slow method of achieving change (1973). To accelerate growth, he introduced the idea of active 'experimentation'. By experimentation he meant encouraging clients to try something out there in the session to see what new awareness or new learning it might elicit. Typically there are two points in the cycle of awareness where experimentation can accelerate learning.

(i) Clarifying the figure of interest

How often have you been listening to a client at the start of a session talking about their situation, without real clarity about what would be of real value to them in this particular coaching session? In Gestalt terms, the figure of interest is hazy and unclear, and experimentation can help locate the *real* locus of interest. Take the following example:

> Client: I often feel uneasy when I am dealing with this particular manager (*hazy, unclear figure*).
> Coach: What is it that leaves you feeling uneasy? (*classic enquiry*).
> Client: Well I'm not too sure really … (*signal that an experiment might be useful*).
> Coach: OK, how about we try an experiment*? Picture that manager here in front of you … notice how he's sitting, how he sounds, what

---

* Personally I often use the term 'experiment', said appropriately I think that it sounds playful and implies a choice of accepting or otherwise the outcome. I know that some find the term awkward. Alternatives I use include 'Are you interested in trying something out?'

he looks like … (*pause to allow the client to focus*), What do you notice in your body as you do so?, (*or … what image springs to mind?/what do you see?/describe what you notice etc.*).
Client: I feel a sinking feeling in the pit of my stomach;
Coach: Stay with that feeling … (*followed by any of the following: Where is that sensation?/What shape/size/colour is it?/If it could make a sound what would it be?/What image comes up?/What words come up? Here the coach concentrates on increasing the client's present awareness through a 'here and now' investigation of their experience, which amplifies their contact with their experience*).
Client: I get the sensation of sinking in my chair.
Coach: OK, stay with that sinking, in the pit of your stomach and in your chair … try exaggerating the sensation (*you might mimic shrinking in the chair, your active engagement offers to support the client's experiment, makes it seem less unusual*) …
Client: It's as if I am expecting him to dismiss my view before I even speak. I know that I won't be able to persuade him.

By staying with the evoked experience and even exaggerating it, it is very likely that the client will have access to a greater awareness of what that manager elicits – a clearer figure with which to work. I find that once the figure is clear, it is important to move out of the experiment and shift the energy from what might have been an uncomfortable recognition into something focused on action, e.g.:

Coach: OK, so it looks as if we have something concrete to work on, the assumptions that you carry into that relationship about your ability to influence. Would that be of interest to you to explore? (*You might actively invite your client to shift their posture, in order to get 'that manager' out of the coaching session.*)

This shift of focus onto what can be addressed is one way of managing the boundary between coaching and therapy. Whilst it might have been perfectly legitimate to have asked, 'Who might this person remind you of?' i.e. checking to see if the client is projecting another authority figure onto this manager, you need to be aware that you are potentially approaching the boundary between coaching and therapy. To remain on the coaching side of that boundary, your focus is on helping the client recognize the pattern and working on how to break it in his *current* relationships. Moving deeper into historical (probably parental) material most certainly constitutes therapy.

(ii) Mobilization of energy into action
Being aware of the need or figure of interest is the essential first step, and many clients will naturally clarify what they want to do next.

However, I experience some clients who know what the issues are but are 'stuck', they don't know what to do next. Resistance to action takes many forms and you will know that you have moved into seeking solutions too soon when you keep hearing the 'yes, but …', 'yes, I did try that but …'. When this is the case, then experimentation is a good way of raising awareness of *their real choices* (rather than the choices you would wish for them).

Example one: Stay with the resistance

Coach: It sounds as though you are really stuck, you don't know what would work in this situation (*in 'paradoxical theory of change' terms you are acknowledging 'what is' rather than pushing to change it*). Are you interested in trying something? I am thinking that it might be interesting to simply explore what it's like 'not to know' (*To make it a genuine choice I usually disclose my thinking, and ask again if they are interested in giving it a go. Assuming consent.*)

Coach: How about starting with what is, and simply saying out loud to me, 'I'm stuck, I don't know what to do'.

Client: (*In a small voice*) I'm stuck, I don't know what to do.

Coach: I'm struck by how quietly you said that, what would it be like to make your voice even smaller?

Client: (*laughs*) No I don't want to be smaller … 'I'm stuck, I don't know what to do (*in a more defiant tone*).

Coach: Try that once again (*you have detected a shift in energy that needs to be built on*).

Client: I don't know what to do … well … actually it's more like I do know what to do but don't want to do it!

I find that it is pretty certain that the client won't stay stuck for long, something will emerge that gives a focus that can be worked with. By 'starting where the client is' (if anxious, exaggerate anxiety; if bored, exaggerate boredom) rather than trying to change the client you eliminate the client's need to push back and resist you, thus making space for something more creative to emerge.

When you are comfortable working in this way, you will find that ideas for experiments flow naturally from the material presented by the client, and you will discover a rich and creative way of working as a coach. I was working with a client whom I knew to be passionate about biographical literature. In one session he was pondering aloud about what Nelson Mandela would do in his situation, so I invited him to say who else's opinion (historical, contemporary, real or fictional) he would be interested in. I then invited him to seat them all on separate chairs (see below), sit in each chair and speak as each of them, to see what 'message' each one would give. It was fascinating how much his physical demeanour and tone changed with each character, and the material that emerged was very rich. When we debriefed his experience, he was absolutely clear what messages he was prepared to act on immediately and which he would need more time to reflect upon.

Example two: The classic two chairs/empty chair approach

This way of working is what most people associate with Gestalt. It is at its most useful when:

- *The client is facing a dilemma* (on the one hand I could stay in this role and hope for a promotion, on the other hand I could move to another department to raise my profile). There are many experiments that you might try. One option is to invite the client to fully express the benefits of both options, sitting in different seats (this physical separation aids the untangling of the thoughts and emotions that usually accompany a genuine dilemma). What you watch for is the client's energy levels as they speak. They often have more energy for one option over the other (of which they are likely to be unaware) which manifests in tone of voice and body language. If you spot a difference, you can invite the client to exaggerate their energy for that option, to see if this brings into consciousness the unconscious decision that they have already made.

- *The client seems to be engaged in an inner dialogue with two (or more) aspects of the self.* Perls identified the fact that most of us have an internal critic which he called the Top-dog and a hopeless, stuck side he called the Under-dog. The internal Top-dog tells us how we 'should be' how inadequate we are and that we ought to try harder to change. The Under-dog in us passively resists, feels guilty but finds all sorts of excuses for not complying, and thus is covertly powerful (Perls, 1969). A battle between the two ensues when neither polarity is being fully acknowledged and owned, which ties up vital energy, leaves us stuck and immobile. The route to mobilization comes when each side of the 'personality' is brought fully into awareness (separation) then brought into contact with each other (integration). Thus it opens up the possibility of finding a creative resolution. A simple example:

> Client: I keep telling myself that I'm being ridiculous, a leader in my position should be able to challenge the senior team about this, but …
>
> Coach: OK … it sounds like you have different voices telling you different things. How about we try something … put them each on different chairs and have each talk to the other, that way we can unpack the issues and understand them better. Want to try? (*wait for*

confirmation) … Which voice do you want to start with? …(*to make sure the client takes charge of the experiment*). Try talking directly to the other part of you here on this chair … (*the client may just need a little prompting away from 'talking about' towards 'talking to' – this makes the experience much more vital and immediate*).

Client: (*as Top-dog*) You are a useless leader, you should push back more, where is your courage … you should stand up to them more!

Coach: OK … try moving to this chair and give this part of yourself a stronger voice in response.

Client: I have got courage. I just don't want to undermine all the good work that I've done developing the team by making enemies in the wrong places. You push too hard. (*It would be usual to swap chairs a couple of times to deepen the dialogue, but in the interests of brevity …*)

Coach: So part of you wants to push harder and another wants to push less hard or push differently, is that right? What are the benefits to you of each of these positions? (*Remember that whatever the client is doing is for a good reason.*)

Client: Well, the critical part has always been a driver, taking me further than I ever thought I'd go, and the other part is the diplomat, making sure that I don't burn bridges along the way.

Coach: So both serve you well in fact, when they are not at war! (*Both laugh.*) So what would be a statement that sums up the best of both of these voices in this current situation that you are in? (*Appreciation of and reinforcement of the healthy functioning aspect of the pattern.*)

Client: Well … it's important that you …

Coach: Stay with the 'I' statements, 'it's important that I …' (*Again by keeping it in the first person the message remains vibrant.*)

Client: It's important that I push myself, take risks, but I also want to make sure that I do this in an assertive, diplomatic way not an arrogant and aggressive way.

Coach: Try that again with 'and' rather than 'but …

Client: It's important that I push myself, take risks *and* I also want to make sure that I do this in an assertive, diplomatic way not an arrogant and aggressive way.

Coach: What's it like to say that?

Client: Really good, it fits, it sounds like how I really am.

Coach: So what can you take from this into the situation we have been talking about with your senior leadership team?

Once again, one of the things you are looking out for is a shift in energy. When there is real acceptance of 'what is' (i.e. the client's real 'truth' as opposed to how they think they should be) they often experience a surge of energy (and relief) that can be directed towards taking appropriate action.

Another word on the difference between this and therapy: in coaching you are always working with the client within the context of their work arena, asking questions like 'what sense does this make for you in *this* situation?'. It may be screaming at you that the Top-dog voice sounds like a critical parent (they may even make that connection for themselves) but the key is that you don't move towards repair of the parental relationship, you use that data to inform the 'now', how they are functioning in their current work relationships.

● *The client is stuck in his/her working relationship with another person.*

This is probably the most familiar use of the 'empty chair' approach in coaching:

> Coach: What would you *really* like to say to your boss/direct report/colleague? Imagine she is sitting here in front of you, try saying it directly to her …

The coach might then encourage the client to make the message stronger, exaggerate it, to bring into sharper focus what is *really* going on in the relationship. You might ask the client what they experience in doing this, what they become aware of. Often the client will become clearer about what the real message is, and then you might say something like:

> Coach: Well I dare say you wouldn't say exactly that or in that way to the real person … so … what would it feel OK to say/do in relation to her?

Another variation is to invite the client to 'be that other person', i.e. to sit in their shoes, and to speak as them. If I do this, I generally invite the client to sit in a posture that is similar to that of the person they are having difficulty with. It is uncanny how much insight someone can get into the other person by stepping into their shoes. Whatever experiment you try the critical thing at the end is to ground their new awareness in their actual situation, help them make sense of their experience and help them clarify what choices they want to make about their situation going forward.

Active experimenting: the integration of the 'whole' personality

A healthy, functioning person is one who both knows and accepts him- or herself, even those aspects of the self that may be more difficult to admit to (e.g. our greed, aggression, spite, selfishness, envy, pettiness at times, etc.). Perls believed that we all have the capacity for any human characteristic, but often disown those that seem unacceptable to us, frequently seeing them in others but not in ourselves. For example, when I hear a coachee describe a colleague as, for example, 'cool and distant', I would generally explore his own 'cool distance' with this particular colleague. Typically I would use the approach described above, i.e. ask him to envisage the colleague and describe what feelings, sensations etc. this evokes in him, listening for signs of 'projection', projecting onto the colleague, the disowned aspect of himself.

There are many ways of working with polarities. Recently I received a call from a very talented woman executive who wanted a coaching session to help her prepare for an interview for a new job she really wanted, but was feeling under-confident about her ability to put herself across well enough. On impulse I invited her to bring along an object or article of clothing that represented an aspect of herself that she would never dream of exhibiting in work. I was curious about what she denies about herself in certain situations such as this interview. She brought to the session a pair of vivid red stiletto shoes, and a black jacket with a luxurious fake fur collar. It didn't take much to persuade her to put them on in the session.

> Coach: See what it is like to move around the room, really inhabiting the place that these items represent for you.
> Client: (*tentatively*) I feel very visible …
> Coach: What's it like to be visible?
> Client: Well, it's a mix of daring, scary and exciting.
> Coach: OK, how about you try saying directly to me, 'I am daring, scary and exciting'.
> Client: (*quite boldly*) I am daring, scary and exciting.
> Coach: What do you experience as you say that to me?
> Client: Strong.
> Coach: Well, how about picturing yourself at the interview, imagine standing or sitting in front of the guy you are meeting and saying that again.
> Client: (chooses to sit) I am daring, scary and exciting … (sounding uncertain) yes, but I am empathetic and good with people … (*a good example of how the more acceptable polarity can seem to 'cancel' out the other: these need to be brought together and both held as true*).
> Coach: OK, yes I agree, you are empathetic and good with people. How about trying on for size 'I am empathetic and good with people, **and** I am daring, scary and exciting'. Try it out.
> Client: I am empathetic and good with people, **and** I am daring, scary and exciting. (*Looking over at me, and showing a lot more energy.*) Well yes, when I am really working well I *am* all of those things.

Ignoring or disowning aspects of the self results in inner conflict or immobility as the dominant and denied parts struggle (remember the Top-dog/Under-dog conflict?). Energy is channelled into keeping the denied polarity out of awareness, but it is a waste of effort because we function much more authentically and effectively when the denied part is integrated into the whole. At this point in the session my client was feeling much more animated, and in Gestalt terms, ready to mobilize her energy into appropriate action, i.e. prepare well for her interview. Says Latner (1986), 'The reinterpretation of polarities is called the "Aha" experience. It is a moment of creative revelation. At this moment we have changed the structure of ourselves … and we will behave and think differently because the field is new, we have reorganized it' (p. 55).

Active experimenting: working with the whole system

Gestalt is essentially a 'relational' framework, i.e. it holds that your coaching clients cannot be understood as separate from their unique context. How they are shaped by their historical relationships is the province of therapy, the relationship with you in the room (as described above) and their relationship with their colleagues in the workplace is the province of coaching. So how do you explore their wider systemic context when you are working one to one? Clearly one way is to 'shadow' your coachee and observe the dynamics of their relationships with colleagues. Another way to do this is to bring the system into the room. My favourite way is to ask the client to select a range of objects from the room in which you are working to represent each individual (and/or sub-systems that he or she interacts with) in the wider team/system.

My first step might be to invite my coachee to use the objects he or she has chosen as a metaphor for the person the object was selected to represent, e.g.:

> Coachee: (*holding a glass paperweight selected to represent the boss*)
> Graham is clear, cold, a bit slippery. You can see something inside, but you can't quite touch it.

This can reveal new insights about how the coachee sees others in the system and how different others might see my coachee. To get a deeper understanding of the more systemic issues at play, typically I would ask my client to place the objects spatially in the room in a way that represents something important in the system (e.g. emotional closeness/distance of the relationships). In itself this isn't unique to Gestalt, but what makes it so is how you then work with the data. I invite my coachee to stand in each place one at a time, and then to speak from that place in terms of what it feels like to be there, how they perceive the rest of the system as they look around, what needs they have, etc. A coachee of mine, Martin, mapped his immediate system of direct reports, boss and clients:

> Coach: OK, so now move to one of the other places, and see what you would say from that place.
> Client: I work for Martin … I feel isolated standing here … I can see my other colleagues, but they are a long way from me … I can see Martin, but he isn't looking at me …
> Coach: OK, which place are you drawn to next?
> Client: (*Moving to his boss's position*) I can see Martin there, I see him looking out beyond the team, he isn't focused on them at all.

Once all positions have been explored (including where the coachee has placed himself), I would ask the coachee what strikes him most strongly about what's happening in the system. This might lead onto a two-chair dialogue between my coachee and other individuals in the system, or indeed between my coachee and the whole system! When the client has placed an individual looking away from another individual in the system, I often stand in for that individual, so that the client gets a physical sense of what the dynamics might be between the two, and I might even say what is evoked in me as I stand-in for that part of the system. Like many coaches I often work in meeting rooms which are starved of interesting objects, so I will ask my client to draw a picture/image that represents each person/sub-group. I have even used chess pieces (doesn't everyone carry a chess set around with them at all times?) which in itself introduces an interesting set of dimensions (the white knight, black queen, the 'pawn in the game', just to mention a few typical archetypes!).

Clearly there are limitations to this way of working, because essentially you are not working with the real system, but with the projections of the client onto the system. Nevertheless, I have found it a very rich and creative way of exploring the wider systemic issues which moves the client beyond their own, inevitably, parochial view.

Some closing remarks

Gestalt provides a rich source of support to the coach. The cycle of experience offers an excellent compass for orientation through a coaching session: where is the client's energy, what's in/not in awareness, how is/isn't energy being mobilized towards action, how is closure being/not being managed, how he or she moves onto the next action without savouring the satisfaction of success etc. The practice of active experimentation brings creativity to the coaching work and the notion of bringing the coach's own presence into the relationship means that the work is both challenging and deeply rewarding.

Finally, there are three points that I would like to emphasize before I close this chapter. The first is that if you are working well as a Gestalt coaching practitioner, your Gestalt orientation will be more 'a way of being' than a set of tools in a tool bag. Your practice is one of continuously moving your attention between your client and your own response, looking to see where the energy is and where it is blocked. You will be paying attention to what is happening within the coaching relationship and checking this out against the context of their system. You will be observing carefully and then selectively sharing observations of what you see, hear, etc. establishing your presence as a coach in so doing. In short, the Gestalt oriented coach is engaged in a continuous process of awareness and skills development, which becomes a way of life.

The second point is that you may have noticed how directive the interventions as described above can be. This way of working is strange territory for most clients, and they need to feel in 'safe hands'. If you are too tentative, they will be hesitant too. The skill of the Gestalt coach is to step robustly into your own authority, whist always ensuring that you are offering your client genuine choice.

My final point is that a truly Gestalt oriented approach is *not goal focused*. Remember that the only goal of Gestalt is awareness and that change flows from being more fully aware of who you really are, not what you are trying to be. Since traditional coaching *is* goal focused, it is unlikely that you would use a Gestalt approach throughout a whole session but that it can guide your choice of interventions and bring vibrancy and creativity to your work.

Suggested further reading

There are many books on Gestalt. If you want a good introductory text with lots of examples of therapist–client dialogue, you can't go wrong with:

Mackewn, J. (1997). *Developing Gestalt Counselling*. London: Sage.
O'Leary, E. (1992). *Gestalt Therapy, Theory, Research and Practice*. London: Nelson Thornes.

For something more comprehensive and still accessible my favourites are:

Yontef, G. M. (1993). *Awareness, Dialogue and Process: Essays on Gestalt Therapy*. Highland, New York: The Gestalt Journal Press.

Zinker, J. C. (1977). *Creative Process in Gestalt Therapy*. New York: Brunner/ Mazel (republished by New York: Vintage Books in 1978).

For those keen to read the 'original' (not the easiest of reads in the world):

Perls, F. S., Hefferline, R. F., Goodman, P. (1951). *Gestalt Therapy: Excitement & Growth in the Human Personality*. London: Souvenir Press (1972 edition); London: Crown Publications (1977 edition).

For more on Gestalt and coaching:

Bluckert, P. (2006). *Psychological Dimensions to Executive Coaching*. Maidenhead, Berkshire: McGraw Hill, Open University Press.

References

Beisser, A. R. (1970). The paradoxical theory of change. In: Fagan, J. and Shepherd, I. L. (eds), *Gestalt Therapy Now*. Palo Alto: Science & Behaviour Books. Available via www.gestalt.org/arnie.htm.

Koffka, K. (1935). *The Principles of Gestalt Psychology*. Princeton, New Jersey: Brace & World.

Latner, J. (1986). *The Gestalt Therapy Book*. Highland, New York: The Gestalt Journal Press (first published in 1973).

O'Neill, M. B. (2000). *Executive Coaching with Backbone and Heart. A Systems Approach to Engaging Leaders with their Challenges*. San Francisco: Jossey-Bass.

Perls, F. S. (1969). *Gestalt Therapy Verbatim*. Utah: Real People Press.

Perls, F. S. (1973). *The Gestalt Approach & Eye Witness to Therapy*. Palo Alto: Science & Behavior Books (republished by Bantam Books in 1976).

Perls, F. S. (1978). Finding self through Gestalt Therapy. *Gestalt Journal*, **1**(1), 54–73.

Chapter 4

The transformative power of ontological coaching

Alan Sieler

> Real learning gets to the heart of what it means to be human. Through learning we re-create ourselves.
>
> (Peter Senge, *The Fifth Discipline*)

Ontological coaching gets to the heart of what it is to be human as the means for generating profound positive change. In times of rapid and disruptive change coaching needs to focus on more than providing new skills and strategies for shifting behaviour. This is insufficient for equipping coaching clients to expand their inner resourcefulness and capacity for living and working effectively. Ontological coaching provides enduring value by positioning clients to not only deal with immediate problematic circumstances but also to expand their resourcefulness and resilience for dealing with future problematic situations.

Coaching to way of being

The word 'ontology' means study of being. The essence of ontological coaching is a focus on coaching to the *Way of Being* of coaching clients. Way of being contains our deeply ingrained attitudes and patterns of perception, which may significantly limit our effectiveness and what

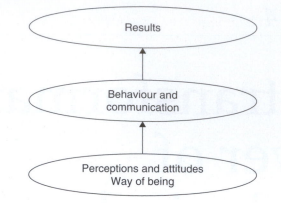

Figure 4.1   Way of being underlies performance.

we are capable of accomplishing. Way of being is the underlying driver of our behaviour and communication, and ultimately the results we do and don't get in all areas of our lives (Figure 4.1).

The transformative nature of ontological coaching is its capacity to generate significant shifts in deep-seated attitudes, perceptions and behaviours through the transformation of way of being. Coaching clients gain lasting value through the development of a profoundly different understanding of themselves, the world and their possibilities in life.

Before considering the specifics of what is involved in coaching to way of being, it is worth looking at the first coaching example.

Case study   **Ontological coaching in action 1**

Karen was a manager in a suburban real estate office and listed some key areas of dissatisfaction in her life. These were: insufficient money, not having a partner and not asking for what she wants. These emerged from a lengthy conversation in which the coach assisted Karen to identify the core issues underlying her dissatisfaction. This is an important technique in ontological coaching called the *Conversation for Clarity*, ensuring that coach and coachee have an explicit mutual understanding of the coaching agenda.

Karen chose to explore the issue of money. After a range of exploratory questions about money and her life circumstances the coach asked, 'What is the story you hold about yourself not having enough money?' Karen said that it meant she could not have fun, and with that her body lurched back slightly and her eyes widened. Although a simple statement, this was a revelation to her as she came to see how life had become serious and heavy for her. The coach then said, 'What else is part of this story?' She replied, 'That I can't have what I want'.

(Continued)

Her last comment opened up a different path for the conversation. She was asked, 'Where did you learn that you can't have what you want? I don't think you were born with that, were you?' She said she had learned in her home life when she was a young child. In particular she said that she had learned from her father that she was a nuisance when she asked for things and she should not expect to get what she wanted. Tears began to well in her eyes and the coach paused and asked if she was okay to continue. Karen requested a glass of water and said she wanted to continue.

The coach then asked, 'What did you learn about yourself from being told that you shouldn't have what you want?' She said that she learned 'You're stupid. You're an idiot'. The coach then offered some thoughts about powerful learning that can happen when we are young. She (the coach) said when we are young the opinions of others, especially our parents, are very important to us. 'Their judgements matter a lot to us, for we want to be accepted and approved by them. None of us wants to feel rejected. In doing so, we grant them a lot of authority, and their opinions carry a lot of weight with us, so much so that we take them on board, not just as opinions but as facts. In essence, we can be very vulnerable to unconsciously making the opinions others have of us define who we are.'

The coach paused and asked Karen what she made of this interpretation. Karen said she could see how she had learned these opinions. The coach continued, 'But something else happens too. It is not only "You're stupid. You're an idiot" that has been learned, but also as "I'm stupid. I'm an idiot." Of course, when we have such strong negative opinions of ourselves, why should we expect anything in life? Why would anyone find us attractive? We certainly may be too stupid to have enough money.'

The coach had been applying a model of language called *Basic Linguistic Acts*. This is a framework that allows the coach to listen to how the coachee is using language to generate their perceptions, and provides important clues about how to support him or her to use language more constructively. Basic linguistic acts identifies six precise ways or processes humans continually engage in to create their reality (see Figure 4.2).

The coach used two basic linguistic acts in the conversation with Karen, these being assertions and assessments. Understanding the role of assertions means recognizing how facts are created and what constitutes a fact. Assessments are judgements and opinions. A common linguistic trap, often with very negative consequences in our relationship with our individual selves and our relationships with others, is that we confuse our opinions with being facts, predominantly doing this outside of awareness, locking us in to a particular understanding of our self or someone else.

Returning to the coaching conversation, the coach explained that Karen's opinions of herself are called negative self-assessments. The coach explained

(Continued)

- Assertions – statements about what exists and the process of deciding what is and is not factual
- Declarations – utterances backed by authority that generate new circumstances
- Assessments – technically a subset of declarations, these are opinions and judgements
- Requests – the means by which we explicitly seek someone's cooperation by asking for support
- Offers – where we take the initiative and put ourselves forward to do something for others
- Promises or commitments – these are agreements we make in accepting requests and offers

Figure 4.2   Basic linguistic acts.

that we all have positive self-assessments and spent some time supporting Karen to articulate some of her positive self-assessments. Karen then asked, 'But why do the negative ones overpower the positive ones?' The coach then said, 'Let's take a look at that'.

With the coachee's permission, these statements became the basis for a deeper exploration to begin to touch on a central feature of Karen's (and anyone's) fundamental way of being. Often there are core negative self-assessments operating as silent tapes in the background of our existence. They play a pivotal role in running our life. Karen came to see that she was living from two interrelated core negative self-assessments – 'I'm not wanted' and 'I'm not loved', leading her to think that she was fundamentally flawed as a human being and that she was a fixed property, unable to change. This is an insidious linguistic trap.

Using a specific questioning strategy called *Grounding Assessments*, the coach and Karen explored the deep meaning behind Karen's negative opinions with a view to investigating if there was any substance to her negative self-assessments. The grounding assessments procedure is an inquiry based on five questions.

1. For the sake of what? What purpose does the negative self-assessment serve for the coachee or how does the assessment take care of the coachee? It is not unusual for the coachee to respond, 'It serves no purpose', which was Karen's reply to this question.
2. In which domain(s) of life? In what specific areas of life does the assessment apply? It is important for the coach to be willing to 'drill down' in this question; for example, if the domain identified is work, to what specific aspects of work is the assessment relevant?
3. According to what standards? Every assessment is always a comparison with standards or acceptable criteria. With negative self-assessments we are not measuring up to our own standards and it is crucial to be precise in exploring this question with the coachee by clearly articulating

(Continued)

their standards, whether these are standards they 'own' or think they should have, how specifically they are not living up to their standards, and whether the standards require revising.

4. What facts support the assessment? The importance of this question is to ensure that the assessment is not based on generalizations and opinions, that solid factual evidence is cited. Karen's reply to this question was typical of most coachee's response – she could not identify any facts.

5. What facts do not support the assessment? This question is designed to provide counter evidence of specific factual instances that contradict the negative assessment. Sometimes the coachee can identify a number of positive opinions that others have expressed of them and, while opinions per se do not count as evidence, the number of opinions cited is factual.

Through the questioning strategy Karen recognized that there was no substance to her core negative self-assessments. She was able to see the possibility of getting out of her linguistic trap when she recognized that she was not born with these ultra-negative opinions of herself and that they were not a permanent part of her existence. They were learned and could be unlearned.

The coach explained that these deep negative self-opinions can have a strong emotional grip on us, and these emotions (called moods) can endure and run our life. This is because moods are predispositions for action – they predispose us to see the world in certain ways, and reveal what is and is not possible for us. Karen said the moods associated with her deep negative opinions were anxiety, depression and resentment. The coach suggested that these are heavy moods and Karen said 'Yes, much of life is a burden for me'.

A central part of the methodology of ontological coaching is the framework *Some Basic Moods of Life*. The framework identifies six common moods as a guide to the emotional world of the coachee and provides a detailed interpretation of the structure of each mood, how it affects perception and behaviour and how it can be manifested in body posture. The moods are resentment, resignation, anxiety, acceptance, ambition and wonder.

When the coach outlined the structure of anxiety and resentment it resonated strongly with Karen's experience, enabling her to gain a valuable perspective on how the moods were an integral part of her perception and behaviour. For example, she recognized the strong tendency in anxiety to imagine worst-case scenarios and believe she would not be able to cope if these eventuated. Consequently, she withheld herself from engagement in many situations that were potentially beneficial and enjoyable. She also recognized the destructive nature of resentment that results from trying to change something from the past that cannot be changed, and in doing so generates negative energy and wasted effort. Both anxiety and resentment place severe limitations on how the future is viewed.

(Continued)

One of the most important coaching strategies in ontological coaching is to utilize subtle shifts in body posture and muscle configuration to assist the coachee move from the restrictions of negative assessments and unresourceful moods. Karen was invited to explore how her negative opinions and heavy moods were embodied; i.e. held in her body. With her permission, the coach provided some observations and invitations to explore making small shifts in her posture. It was observed that she was slightly tilted forward from the shoulder blades to the neck and the top of the head. It was also observed that her hips were pushed back and that her knees were locked tight, as well as tightness in her jaw. Karen commented she often required chiropractic treatment to have her back adjusted. With her permission the coach adjusted her posture so that she became more upright. She was invited to imagine having a string attached to the crown of her head that was being pulled upwards so that her neck vertebrae gently stretched, whilst her chin remained parallel to the ground. Suggestions were made to adjust the position of her hips and to 'take a breath and exhale down into soft and flexible knees'.

Karen was asked how this different posture was for her. She found it amazing that she felt so much lighter and things seemed so much clearer. She was invited to walk in her 'new posture' and then go back to her 'old posture' to appreciate the difference. The world was a very different place for her, including the world of possibilities, from each posture. The coach observed that her face had opened up and there was more sparkle in her eyes – she 'showed up' differently to the world! Karen reported that from her 'new posture' that she was not stupid and that it was legitimate for her to ask for what she wanted. She was provided with some gentle exercises to continue re-educating her body into a more supportive posture.

In a follow-up conversation Karen reported feeling 'relieved, being worthy of a place in the world, and having a new direction and sense of purpose'. Ontological coaching can be extremely powerful in respectfully and caringly touching the coachee's soul. When this occurs the coach is like a poet (from the Greek, *poiesis*, which means to create), generating new meaning. The coachee is able to view him/herself and the world differently, so that new possibilities and avenues for creating a better life can open up.

Way of being

Way of being consists of three interrelated spheres of human existence (Figure 4.3). These three spheres are language, emotions and physiology (body posture). Our way of being can be thought of as the internal reality we live in, which especially includes the relationship we have

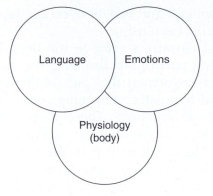

Figure 4.3   Constituents of way of being.

with ourselves. It is from this internal reality that we form our reality about the external world and how we participate in it.

The coaching methodology contains a set of tools for observing and shifting way of being. These can be divided into the three 'tool kits' of language, emotions and body.

Language

The methodology is based on a new understanding of language and communication developed in the latter part of the 20th century. The essence of this new understanding is that: (i) language consists of listening and speaking and (ii) that language generates reality. Listening is language because it consists of our self-conversations (internal dialogue), as well as our often deeply held and out of awareness beliefs and assumptions about how the world is and should be.

Language is regarded as the fundamental human technology, for we use it to produce outcomes and generate realities. People act (behave) from what comprises reality for them. Effective leadership, management, coaching and team behaviour depend heavily on how people use language. What is done, and how well it is done, is shaped by how people do and do not use language.

Using such models as Basic Linguistic Acts, Conversational Typology and Cultural-Historical Narratives the coach is able to facilitate the coachee using language differently to generate a more constructive sense of the present and the future. Conversational typology refers to specific types of conversations, each of which has a specific purpose and generates specific outcomes, such as Conversation for Clarity, Conversation for Coordinating Action and Conversation for Accountability. The coach listens for how effectively specific conversations are being used and may suggest the relevance and benefit of certain types of conversations that the coachee has not been using.

Cultural historical narratives refer to the deep background stories that are such a critical part of our listening, for they contain the basic assumptions (core assessments) that are subtle yet powerful perceptual and behavioural templates, informing people how to understand and behave in different situations. These are narratives about gender, religion, ethnicity, age, socio-economic situation, professional class, organizational, etc. The coach is alert to the influence of one or more narratives and sensitive about to how to bring their presence to the coachee's attention and explore their influence with him or her.

Moods and emotions

People are always in some mood or emotion. Moods and emotions are an integral part of human biology, occurring throughout the nervous system, permeating everything people do and are an inescapable influence on behaviour. If business is about getting things done, involving people's behaviour, and moods and emotions are inextricably part of behaviour, it can be argued that they are a core business process.

Ontological coaching has specific tools for recognizing, managing and shifting moods and emotions. The power of moods and emotions is that they always predispose people towards specific ways of perceiving situations and behaving. Thinking, speaking and listening, and engaging in conversations, are indispensable forms of human behaviour. How effectively people think, speak and listen cannot be separated from moods and emotions.

Unfortunately, moods and emotions have not been seen as a crucial area of learning for performance improvement. They are an integral part of the effective use of language for effective communication in leadership, management, coaching and team building. In short, they form a crucial dimension of morale and organizational performance.

Physiology and body posture

This would seem to be an unlikely area of attention in the context of organizational performance and improvement. Like moods and emotions, the body has largely been ignored as a key area of learning that impacts on individual and organizational performance. The importance of the body can be expressed in the following way: our way of being is embodied.

The body is always present in how people listen to each other and speak with each other. Speaking is not limited to the vocal chords – it occurs from the body. (This is well known for actors and singers.) An individual's posture consists of the subtle configurations of muscles and skeleton that have been learned throughout life. In many subtle and powerful ways, posture can keep people trapped in negative moods, and negatively impact on listening and speaking.

Specific tools that are part of this aspect of the methodology are:

- How to use the body to get into more constructive and productive moods.
- How small shifts in body posture can generate a more positive outlook and produce more effective communication.

The coach first invites the coachee to observe and comment on his or her own posture and muscular tension and asks them what shifts are likely to be beneficial. At the same time the coach attends to how the coachee is holding specific parts of their body, such as jaw, neck, shoulders, chest and torso, pelvis and knees to assess if postural integrity and muscular tension can be improved. Using the coachee's suggestions and their own observations the coach ensures permission to suggest postural shifts and their effects on the coachee's perceptions of him- or herself and problematic situations. Repetitive 'rehearsing' or continual experiencing of postural shifts is vital for the coachee gaining a first-hand appreciation of the role of the body to consolidate a shift to a more resourceful way of being.

Ethical considerations

Ontological coaching has a clearly articulated ethical stance. While ontological coaches are able to generate powerful interpretations that benefit coaching clients, the coach does not hold 'the truth' about what is best. A crucial aspect of the coach's way of being is to continually hold the coaching client as a 'legitimate other'. This occurs when there is deep respect for the coachee as a person and a learner, best exemplified by continually ensuring that the coachee grants permission for where the coach may want to take the conversation. It does not matter how powerful the coach thinks his or her methodology is, it is only as powerful as the coachee will permit.

There is always a risk that coaches become arrogant, seduced by the perceived brilliance of their own ideas, and blind to how they can be as impeccable as possible in effectively serving the coachee. Indeed, the coach is privileged by the opportunity to join in a learning partnership with a fellow human being, and explore the potential of ontological learning for facilitating profound positive change.

With the specifics of the coaching methodology and ethical considerations in mind, let us now look at the second coaching example.

Case study   Ontological coaching in action 2

Stella worked as a middle manager in a large global information and computer technology company. She was identified as having leadership potential yet encountered difficulties in realizing this potential. The company offered to employ a coach for Stella to provide an opportunity for her to move to senior management level, and perhaps beyond that to executive level.

After an initial conversation with Stella, and then a conversation for clarity with Stella and her line manager, the following coaching outcomes (learning agenda) were identified:

1. First and foremost, greater self-confidence and an enhanced sense of self-worth.
2. To be more able to deal with, and express, how she is feeling, rather than keep it inside and get to a breaking point.
3. To not to take things personally, which is associated with becoming more resilient.
4. To have a more strategic mindset, and not be as operationally oriented – to be able to stand back and observe the bigger picture.
5. To express her point of view clearly and firmly in meetings, including having another perspective to senior people present at the meeting.
6. To delegate and not be caught up in completing the details of various tasks – to know the deliverables required, where they fit in the larger schemes of things and to delegate to others in the team.
7. Through delegation to gain more from the variety of specialized expertise within her team.

The coach also ensured there was a shared understanding with Stella's manager about observable changes in Stella's behaviour that would be evidence of the fulfilment of the coaching outcomes. These were:

- 'Doing less doing', with her team doing much of the detailed work;
- Asking the appropriate questions – ones that indicated a strategic focus, such as 'How does this relate to the business objectives?';
- Being prepared to express well-thought-out 'push-back' or alternative opinions in meetings, especially where more senior personnel were present; and
- Coping effectively with setbacks – rather than getting down or despondent and dwelling on what 'went wrong', she would move forward to different issues.

Before the start of coaching, Stella said she thought that it would take a long time for her to work through her issues; she estimated at least 9 months.

(Continued)

The coaching engagement was completed after four 90-minute sessions over a period of 3 months. At the completion of the fourth session, both Stella and her line manager agreed that all coaching outcomes had been accomplished and were evidenced in her behaviour. Asked to rate where she assessed herself to be on a scale of 1–10 for each of the seven points in the learning agenda, Stella rated herself 2–3 before the coaching. When asked how she rated herself after the coaching, she indicated she assessed herself to be 8–9 for all points.

From an ontological perspective, the essence of the coaching was:

● Moving beyond a core negative self-assessment;
● Shifting from the debilitating effects of a mood of anxiety; and
● Developing a posture of legitimacy.

Despite her high conceptual intelligence, Stella's lack of confidence and self-worth revolved around living in a core negative self-assessment of 'not being adequate'. This produced on-going self-doubt about her ability. She constantly imagined others were making negative assessments of her, which she could not ground yet was living as a true assertion. When the grounding assessment procedure was applied to her self-assessment, she was surprised that it was not grounded and it became clear to her that this assessment was not serving her and was holding her back.

Not surprisingly, Stella's core negative self-assessment was associated with a mood of anxiety, which is a pervasive deep emotional space of not feeling safe and continually perceiving 'worst-case scenarios'. An important part of her anxiety was 'waiting to be invalidated'. Being sure that others knew she was not competent meant she feared that one day she would be 'found out' and her incompetence 'unmasked'. Her ungrounded assessment of others making negative judgements about her was lived as a constant threat, which she had to be prepared for. Two important ways her anxiety was manifested in her behaviour were (i) taking work home, especially on weekends, to ensure she was 'across everything' and (ii) needing to be involved in the details of just about everything and not delegating to her team members. Her behaviours were indicative of an important behavioural component of anxiety – a focus on self-protection to guard against all possible threats.

Stella was gradually introduced to the domain of the body as an important area of learning. The body learning aspect of the coaching had two components. The first was developing an awareness of how she had developed posturally in response to living in her core negative self-assessment and a mood of anxiety. The coach encouraged her to become aware of how she held her head and neck, her shoulders, her chest and torso and

(Continued)

her hips, and asked her how the world was for her from this posture. The essence of her response was that her focus was short term and anticipating negative consequences, which she had to prepare for. Very unlikely to be the posture of leadership!

The coach asked Stella what would be a more resourceful and beneficial posture for her. This is an important question, for it is designed to begin to engage the coachee in learning about the body as a key avenue of change. She identified a number of aspects of her posture that could be shifted and the coach asked her to 'move into the posture' that represented those shifts. With Stella's permission, the coach shared some additional postural shifts that she was willing to adopt. When asked by the coach how the world appeared to her from a different posture, she replied, 'Much more positive and less threatening'.

The coach then suggested that she had a less resourceful posture and a more resourceful posture. He asked her to move from one posture to another a number of times to ensure that she had a 'good feel' for each and the different view of the world both postures provided her. This activity was designed to encourage the coachee to become a close observer of her own posture, and to be able to 'catch' herself if she were to revert back to her less resourceful posture.

The second important piece of body learning was to support Stella in living from a 'body of legitimacy', as a way of ensuring that the limiting effects of her core negative assessment and the associated mood of anxiety would be negligible or eliminated. She was invited to stand in a relaxed and upright posture, with her arms wide open and the palms of her hands and fingers open and relaxed, and to say in a voice that had depth and resonance, 'I am a legitimate and worthy person'. Stella was also introduced to the distinction of speaking a declaration from her personal authority. The coach emphasized that she was not asking the world for permission to be legitimate. Rather, she was informing the world that this is how it is going to be with her from now on. She was encouraged to speak the declaration a number of times to ensure that she was speaking with conviction. The coach also asked Stella to walk around the room they were in saying, 'I am a legitimate and worthy human being' in a voice that meant what she was saying. Stella's response to the above experiences was, 'That's amazing – I feel so different and much more positive about myself'. When asked about the effect this different sense of herself might have on her work, she replied, 'Much more confident and far less intimidated'.

Three months after the fourth coaching session, the coach unexpectedly received a request from Stella for another session, and wondered what issue she wanted to explore. Stella did not have another issue for coaching. She wanted to report an extensive range of positive experiences and shifts

(Continued)

that had occurred for her, which she attributed to the coaching. The coach suggested that their conversation could consist of conversations for self-appreciation and accomplishment, to which Stella agreed. The coach took notes and filled a page with Stella's report about positive developments and positive self-assessments. A noteworthy point for the coach was the improvement in Stella's performance rating from the organization, and more importantly the increase in her potential rating (an assessment of her capacity for more senior leadership). Stella commented that it is very unusual for someone to receive a higher potential rating.

Stella experienced a significant ontological shift from having a limited sense of her own power and experiencing herself as being 'at the mercy' of others and work circumstances, to developing a robust embodied sense of her own legitimacy and competence. From a different way of being, Stella was able to engage in behaviour that was consistent with the company's criteria for effective leadership.

Suggested further reading

Flaherty, J. (2005). *Evoking Excellence in Others*, 2nd edition. Oxford: Elsevier/ Butterworth Heinemann.

Sieler, A. (2003). *Ontological Coaching and Deep Change*, vol. I. Melbourne: Newfield Australia.

Sieler, A. (2007). *Ontological Coaching and Deep Change*, vol. II. Melbourne: Newfield Australia.

Winograd, T. and Flores, F. (1986). *Understanding Computers and Cognition*. Reading, MA: Addison-Wesley.

Chapter 5

Developing intuitive awareness

Megan Reitz

I have noticed that many articles and books on intuition quote Einstein at some point or another. So for good measure; Einstein reflecting on the way in which he developed his theories explained that 'there are no logical paths to these [natural] laws … only intuition resting on sympathetic understanding of experience can reach them' (Rowan, 1987). Because intuition has, generally speaking, been regarded as both different from, and then marginal to the rational mind, quotes from such highly respected *scientific* individuals are deemed necessary to rationalize the focus on intuition. This, when you think about it, is rather ironic.

In the business world executives have been taught predominantly to be objective, to think logically, to apply theory, to make sense out of situations and to act in a defensible way. In recent years however the focus on using intuition in decision making has risen, warranting discussion, and on a number of occasions appreciation, in the higher echelons of the *Harvard Business Review* (e.g. see Hayashi, 2001). Admitting the use of intuition in the coaching world has, I think, been much more acceptable, in fact it is often encouraged, although surprisingly little has been written about it.

When I have asked coaches whether intuitive abilities are important in their coaching, their resounding reply is 'yes!' Where the responses start to differ however is around the definition of intuition and the degree to which it can be developed. And the debate really heats up when you start talking about how it is that we have intuition in the first place. We need to explore all these questions in order to enable us to devise techniques which may be valuable in improving our abilities as coaches for tuning in to our intuition. Then, as we consider *how* we use intuition in our coaching sessions, we must also acknowledge the 'shadow side' of intuition; the variety of reasons that intuitions can become mixed up with our own wishful thinking, desires, beliefs and egocentric needs.

What is intuition?

Pause a moment and before you read on, ask yourself these questions:

1. When have you personally experienced intuition?
2. How would you describe it?
3. Why do you think you knew what you knew?

Most people's definition includes a number of the following:

- 'I know, but I don't know how I know!'
- 'A synthesis of ideas.'
- 'Immediate, in the moment knowledge, sometimes really unexpected.'
- 'A strong sense that my intuition is correct.'
- 'Difficult to articulate.'
- 'It's not rational.'
- 'It's accompanied by a physical feeling', this is often a 'gut feeling' which feels significant.
- 'It's not always verbal; in many cases it seems to come as an image or through metaphor.'

In terms of how we come to have intuitive abilities, opinions can be summarized into two main camps (and of course one can agree with both). I refer to these as the expertise camp and the connection camp. Which camp you follow drives which methods you might use to improve your intuition. In both cases the way in which you use intuition in the coaching session is vitally important and some examples of this are drawn out from the case studies.

The expertise camp

The expertise camp proposes that intuition is a result of our mind grasping a pattern in a situation which is similar to one we have encountered before. Our mind has an ability to 'chunk' meaningful pieces of information and store these in memory, and sometimes, faced with a similar situation, we are able to access this knowledge in an immediate synthesis – we just know what to do without having consciously gone through the logical process of connecting past experience to current circumstances. Even if the intuition seems to come to us at a magical moment, it may in fact be that our subconscious mind has been busy pondering the problem and our intuition is the conscious outcome of this process. Then the coach needs the added ingredient of confidence and trust in their own intuitions in order to act. Herbert Simon who has researched this 'chunking' process states that 'intuition and judgment are simply analyses frozen into habit' (Simon, 1987).

William McGinnis, a senior executive interviewed by Weston Agor, sums up this aspect of the expertise camp well saying 'I believe that good intuitive decisions are directly proportional to one's years of challenging experience, plus the number of related and worthwhile years of training and education, all divided by lack of confidence or the fear of being replaced' (Agor, 1984).

Also in the expertise camp is the view that intuition is a result of exceptional perceptive abilities. In each moment our brain filters and files an enormous amount of data about our surroundings. Sometimes we experience a hunch which we can't explain but in hindsight can be accounted for by our ability to pick up minute changes in our environment. Eugene Sadler-Smith, writing in *The Times* newspaper in August 2007, describes a very famous case of intuition in sport, that of Juan Fangio, the Argentine racing driver who, in the Monaco Grand Prix in 1950, avoided a major accident by braking more than normal before going round a bend beyond which a crash, which was out of his sight, had occurred. Now, did Fangio have a 'sixth sense' that he needed to slow, or did he, unconsciously, notice that the crowd were unusually looking away from him, or were wearing different expressions on their faces?

> **Case study**   **Alex**
>
> Alex has coached the paralympic rowing team and describes the challenge that he and the other coaches face with one particular team member who suffers unexpected seizures. They obviously need to be immediately on hand as soon as one of these occurs whilst out on the water. When asked about his 'sixth sense' in being able to anticipate a seizure, he explains how he now has an acute ability to judge from aspects such as the puddle left from the oar after a stroke, and the movement of the oar into, and out of the water, when a seizure is about to happen.

Alex allies himself to the expertise camp. He argues that your intuition is a result of your level of experience, the degree to which you have effectively learnt from your correct and incorrect judgements in the past, and your ability to be totally focused on the coachee in the moment so that you are able to pick up acute changes in them. Methods of improving in these areas are discussed later in the chapter.

The connection camp

In the connection camp I put a number of explanations for intuition which contemplate our connection as a human being to our surroundings and to other people, and which conclude that we are able to communicate with, and 'read' our environment in ways which we may not even realize. My own research has examined occasions when coaches have had 'peak experiences' in connecting with their clients; where they have felt truly in flow with each other and they often report that in such situations they have a greater intuitive understanding of their client's issues. They feel a sense of resonance; being 'in tune' with their client. In medical research, phenomena such as entrainment, where brain waves from two different people synchronize during good conversations, inform our understanding of the possibilities of 'being on the same wavelength' as our client. In such flow experiences, as well as having acute perception and an expertise in relating to people, it may be that we are able to tap into what Jung would have described as 'the collective unconscious'. David Bohm explains, in relation to his concept of the 'implicate order', that 'in a holographic universe … everything is connected, and time and space are not barriers … Human consciousness would be part of that web and when properly tuned could resonate with any portion of it' (Bohm, 1980). Rupert Sheldrake's (1981) scientific research into telepathy and morphogenetic fields gives another possible description and explanation for some experiences which might be referred to as intuitive. Stories that sit in this camp are often less clearly rationalized through hindsight, as Paul's account illustrates.

Case study   **Paul**

Paul is an experienced coach who was meeting a client, Isabel, an MBA student. Paul had been working with Isabel for a year and she was nearing the end of the course and had been in high spirits. She had asked to meet with him to talk through her thesis. In the meeting, however, Paul had a sense of discomfort; 'an invisible distraction', and asked her 'is that really what you have come for?' 'Yes' was the resolute reply. Paul explains that with such a response, and with no other obvious sign that there was an alternative need, he would normally leave it at that and follow on with the client's stated objective. However, he had an extremely strong 'overpowering' feeling that he needed to push again. When he did, Isabel began to describe a family crisis that had hit the previous week and which, it turned out, was an extremely important event to discuss. Paul cannot rationalize his intense knowing with anything that he saw externally from Isabel's behaviour or body language.

Paul's confidence in trusting his own intuition is critical, particularly as there is no obvious rational explanation for his hunch. The way in which Paul then chooses to share his intuition with the coachee becomes extremely important as we explore below.

How do you use your intuition in a coaching session?

Case study   **Angela**

Angela had told me that she often draws on her intuition in her coaching. When I asked her how she uses her intuitive ability she said she uses it:

- *To assess her client's situation*, in tandem with her rational analysis, for example, she may ask herself, 'I get the feeling that the client is in this position; does that align with my rational analysis of the situation?'
- *When there is a problem* which the client may not be explicitly telling her – for example when the client feels upset or is scared. In this case Angela 'gets a sense' of incongruence in the coachee's behaviour which she cannot explain.
- *To synthesize lots of data*. Rather than trying to logically draw out each separate aspect of the coachee's complex situation, Angela actively 'asks' her intuition to sort through the complexity and has confidence that it will draw out the most relevant line of enquiry which usually emerges to her in the form of a question or an image in her mind.
- *To determine the next appropriate intervention*. Angela speaks of finding a moment of silence in a coaching session when she allows her intuition to reveal the way forward to her.
- *When she needs to react quickly*. In this instance there is no time to sort through rational analysis; Angela has the confidence to go with the clearest message that her mind and body transmit to her in the moment.

Recognizing an intuition is only the first step to using it in a coaching session. A coach then needs the confidence to do something with it which may mean sharing it explicitly with the coachee, or might mean asking certain questions in order to check it out.

The manner in which Alex and Paul communicated their hunches to their coachees was very important. They both took care in ensuring that they did not inform their coachees that they thought they had a problem! They knew, firstly that their hunches may prove misguided; and secondly that the coachee can react defensively to the coach presuming to tell them what they are thinking or feeling.

In Paul's case working with Isabel, the MBA student, the worst possible way of dealing with his hunch would have been to say 'Isabel, I don't believe you', or even worse 'I think you are lying'! Some alternative ways of voicing the hunch, depending on Paul's relationship with Isabel, might be:

- 'I hear that it is important for us to discuss your thesis. Could it be that there is something else important on your mind? If there was another matter concerning you at the moment, what would it be?'
- 'Isabel, I asked you again whether your thesis was the real reason because I have a sense that there might be another matter which is important for us to discuss. If there is anything else, I would love to help.'

In Alex's case, he asked the rowers to stop, then questions the individual by saying 'tell me how you feel, I noticed that ...' He did not say 'I think you are about to have a seizure' which might provoke anxiety in the individual and generate a defensive reaction.

Can you improve your intuitive abilities?

Do you think that people are 'born intuitive'? Or do you think you can improve your own use of intuition? Most people I have spoken with agree that everyone has access to intuitive abilities; however we may block this access in a number of ways. To find out how accessible your intuition might be ask yourself these questions:

- How confident are you in using your intuition?
- How might the context in which you coach affect your confidence in using intuition? (For example do you coach in an organization which heavily favours rationality and logic and therefore may temper overt use of your intuition?).
- How able are you to recognize intuition and separate it from your own wishful thinking and bias?
- Do you find it easy to focus and remain relaxed and present with your coachee?
- How prepared are you to wait? Intuition doesn't necessarily come on demand.
- What methods do you employ to actively learn from experience and so improve your perception and expertise over time?
- Are you comfortable using intuition as data or do you prefer specific facts and data? A proxy for this would be the Myers-Briggs Type Indicator dimension on Sensing and Intuition.

How do you improve intuition?

There are a variety of methods which can encourage our intuitive abilities; the ones you choose will depend in part upon your beliefs around how we come to have intuition in the first place (the expertise and the connection camps). The techniques developed below are categorized into three groups:

- Clearing a path for intuition.
- Learning from experience.
- Thinking differently.

The techniques in the first category are broadly aligned to the connection camp; those in the second category to the expertise camp; and those in the final category apply across both.

Clearing a path for intuition

Frances Vaughan explains 'there is nothing you can do to make intuition happen, but there is much that you can do to allow it to happen' (Vaughan, 1979).

When coaches have told me about times when they have experienced intuition they rarely tell me about times when they have been anxious, very busy and preoccupied. Often they notice that their mind is calm and quiet. They also hold a belief in intuition and therefore 'invite' it in and listen to it.

So the first step is what I call 'lowering the force field', a phrase I coined after meeting Peter.

> **Case study**   **Peter**
>
> Peter is a very experienced coach and trainer and has a particular interest in the connection between himself and his clients. When I talked to him about 'peak' moments of connection, what I call 'empathic resonance', he explained that 'when I experience empathic resonance (see Reitz, 2007), one outcome seems to be an increase in my intuitive understanding. This is brought about by lowering my force-field and being open. I tend to have this shield out in front of me to protect me – I think many people do – what I do is I turn the "dimmer switch" to lessen the field.'

To Peter, dimming the force-field was a matter of lowering his personal ego, inviting greater connection with his client, valuing and welcoming intuition in, and having the confidence to trust in his intuitive abilities.

Once the force-field is turned off, another way to clear a path for intuition is to tune out any interference. Staying with a radio analogy, I sometimes find the volume control of my own internal dialogue can get stuck on loud and make it near to impossible to sense any intuitive signals. This is where the practice of meditation can be enormously beneficial.

Michael Chaskalson is a Buddhist practitioner who, under the name Kulananda, has published a number of books on Buddhism and mindfulness. He is now a personal coach and believes that intuition can be sharpened by the practice of mindfulness meditation. He advocates a daily practice of between ten and twenty minutes to improve coaching effectiveness – and one's life – by helping to develop a more continuous awareness of what is actually going on in one's thoughts, feelings and body sensations. Michael teaches coaches to use a 'three-minute breathing space' to set themselves up before a coaching session. There are three phases to this practice, each lasting more or less one minute:

The three-minute breathing space
1. Acknowledging
Bring yourself into the present moment by deliberately adopting an upright and dignified posture. Then ask yourself: 'What is going on with me at the moment?'

Acknowledge your current experience. As best you can, accept whatever you're experiencing – in thoughts, feelings or bodily sensations – staying with these experiences for a few moments, allowing any negative feelings or experiences to be just as they are.

2. Gathering
Gently focus your full attention on your breathing. Experience fully each inbreath and each outbreath as they follow one after the other. Let the breath be an anchor to bring you into the present and to help you tune in to a state of awareness and stillness. When the mind wanders, as it will, gently bring it back to the breath.

3. Expanding awareness
Expand your awareness around the breathing to the whole body and the space it takes up. Feel your whole body breathing. Have a sense of the space around you. As best you can, hold your body sensations, feelings and thoughts in a broad awareness. Let things be, just as they are.

Regularly practising in this way, Michael argues that coaches can stay more closely attuned to their 'gut feeling', their intuitive sense of what is most significant in the constantly changing flow of the coaching situation.

Once the mind is quiet and one feels very present in the moment, another exercise which I use, inspired by John Heron, is called 'gazing' and is one way in which a coach and a coachee can experience profound levels of connectedness between them and with the environment around them, thereby often encouraging intuitive insight.

Gazing

After a period of meditation I ask a coach and coachee to sit opposite each other and close their eyes. I ask them to visualize an occasion when they felt truly connected to another person; in 'flow' with them. I ask them to visualize this in great detail and focus in particular on the physical sensations they experience when in flow. I then ask the pair to open their eyes and make gazing eye contact with each other. I ask them to hold this gaze, in silence, for about five minutes, or more if wanted. It is common initially to feel uncomfortable in this exercise; our minds often suddenly go into anxious overdrive as we are so unused to making such a deep connection with someone else. However over time, both partners usually relax into each other's gaze and I have observed deep levels of flow experience where coach and coachee feel extremely connected with a consequent deeper level of intuitive understanding between them.

Although the techniques in this section are perhaps more aligned to the connection camp view of intuition, abilities such as quietening the mind are also helpful to aid recollection of past learning, and therefore intuition via the expertise camp.

Learning from experience

You may well be familiar with David Kolb's research into the way we learn (Kolb, 1976). One inference from Kolb's work is that people learn most effectively when they touch all the bases, i.e. experiencing, reflecting, thinking and acting. So if intuition is, in part, expertise, unconscious competence or tacit knowledge, a coach can improve intuitive abilities by effectively learning from experience by taking time to reflect, think and practise application. Five methods for facilitating this learning are discussed below.

1. Journaling

Keep a journal close by to record the moments where you experience intuition. Write down what you thought and felt, and what you did with the information.

- Did you ignore it?
- Did you test it?
- Did you make a decision based upon it?
- What did you learn?

One interesting question which I have asked coaches is 'if your intuition turns out to be wrong, was it really an intuition?' Most, but not all, reply no as they believe an intuition is by definition a 'correct' insight into a situation. Regardless of your response to this question, if you felt your hunch turned out to be 'wrong', analyse why that might be the case so that over time you can build up your own awareness about your use of intuition and how it might become entangled with your own assumptions and bias.

2. Supervision
Where I work, at Ashridge, all accredited coaches must attend supervision (either individually or in a group with other coaches) with an external coach/supervisor at least quarterly (more frequent for those coaches providing a higher volume of coaching). During a supervision session you will be able to discuss your coaching experience and in turn be coached on it, hence it is strongly recommended both for the coach's learning and renewal. It is intended to be:

- Formative – developing skills, learning from others and expanding practice.
- Normative – establishing and reinforcing best practices across the group of coaches and becoming a community of best practice.
- Restorative – supporting coaches to enable them to work with very difficult issues and with people's anxiety. It should be a place to let go of difficult clients, and to unhook oneself from personal patterns or projections.

It is therefore an ideal forum for exploring intuitive experiences and learning from them.

3. Mentoring
A mentor is someone who has experienced (and therefore hopefully learnt) a great deal, and who is able to effectively share some of this learning with others. Although perhaps not as impactful as experiencing something yourself, discussions with someone who has 'been there, done that', can be very useful in building up your own expertise.

4. New situations – broaden the mind
If, as Herbert Simon claims, intuition is, in part, the mind's ability to chunk information from different experiences and then draw upon these 'chunks' as desired in new situations, then the more chunks one can file away, the more likely it is that in a new and perhaps complex situation we will be able to retrieve the chunks required to see a way through.

I find that I experience intuitive insight frequently when I am in new situations and encouraged by new learning. Given this, and given the research we have undertaken at Ashridge which indicates that successful leaders are often those who have had a diverse range of experiences, it appears that coaches who expand their variety of experiences can only aid their ability to draw on intuition when a new situation presents itself. These new experiences might be accessed through:

- Attending seminars and training workshops.
- Reading books.
- Changing your routine.
- Meeting new people.

So you could ask yourself the following:

- When was the last time you attended a talk or a workshop on something completely new to you?
- Do you tend to read very similar books or do you occasionally read something very different or critical to your own preferred view?
- If your work involves routine, for example, you always hold coaching sessions in the same place, in the same room, have you thought about altering this and seeing what happens? For example, what would it be like to conduct a coaching session outside?
- We often prefer to spend time with people who are similar to ourselves. How frequently do you get to meet new people properly outside the coaching relationship? Do you prefer to take on similar coachees? Could you benefit from widening your coaching practice?

5. Practice in simulated environments

We know that executives and coaches learn enormous amounts through experience. We also know that very few want to wait for such experience! A simulated learning environment enables participants to experience new things in a safe setting.

Case study   **The future leaders' experience**

A few years ago, Ashridge faculty members Eve Poole and Melissa Carr undertook some research with leaders asking them what critical incidents they felt were instrumental in developing their leadership career. I am continuing this research today and building up a comprehensive picture of the events that our 'future leaders' are likely to experience. We have created a simulation which contains within it many of these critical incidents. The hypothesis, which appears to be working, is that if participants experience these critical incidents in a safe environment, when they encounter similar situations in 'real' life, they are able to draw upon their experience to cope with the event more effectively; we have heard past participants explain that they 'intuitively knew what to do'.

(Continued)

In a coaching context you could practice different scenarios as part of a formal training programme, or arrange this practice yourself with colleagues.

Thinking differently

Intuition is not the opposite of rational thinking; the two are better described as closely connected twins. We often, in fact, make decisions, however apparently logical in conjunction with our intuition, in particular our felt sense of the situation. However, many people report that they find it easier to enable intuitive thought when they shift out of rational thinking (colloquially referred to as left-brain thinking, although more recent studies show that the lateralization of the brain is much more complex). This is particularly because intuition has a number of different 'voices'. The methods below enable us to think differently and to give our intuition an alternative outlet.

1. Felt sense

Many people experience intuition as a physical sensation in their body. Given that we are experiencing physical sensations all the time, it is surprising that we often don't pay them much attention. Csikszentmihalyi advises us that 'the body is like a probe full of sensitive devices that tries to obtain what information it can from the awesome reaches of space. It is through the body that we are related to one another and to the rest of the world' (Csikszentmihalyi, 2002). Try paying extra attention to how you feel during a coaching session. Journaling or discussing these feelings in supervision can then help you learn from these experiences.

2. Symbols and metaphor

If you were to describe the relationship that you have with your client as a symbol, what would it be? Why? What would it be if you described it in terms of an animal/a film/a car/another metaphor? Many coaches I have spoken to find their intuitive take on a situation through this, more creative thinking.

Case study   **Ben**

Ben was meeting Patricia for the first time. Patricia was a successful management consultant and they were discussing whether she should commit to attending a development course.

(Continued)

At the start of the conversation Ben had a sudden, vivid image come into his mind of a snake shedding its skin. He later said he was struck by just how clear the snake appeared to him. When he shared the image with Patricia she responded enthusiastically. What she had been trying to explain to Ben was that she felt like she had reached a stage in her life where she needed to shed some of her habitual ways of being and reveal a new self. The image of the snake shedding its skin was a metaphor that really summed up how she was feeling.

Images like the one Ben describes, seem to come to coaches more frequently when they are very focused on the coachee in the present moment. Again, voicing these images in an appropriate manner is important. Saying 'I see a snake' might not go down too well with a coachee you don't know well! In the instance above the coach might say 'As I listen to you talk Patricia, I have an image which comes into my mind. I would be interested to know whether this image helps to explain some of the issues you are talking through. May I share it with you?'

Complementing the use of symbols and metaphors, you could try drawing or sculpting your relationship with your client, or your client's specific issues.

3. Physical

Many people report that if they go for a walk, or do some form of physical exercise, they clear their mind sufficiently to allow in a more intuitive perspective. The healthiness of our bodies and our minds are intricately linked, and additionally, a change in environment and a forced focus on something else can give our mind the space to think differently.

4. Poetry

William Wordsworth thought that 'poetry is the spontaneous overflow of powerful feelings'. Many poets find it easier to express or make sense of an experience using poetry and through poetic language discover intuitive insight. One coach I know well regularly puts pen to paper, without any prior planning, and finds that in this way she can come to a new understanding about her experience.

5. Dreams

We have probably all at some stage tried to interpret our dreams. Certainly throughout history dreams have been lauded with amazing powers of insight. Freud and Jung explored dreams, facilitating the dreamer to interpret their dreams and make meaning from them. Whatever the level of credibility you place on dream interpretation, it is widely believed that dreams bridge unconscious and conscious processes. Given that some people think of intuition as tapping into unconscious thought, dreams may indeed be interesting to interpret. Some people believe they are able to 'seed' dreams, for example by asking themselves a question and inviting their dreams to explore the issue and inspire them. The best time for seeding dreams is that 'just wakefulness' stage in the morning when you bridge the waking and sleeping worlds.

If you want to experiment with this method, you may find it useful to have a 'dream diary' by your bed so that you are able to write down your dreams immediately on waking; dreams are notoriously difficult to remember unless you catch them by the tail before they slip away.

The shadow side of intuition

It's quite impressive isn't it when you hear that someone is 'an intuitive'? Probably most of us would like to describe ourselves as intuitive. That's in part because the word 'intuitive' has kudos. It is slightly mysterious and has a somewhat supernatural air to it. The allure of intuition in the business environment has been examined by Bonabeau and certainly some of the high profile stories he relates to intuition are impressive; George Soros' ability, for example, to sense an impending movement in the currency markets and make an enormous profit as a result. However, Bonabeau warns that intuition is seen as romantic and sexy and 'makes us feel special'. 'What better way to justify a high status – and a huge salary – than to claim the superhuman power of exceptional instinct' he says (Bonabeau, 2003). And to a degree this is a risk faced by coaches also. If someone remarks that we are intuitive, there is no doubt that our ego is massaged. This is not in itself worrying; however we need to take care of the following:

- 'Revisionism' refers to our tendency to remember clearly and talk about those times when our intuitive insight proved correct, and ignore the times when it turned out to be 'wrong'.
- It can be easy to mix up intuition with personal bias, fears and assumptions.
- If I say to a client 'my intuition is telling me that underneath everything, you are scared', there is a risk that the client feels like they must affirm due to a lack of confidence, or due to projections put onto me as 'an expert'. Our 'intuitions' then become self-fulfilling, particularly if we feel a great level of attachment towards them. These subconscious changes in behaviour resulting from a coachee's interpretation of their coach's intervention are known as 'demand characteristics'.

To help mitigate these risks associated with intuition there is no doubt that the coach needs to continually develop their own self aware-ness in relation to their use of intuition by:

- Testing out intuitions and learning from them, when they are wrong as well as when they are right.
- Checking out their intuition with the client by using careful wording, as shown in the case studies for Alex, Paul and Ben.
- Exploring in the session and in supervision how their own wishful thinking, fears, projections or transference might affect their thought processes and potentially get mistaken for intuition.

Our intuitions serve us well if we hold them lightly. But ignoring intuitions can be just as dangerous as some of the shadow elements mentioned above.

There is still so much about intuition that remains undiscovered which is perhaps why it is such a beguiling topic. However, it does seem from my own experience and from the experiences of the many coaches I have spoken to, that intuition plays a crucial role in the coaching relationship. We are capable of holding only a relatively small amount in our conscious mind. Intuition enables us to tap into our unconscious expertise as well as perhaps giving us access to a wider, collective or universal unconscious.

References

Agor, W. (1984). *Intuitive Management; Integrating Left and Right Brain Management Skills*. New York: Prentice-Hall.

Bohm, D. (1980). *Wholeness and the Implicate Order*. London: Routledge and Kegan Paul.

Bonabeau, E. (2003). Don't trust your gut. *Harvard Business Review*, **80** May, 116–23.

Csikszentmihalyi, M. (2002). *Flow*. London: Rider.

Hayashi, A. (2001). When to trust your gut. *HBR at large*, **79**(2), 59–65.

Kolb, D. A. (1976). *The Learning Styles Inventory Technical Manual*. Boston: McBer.

Reitz, M. (2007). Leading in the moment. *Ashridge*, **360,** Spring, 24–9.

Rowan, R. (1987). *The Intuitive Manager*. New York: Berkley Books.

Sadler-Smith, E. (2007). When you just know … . *The Times*, August 13, Times **2**, 4.

Sheldrake, R. (1981). *A New Science of Life: The Hypothesis of Formative Causation*. Los Angeles: Tarcher.

Simon, H. (1987). Making management decisions: the role of intuition and emotion. *Academy of Management Executive*, **1**(1), 57–64.

Vaughan, F. (1979). *Awakening Intuition*. New York: Anchor.

Chapter 6

The discovery of 'writing as inquiry' in support of coaching practice

Daniel Doherty

Introduction

'Writing as inquiry' is best understood as a method of writing in a free way that allows the writer to tap into their stream of unconscious ideas, into those thoughts and feelings that flow in all of us, just below the surface. Known also as 'free writing', 'discovery writing' or 'creative writing', the term 'writing as inquiry' was first coined by Laurel Richardson, a sociologist, who, like many of us was taught 'not to write until I knew what I wanted to say' (2005, p. 960), and who passionately believed that there was another approach to writing. Writing as inquiry takes the opposite direction to the planned approach, encouraging the writer to write into the text, to break away from the essay plan and to be prepared to be surprised and often delighted by what appears on the page. Writing as inquiry requires that you start writing before you have the slightest idea of what it is that you want to say on any given subject. The product of writing as inquiry, in the form of reflective written accounts, serves as a record of this creative endeavour and can be put to all manner of purposes as the inquirer seeks to broaden their range of reflective practice.

Within the academic world the support for the use of writing as inquiry is to be found in the work of Richardson (2005), Ellis and Bochner (1996) and other likeminded scholars. Writing as inquiry makes claims to interpretive academic validity, positioned as it is within the broader 'autoethnographic' tradition, where the researcher uses 'self as instrument' to write into personal experience and in that way attempts to make sense of the social world around them. This interpretive academic tradition includes the practice of making public one's research diary, where the account of one's researching is given equal status to that of the research product, and is sometimes offered as a parallel interpretative text. In terms of locating this practice within the field of management learning, it nests within the emergent rather than planned learning approach (Megginson, 2004).

The use of writing as inquiry is by no means confined to the world of academic inquiry. Indeed there has been a proliferation of self-help style publications over the past fifteen years or so that actively promotes the use of free-style journaling as a tool for personal development. Books with titles such as *Journal Keeping: How to Use Reflective Journals for Effective Teaching and Learning, Professional Insight and Positive Change* (Stevens and Cooper, 2008), or more simple titles such as *Restless Mind, Quiet Thoughts: A Personal Journal* (Eppinger, 1994) abound in bookshops and on internet book sites. The other internet phenomenon that chimes with this upsurge of interest in the keeping of journals is the explosion in the production of personal web-based journals or 'blogs' that invite readers in for a glimpse of certain aspects of the writer's private world, be it confessional revelations or an account of a personal development endeavour.

Writing as inquiry in support of coaching

Writing as inquiry in support of coaching relates to the practice of using free writing as an aid to coaches, coachees and also coaching supervisors in their preparation for and reflection on their coaching practice. We have found that this practice can be used to assist in development of the substantive issues and themes that arise during the course of a coaching assignment, where both the coach and the coachee take time out after a coaching session to write into their thoughts and feelings, thereafter to share (within limits of that which the writer feels it safe to disclose) these written impressions with the other party in the coaching conversation. Equally these accounts can be shared outside the coaching dyad – say, with key players in the coachee's world – to assist those involved in the issue under reflection or to understand more of the protagonist's inner reflections.

In addition to shining light on substantive themes, writing as inquiry can also be deployed by those engaged in the coaching process – including the coach's supervisor as well as the coach and the coachee – to address underlying issues relating to the coaching process. We have found that this written form of reflection upon the dynamics of the coaching process has proved to be of considerable value in surfacing the 'undiscussables' inevitably attached to coaching practice – issues such as power in the coaching relationship, or the extent to which access to the coachee's private space is volunteered or mandated – and has been valuable in ensuring that both parties to the coaching relationship engage in robust two-way contracting rather than proceeding tentatively along an uncertain coaching ground that is highly likely to exert an inhibiting effect upon open and free expression.

Our early experiments in application of writing as inquiry to coaching

Throughout the course of 2005 and beyond, Dan was engaged on two immensely steep learning curves, one relating to becoming an academic researcher, and the other to becoming an academic teacher. He chose as his mentor Ann Rippin who is an experienced reflective practitioner. Not only did she fully support the construction of his mandated 'new teacher's' reflective portfolio which was a requirement of the course, but she also joined with it in two ways. One was through asking that he write up their post learning event review conversations as learning journal entries. She then went further than this and wrote a number of pieces relating to his teaching and to their co-teaching. Dan's accounts were to prove an invaluable springboard for their coaching sessions, and her accounts as they developed this method were to further nuance and heighten these developmental conversations. In this way, they proceeded to further experiment and embed a practice that is an example of the integration of coaching and writing in practice.

Just as writing as inquiry was to enlighten Dan's development as a teacher, so too did it prove pivotal in his development as a researcher. His research supervisor was privy to his research journal, much of which in modified form was to make it into the substance of his PhD. And once again the content of the same journal was to enrich and enlighten their research conversations, to the extent that they needed only to focus in this coaching and supervision on the content of his journals, rather than to become bogged down in the detail of his research findings. They concluded that the process of writing as inquiry as a complement to face to face coaching both dramatically deepened and accelerated the coaching process, which further reinforced the belief that reflective writing and coaching practice are highly complementary one to another.[*]

---

[*]This interest in the application of writing to coaching has since manifested a number of coaching related initiatives and inquiries, including the establishment of the Critical Coaching Research Unit at the University of Bristol Management department.

The emergence of the professional requirement for reflective practice

At the same time as we were considering the power of free writing for the enhancement of coaching, we were confronted by the somewhat uncomfortable fact that while we demanded of our mid-career professional part-time masters students that they engage in reflective practice for a significant proportion of their management learning assignments, we gave little support to the development of their reflective practice skills. Some students seemed to 'get it' and took to the genre effortlessly, or at least with some practice; while others were simply a little bewildered and felt inadequate, unless by chance they stumbled across 'their voice' and stuck with it. Many of these students needed a great deal of encouragement and persuading before they felt confident to put fingers to pen or keyboard and commit their reflections to paper.

When we discussed this difficulty with them, they reflected that not only were they confronted by the need to keep reflective accounts for their masters degree work: it emerged that – driven by the publication of texts such as Donald Schön's ground breaking *Developing the Reflective Practitioner* (1982) and the trend towards the production of evidence based accounts at work – they were also increasingly required to produce reflective practice documentation for continuous professional development (CDP) by their professional accrediting bodies. This requirement proved true in particular for those in health, education and human resources, but we found that it is also increasingly being demanded in traditional disciplines such as engineering. While the advocacy of the use of reflective practice has grown in volume, the reception of the use of it among learners, and also among some educators has been mixed. Some have warmly embraced it, while others have accepted it with an inner groan. Part of the fear we heard expressed was that authentic reflective practice could descend into becoming yet another tick-box exercise, where the products are duly filed away by administrators but rarely dwelt upon in any meaningful fashion by anyone that matters. It would seem that a key to the acceptance of reflective practice is that learners and coaches/teachers feel sufficient confidence to practise and gain familiarity with this method. They also need to 'make it their own'. It is not the type of skill that can be developed through following a set of mechanistic guidelines.

Adventures with students in writing as inquiry

This realization that students needed support in developing reflective practice resulted in us offering our students, on a volunteer basis, weekend classes in reflective writing skills. Simply stated, at these writing classes we encouraged our students to practise their free writing through offering a writing prompt – such as 'something that I noticed on my way to this class was' – and thereafter encouraging them to allow the words to flow freely onto the page, without pause for thought for ten or fifteen uninterrupted minutes. We the facilitators engaged in this writing activity alongside our students. Once this intense and concentrated writing period was concluded, we then invited the students to share their pieces by reading aloud from them. We typically found that, after some initial reluctance, students took to this sharing and giving of feedback with enthusiasm. (The 'right to remain silent' should the student not want to share their text was of course sacrosanct.)

We were all surprised by what came out of our writings, remarking on the quality of writing achieved in such a short space of time which, although not the purpose of the exercise, was a pleasing byproduct all the same. We – the students and the facilitators – became progressively aware of the power of the prose as the flow of our stories gained momentum. We noticed the weaving of the interplay of thoughts, impressions and ideas that shone through our scruffy texts, and were fascinated as we listened to each other's prose to gain a glimpse into the webs of thought, into the stream of consciousness that represents our elusive inner dialogue, our moment-to-moment sense making.

When we started to write about coaching, many of our stories had an element of journeying to them. We travelled on the page, and as we travelled, so too did we find that we transported our readers with us. The descriptions of kinetic power served us well, also, where physical movement was used in our narrative as a device to capture reflections on our early experiences of cycling, walking, running, boxing, piano playing, driving a car, all of which were analogies used in our students' reflective accounts of being mentored and coached.

We talked of writing blocks, and of how we can get in our own way as writers. We alluded to the insidious, undermining role of the 'inner critic', and we reminded ourselves of the need to release the 'inner angel', to counteract this dominant critic, and to nurture the development of our product. One thing that did not work for us, we decided, was aiming for written perfection. That is not to say that perfection on the page is unattainable. But it is unlikely to occur through attempts to force it into existence. It would seem that perfection is more likely to manifest itself when we are 'in the flow', rather than trying to force it along.

We noticed how the writing stirs surprisingly deep emotions, in ourselves and others. In fact at times these feelings were so powerful that sometimes we stopped short during our writing and reciting process, hesitating, somewhat dumbstruck in the face of these emotions. But it was also clear that when we wrote through these emotional impasses, then breakthroughs occurred. There was a therapeutic quality to these breakthroughs, where we experienced a palpable sense of emotional release as the words flowed onto the page. When we became stuck in the feelings that were surfacing, one strategy that seemed to work was that of writing through the emotional material until clarity began to emerge. It proved possible to achieve a high degree of intimacy and personalization through letting things flow.

We compared the richness of this prose with the normal 'objective' standard of writing that we endeavoured to achieve for our academic pieces. We contrasted what we sometimes experience as the moribund quality of some of the academic writing that we normally encounter with the sparkling quality of these spontaneous pieces. This was not to discard academic writing wholesale, but to notice how our alternative approach was to yield such engaging prose. We learned that as much as we were developing a new type of writing, so too were we being required to unlearn how we were taught to write at school and else-where, and to liberate ourselves from old injunctions that habitually cramp our free expression even before it begins.

Some of us seemed unable to get off the hook of writing into the normal narrative convention of beginnings, middles and endings. For others it came naturally to write with less linear structure without recognizable endings or beginnings, discovering a life of perpetual middle. We reflected on what might be driving this beginning–middle–ending ritual, especially for those of us who seemed unable to move away from it, and concluded that it seemed deeply installed in our hard wiring, despite the indeterminate evidence of life to the contrary. When reflecting on travelling through our life course, we concluded that all of us need to deal with a degree of 'stuckness', of indeterminacy, of unwelcome interruption. We concluded that our lives were not all about neatly tied up three part dramas of identifiable beginnings, middles and endings. This acceptance of indeterminacy certainly challenges the notion prevalent in the way many organizations set up their approach to adult learning that it can be tied together neatly, with a bow, with learning objectives duly set and met, without encountering too many hindrances on the way.

Later reflections on the mental models that we take with us into coaching situations suggested that breaking away from beginnings, middles and endings could be an important point of departure if we were to escape the unthinking goal driven nature of some of the more mechanistic approaches to coaching. And that a reflective practice approach could be of powerful assistance to coaching dyads wishing to break away from such mental models.

Towards a critical meta-level perspective on coaching

We chose reflection on the theme of coaching as one of our writing exercises, on the basis that most of our students were touched by coaching in their professional and personal lives, and had expressed a whole range of feelings with regard to their coaching experiences. To warm up this series of written inquiries into coaching, we set the prompt 'My earliest experiences of coaching were … (finish that sentence).'. This invitation, which was deliberately vague, was subject to a wide range of interpretation of coaching, releasing insights into coaching that we believed would not have occurred if we had asked students to write a purely professional, detached view of the subject. Much of this writing was transgressive of the received managerialist view of the benefits and power of coaching, and was clearly written from the heart. It is our hypothesis that this transgressive writing stimulated a revelatory critical view of coaching that would not have emerged had we pursued a more conventional invitation to comment on coaching at work, or had we asked our students what human resources professionals' perspective on coaching might be.

This spontaneous discovery of a rich critical perspective on coaching gave rise to the exploration of the 'meta theme' of how professionals become attracted towards, and grow to accept without too much question that which is managerially fashionable and faddish. This exploration additionally exposed the related theme of the tendency of professionals towards unthinkingly seeking 'how to' solutions, without fundamentally asking the questions 'What is going on here?' and 'In what way am I being manipulated now?' We noticed that the surfacing of this subtle, unconscious process through reflective writing helped explain how professionals are so often grabbed and then trapped by shiny new management ideas in the first place, seduced by the 'how to', by getting it right, rather than asking, at a deep level, the question 'Why?'

The insights from this student based writing experiment were consistent with our own accidental stumbling upon the power of writing as inquiry, and also resonate with the theoretical findings of Ellis (1996) and Richardson (2005), but were discovered naturally, and experientially, in a learning group. These insights included discovering the power of interruptions to business as usual, of breaking away from formulaic beginnings and endings; the powerful aesthetic of weaving together thoughts and feelings past and present; and of discovering a transgressive view of the management practice of coaching through freely writing into it, rather than intellectualizing about it. We had not imposed these ideas on our students, and it was fascinating that they discovered parallel insights for themselves, and that they were eager to pursue this further through applying writing as inquiry in other domains of their lives, including in the coaching situation, both at the substantive and the processual levels.

Applying lessons learned to the coaching situation

These breakthroughs encouraged us to think more widely about the usefulness of reflective writing to coaching practice. We noticed with interest the conjunction of the institutionalization of reflective practice as a staple of CPD and coaching as the successor to packaged management training solutions which in the past were often delivered on a one size fits all training basis within organizations. (Even if this training was sensitively customized, the assumption still seemed to apply that if you needed to learn, then the way to do that was to be packed in a conference room with other managers facing broadly similar issues.) Both coaching and reflective practice seem manifestations of a trend towards personalization of learning, and of the recognition and legitimation of the learners' inner worlds in which the learners' reception of experiences is privileged every bit as much as their capacity to absorb technical skills and external competencies.

This intersection excited us, as we believe that writing as inquiry, if used judiciously, can play a vital part in the deeper development of both personal reflection and of coaching practice. One particular benefit which has emerged in our various experiments is that writing as inquiry provides a written tangible record of reflection, in a way that conversational coaching does not. This documentation need not be in the public arena for it to be of service to the learner, though there are times when the sharing of the writing can powerfully accelerate the coaching process.

The discussion of the degree to which this sharing can be demanded by the organization has provoked much reflection on our part on the extent to which it is legitimate to require the coachee to extend the private–public boundary beyond their own comfort zone. On the other hand, discovery writing can be of material assistance in finding where that public–private boundary lies in the first place, and puts the coachee in charge of the process of managing those boundaries. At a simple yet profound level, we believe that this process of written inner reflection causes the learner to take themselves and their personal experiences and deeper beliefs seriously, as seriously indeed as they take the predominant discourse of the enterprises that they inhabit.

| **Case study** | **A coachee experience of writing in support of coaching, captured through excerpts from their coaching journal** |

Oh well, here I am once more sat at the kitchen table writing my coaching journal. Strange how normal this all feels when once it felt one of the strangest activities on earth. I remember it vividly the day my coach first suggested that I try to do some 'free writing' in support of our face to face coaching work. He said that it was something that he and others had found useful, recounting that they found that it somehow really solidified the ideas and thoughts that has been floated during the coaching session, and that it also provided an interesting and durable account of that conversation. I could see what he was getting at, but I also felt it was fine for him to say that and believe it. He is probably a skilled writer, while writing is something that I would normally travel a long way to avoid. However, he is nothing if not persistent, my coach, and so it was, just a few months ago, that I first sat here contemplating putting pen to paper. I must say that it all felt quite embarrassing at first. In fact I felt almost furtive about this alien activity. After all, keeping a diary was something that I associated with angst-ridden teenage girls clutching small strangely patterned books with flimsy locks barely containing within them the deathless detail of their many unconsummated crushes. It simply did not feel like the kind of thing that I did.

I found that getting started at first was a really painful process. I recall at one point feeling virtually paralysed with pen in hand, numb to the page, until I remembered my coach giving me some 'prompts' to use in case I got stuck. So I dug these out, chose one at random, then got writing. The initial prompt that I chose was entitled:

Prompt 1: The things that I forgot to say to my coach during our last coaching session were … (finish that sentence … …).
I well remember that, after a moment's hesitation, I wrote down the prompt then launched into about twenty minutes uninterrupted writing. It was as if a veritable tsunami of responses had been released, crashing onto the beach of my virgin page in wave after wave of unbroken expression. What I found myself writing down was a scribbled record of things that I had thought about bringing up during the coaching session, but which, for one reason or another, I had held back on. In fact I wrote beside some of them the category 'things that I didn't pluck up the courage to mention', implying that I had avoided them in the coaching conversation, which was probably true. This list of shame included things that I had neglected to do; conversations at work that I had chickened out of having, even when I knew that there were issues to be faced with people that I do not find it easy to have

(Continued)

things out with; commitments to myself that I had not followed through on, and also a noting of occasions where I felt I had let myself and perhaps others down. So I wrote all of this down and do you know, when I had finally exhausted myself I cast an eye over my handiwork, and I was really quite impressed with the quality of the writing that had made it onto the page. I was expecting it to be nonsense, but it wasn't. Don't get me wrong it was by no means velvet prose, but I felt that it did the job for me, capturing the things that were on my mind with all manner of light and shade that I did not even know I was thinking. It also included feelings that had never found a conscious voice before.

Such was the impact of all of this upon me that I distinctly remember putting my writing pad down, while gazing in a dreamy way out of the window at the garden, without really seeing the garden then at all. And then, unconscious that I had made a decision to move, finding myself out in the garden itself, kicking the occasional log and caressing the odd leaf in an absent way while allowing what I had written to settle in my mind. And again, without really realizing that I had done it, there I was indoors and at the table once again, writing. It was as though a second wave of revelation was washing though me, bringing fresh perspective on the issues that I had been identifying and wrestling with during my first outpouring on the page. I found myself feeling really excited as this second wave revealed itself. There were within it nuggets of useful if un-worked through ideas and even of viable solutions to some of the tricky issues I was then facing. I even starred one or two of these ideas for immediate action.

Pleased with what was unfolding in front of me, I then decided to take things a step further forward by writing up some of the ideas and conclusions on my laptop, carefully securing it in a folder firmly labelled 'private'. Part of the reason for doing this, I told myself, was because these notes would prove really useful in the planning for my next coaching session the following week, and that keeping them on my hard drive would mean that they were easily accessible. If nothing else, I reasoned, the existence of these notes might help stiffen my resolve not to avoid mentioning issues that need facing up to during coaching next time around. Then a penny dropped. It occurred to me that instead of relying on my own wavering courage to bring some of this stuff up, why not instead send on some edited highlights to my coach, with a view to accelerating our conversation, and also to ensure that we spend our precious time addressing the issues that are big for me, rather than skirting around the interesting but probably diversionary periphery?

As I weighed the option of sending something through to my coach, I dimly remembered my coach reflecting that while our coaching conversations only occupied one hour of our time each week, that if the process

(Continued)

worked well, that the thread of these conversations should continue to play out somewhere in my awareness during the course of the intervening week. Well, this had been somewhat true in my experience, though in all honestly the pressures of deadlines and sometimes the sheer volume of decisions I have to make on a daily basis would more often than not drive out any possibility of sustained reflection time. It occurred to me that committing myself to the discipline of journaling, of writing up my coaching follow-up might just provide the means to circumvent the tyranny of the day to day.

I have noticed that as I have proceeded more deeply into my experiment with incorporating reflective writing into my coaching and learning experience, that the writing process has somehow deepened as I have become more accustomed to the writing habit. The more familiar I have become with this process, then the more it seems that my concerns for the mechanics of writing or grammar or whatever have fallen away. These have proven of lesser and lesser significance compared to my allowing some of my inner thoughts and disquiets and hopes as well as nagging anxieties to find expression in my journal. Without this expression they would not go away but instead remain in the shadows, grumbling around to God knows what undermining effect on my daily life. In fact I am not at all sure how the writing process works, but since doing it I have felt that I have somehow been more in charge of my job, and of my life. It has felt as though I am running the show, the show of my life, rather than surrendering that to someone else, to some unknown someone else.

A later journal entry, written after a particularly intense coaching session.

Gosh that was quite a coaching session, was it not? We seemed to cover so much. I feel at one and the same time empty, exhausted yet also brimming full of semi-processed ideas and suggestions. I feel a little giddy with it all. I am glad that I have gotten in the habit of doing this coaching writing as soon as I can after the session as I am possibly able, before the spell of what we have created between us is broken, before the bubble is punctured by the vibration of my Blackberry in my pocket or the flicker of the 'you have mail' prompt across my screen.

Talking of prompts, I remember my coach creating a couple of coaching prompts for me before the session ended, which might help me sort my head out. What he does now – and I find this quite intriguing – is to create customized prompts for me at the end of each session, depending on the subject matter we have covered, rather than pulling prompts that he has made earlier out of some magic coach's hat. At the time they seemed like great prompts. But do you know what, I am not quite ready for a prompt

(Continued)

yet. I need to bide my time, wait for the thought to dawn. One thing I have learned from this writing business is I need what I call a 'writing warm-up', as much as a sports person needs a warm up before they perform. I need to write this kind of gibberish to myself before I am really ready to get going. In fact I notice as I write that it is as if I am writing to someone, yet the person that I am writing this to is myself. How does that work? Is it some kind of inner chatter that I capture when I write to myself? Or is it to some unknown audience out there that I address, patiently reading and waiting for wisdom to spill onto the Basildon Bond? The funny thing is that while you can't predict when it is that you will be ready to write the real stuff, the stuff that matters, you know that moment when it comes, and then you let the real material flow, discarding by and large the writing generated during the warm up. And just as I write this I sense that that feeling, that feeling of writing the real stuff, is imminent. The kids are in bed if not asleep. Newsnight rumbles on somewhere in the background, and I know now that I have the kitchen to myself for half an hour or so. Where did I leave my list of prompts? Now is the time to pick one.

Prompt 3: 'What will happen when I get found out?'

God that is a biggie! Why did I ever pick that one out? The reason it features on the prompt list is that during the coaching session I discovered that I have a deep underlying fear that at some moment, when I least want or expect it, that I will be exposed, found out, revealed for the fake that I am. And in the revelation it would be one of those moments like in one of my recurrent dreams when you wake up in terror covering your bits because in the dream you have been exposed stark naked for all to see and giggled at in remorseless mockery. Well, the exposure I fear would be like that dream except in real time. So what is it that I actually fear being found out about? There is a list in here somewhere. I am afraid of being exposed for the fact that I skate upon thin ice financially, that shamefully enough I am not very good at adding up. I am afraid that someone somewhere will find out that last year I fired someone whom I now think, with the wisdom of hindsight, that I should have given the benefit of the doubt to. I fear someone will discover that I am in occasional unguarded conversations disloyal to my boss, even though I am fully supportive of her in meetings. Or I am exposed for the fact that while I proclaim my commitment to my family and to planning my time to ensuring work–life balance, that the truth is that most of the time, in my mind and in my actions, work actually comes first.

So what could all of that mean? What is the pattern here? How would it be if any of these things – or anything else in the seemingly endless list that I could create – what if any of these things were to be exposed? Well as

(Continued)

I think about it the reality is the consequences would be very few. So why do I make such a big deal of it? Does this fear serve me?

   You know I don't think it serves me at all. In fact I think it gets in the way. And in the future I plan to be far more mindful of it, do what I can to defend against it rather than let this fear sabotage my performance time and again. This issue needs further work with my coach now that it is out there. And maybe, just maybe, it is all far less scary than it first seemed when I first 'fessed up to it.

Implications for the coach

- You could find yourself with a different level of coachee self-awareness to deal with, so be alert to the expression of that.
- Be prepared for the session to take off in all sorts of unexpected directions.
- If you choose to go down the customizing prompts route, then be prepared to work on your feet, designing the prompts from the material generated during the session.
- If you would rather offer pre-prepared prompts, then ensure that you have a wide range of these in your toolkit.
- Do not be afraid to ask for journal material to be included in the coaching session.
- Consider keeping your own coaching journal, mirroring the reflecting that the coachee is engaging with. This may or may not be shared with the coachee, depending on your comfort levels around so doing.
- Also consider sharing your journal, or excerpts from it, with your coaching supervisor.

Implications for coachees

- Be aware that engagement with the writing process is likely to deepen your understanding of the issues you face.
- Be prepared to discover unexpected angles and insights on issues that you previously thought that you had a thorough understanding of.
- It is important to understand that this process might bring up some difficult emotional material that may at first sight appear unwelcome.
- Ensure that you commit the time to doing this journaling properly. You will find that you speed up as you grow habituated to the process.

- You should find it highly beneficial to keep a record of the coaching process; and enjoy referring to this for years to come.

Implications for coaching relationships

- The use of writing as inquiry in support of the coaching process is likely to deepen the quality of relationship
- A result of this deepening is that the coaching process could be more demanding of the relationship, and of each party's commitment to it.
- Each party keeping a journal of some sort or another is likely to bring balance to the depth of the relationship, and the degree of personal disclosure.
- It provides a written record of issues covered, which prove highly useful for historical reference.
- It is likely that the use of writing means that there will be an additional element to the contracting process, with regard to disclosures and commitment to the process.
- Both parties – in particular the coach – will need to be sensitive to the ethical implications of the use of writing, especially with regard to the protection of disclosures from either party.

Cautions about the application of the writing as inquiry approach to coaching

One caution relating to the use of writing as inquiry in coaching is that in our experience it is desirable for the participants to have some skills development in reflective practice. The organization of such skills development would need to be approached with care, and our experience suggests that convening group sessions over a number of half days is enough to allow participants to work effectively. It is worth bearing in mind that the volunteer principle was important in our experiment, which may cause difficulties in an imposed organization system. Our recommendation would be to work with volunteers in the first instance, and to notice what kind of critical mass builds from there.

A criticism of writing as inquiry and similar such reflexive approaches is to charge them with self-indulgence. The bases for these charges are fully understood, though they are well countered in the literature by Ellis and Bochner (1996), and also in Sparkes (2002). It is not our intention to rehearse those arguments here, though we would conclude that reflective writing, at its best, transcends the personally indulgent to inform issues and causes at a wider systemic and often political level, not least in giving expression to those voices that typically go unnoticed and unheard.

Concluding reflections

Even given these reservations, it was our experience of working with managers dealing with the operational realities of commissioning, managing or experiencing coaching, that a reflective exercise using free writing enabled them to scrutinize their practice in a more profound, accelerated way, than simply by conducting a standard evaluation report. Although using writing as a way into reflective practice requires some time and effort to be spent on skills training and development, we believe that these are transferable skills and would be a wise investment for any organization with a genuine wish to transform its practice.

References

Ellis, C. and Bochner, A. P. (1996). *Composing Ethnography: Alternative Forms of Qualitative Writing*. New York: Sage.

Eppinger, P. (1994). *Restless Mind, Quiet Thoughts: A Personal Journal*. San Francisco: White Clouds Press.

Megginson, D. (2004). Planned and emergent learning: consequences for development. In: Grey, C. and Antonacopoulou, E. (eds), *Essential Readings in Management Learning*. London: Sage, 91–106.

Richardson, L. (2005). Writing: a method of inquiry. In: Denzin, N. K. and Lincoln, Y. (eds), *The Sage Handbook of Qualitative Research*. Thousand Oaks, CA: Sage, 959–78.

Schön, D. (1987). *Developing the Reflective Practitioner*. San Francisco: Jossey Bass.

Sparkes, A. (2002). Autoethnography: self-indulgence or something more? In: Bochner, A. P. and Ellis, C. (eds), *Ethnographically Speaking*. Lanham, MD: Altamira.

Stevens, D. and Cooper, J. E. (2008). *Journal Keeping: How to Use Reflective Journals for Effective Teaching and Learning, Professional Insight, and Positive Change*. Vernon, VA: Stylus.

Chapter 7

Mindfulness mentoring and the listening coach

John Groom

Introduction

My son Christopher turns thirty this month. It's been a useful occasion for me to reflect back on the last thirty years, with questions around the nature of learning, the nature of coaching and the nature of mentoring. When I look at Christopher now, I realize that there are some small parts of what I have told him that he has taken on board and things that I have shown him that are now an integral part of him.

What he has learnt mostly however, through his thirty years with me, is who I am. It is disconcerting sometimes as a parent to have ourselves mirrored back through our children, warts and all.

This process has started me reflecting more specifically on what we are doing as coaches. What is it that our clients are learning from us, not just through the increasingly sophisticated techniques we are able to employ, but from the nature of our presence, the nature of our relationship with them and ultimately their sense of who we are? It started me reflecting on what I have called Mindfulness Mentoring.

What do I mean by this? Following our current thinking and literature, I will be using the term mentoring interchangeably with coaching. I have used the term 'mentoring' in the first part of this chapter not only because it has a nice ring with the word mindfulness, but more seriously, to suggest a particular quality of relationship. The quality of relationship that I am suggesting is about being centred, open, present to the moment and committed to long-term involvement. It is ultimately more of a true partnership rather than a directorship. When I turn to mindful listening I switch to using the term 'coaching'. This is because I see coaching as more goal-oriented than mentoring and thus offering a somewhat different set of challenges to a mindful approach.

Mindfulness meditation

What I am suggesting is by no means new. I'm drawing heavily on the teachings of Carl Rogers, with the well-known client-centered approach (Joseph, 2006). I am also influenced by the fact that soon after graduating I trained as a Gestalt therapist. In the American Gestalt tradition under the influence of Fritz Perls, there was an emphasis both on relationship and also challenging the client in the immediate moment of the therapeutic interaction. Later I became aware of research from the early 1980s onwards which compared many counselling and therapy approaches. It became clear that the effectiveness of therapy is not dependent purely on the specific skills, theory or nomenclature of the approach. The effectiveness of the interaction was shown to be held in the nature of the relationship.

Bringing these perspectives to the present moment and to coaching psychology I would refer you to the work of Steven Joseph in the first edition of the *International Coaching Psychology Review* (2006) where he argues strongly that the person centred approach gives us an effective meta-theoretical perspective. My own modest contribution to this area has been an article in the *Coaching Psychologist* (Groom, 2005). In its first edition I argued for the importance of effective listening. In fact I am suggesting a mindful type of listening. Instead of spending time defining mindfulness I will attempt to bring in the experience of mindfulness as this is more likely to be what you will take away from this chapter. For those of us with more of an academic bent, a definition from Steven Hayes appeals to me (Hayes, 2005) from his book *Get Out of Your Mind and Into Your Life*, where he suggests that mindfulness is to 'bring your attention more completely to your life, fully, without defence, non judgmentally, defused and accepting' (2005: 105). When applying this approach to the difficulties in our lives (e.g. our pain), Steven recommends 'learn to look at your pain rather than seeing the world from the vantage point of your pain' (2005: 105).

In some ways mindfulness is difficult to define and in some ways it's extremely easy. The child does not need to be taught mindfulness. As a very young child we live constantly in an experience of the ever present moment. There is little behind us and certainly nothing in front. We are fully aware of, if not consumed by, our feelings, sensations and our increasing thoughts.

Hayes has argued quite cogently that it is this well developed brain of ours which in fact creates many of our own psychological problems, in that we appear to be probably the only sentient being who can be aware of its own mortality. It is this capacity, ironically, that pulls us away from living in the moment.

Using mindfulness mentoring: to follow the client's focus

Recently one of my long-term mentees returned after a month. He was looking tired, ill and preoccupied. Bob is in his early fifties, and carries a responsible management position with those who work with the intellectually handicapped. He came originally from the forestry industry before he retrained as a social worker. He began the session by noticing for the first time, the two striking New Zealand abstract landscape paintings hanging on the walls of my office. (I have been seeing him for a year). His attention was drawn first to the dark abstract behind him, which we agreed captured so well some of the more malignant qualities of the New Zealand literal and figurative landscape. He was also drawn to the bright, uplifting abstract landscape on another wall.

In my early work as a coach I would have noted these things but taken them as breaking the ice and moved on to inquiring how he was progressing with his goals. Being mindful of the moment however, I simply asked him what this was saying about himself and his work. He was able then to open up two of the darker issues with staff and the board that had been clouding his perceptions. By the end of the session he came full circle and returned to his core values. He referred again to the light represented by the other abstract picture. There were moments of real contact and communion in our sharing, made possible by my providing the space for this to happen, and by being mindful of a larger meaning that was coming through.

When using mindfulness mentoring with body sensations, much of what I draw on from both counselling training and Gestalt, is about being as fully present as possible to the other. I'm listening to what people are saying while also noting their breathing patterns, facial expression, nervous ticks, moments of anxiety and their own reactions to me. In a similar way as a mentor I'm using myself as a litmus test for the things they are not able to express. In being mindful, I am mindful not only of the other, but also of myself. For example, in discussing a work issue, if I'm finding my stomach is going tight or I'm feeling a sense of heaviness in my shoulders then I reflect this back and ask if that is how they are feeling. Our own bodies, minds, thoughts and feelings became an accurate mirror of those things that the mentee is having problems articulating.

Sometimes I do work with breathing, and this is often part of working mindfully with people. New Zealand has some of the highest asthma rates in the world and similarly, fortunately for us, has some of the most advanced treatments for hyperventilation. In drawing people's attention to their breathing, I have found great recovery in many of the people I see. I use a simple technique of inviting the person to put their hand on the solar plexus and to breathe deeply and gently into that area while maintaining their awareness of their breathing. Inevitably this leads to a huge shift in the breathing itself though this is not the focus of the exercise. If people are ready, I will also introduce them to the body scan technique, inviting them to close their eyes and imagine that they are going slowly down through their body doing a scan from head to toe, and becoming aware gently and in an accepting way, of all sensations, anxieties and feelings present within the body, down through the head, thorax, abdomen and extremities. This becomes a very settling experience for people and something they can take with them into their day-to-day lives.

Mindfulness and meditation

Mindfulness is not the same as meditation, although they have often been equated in the literature. It would be very rare for me to teach formal meditation in the context of my mentoring practice. I have done this at times, but mostly I am inviting people through the techniques to be in a relationship with themselves in a way that is present to the moment. How they breathe. How they feel. How they sit. What I am inviting people to do is be in a position of observing the experience rather than of being dominated by it. I am finding my recent retraining as an ACT therapist (Acceptance, Commitment Therapy) is having a profound effect on my mentoring practice. Central to the ACT approach is the concept that, at any moment, we can be dominated by our thoughts, feelings or experiences and that each of these can in effect consume us, so that we can at worst become fused with these sensations, thoughts or feelings. ACT is the process of defusing from these into an observer position; a mindful position; even an elder, or wise person position. In this approach I sometimes use the analogy of the movie director. Most of us can relate to feeling as though we are the central player in a drama. Mindfulness mentoring is about getting the person to stand back and watch that drama from the position of the audience or the camera operator or, better still, the director or even the script writer. People have found these concepts valuable in enabling them to move on to more active or positive parts of their lives. The publications of writers such as Brantley (2003) and Eifert and Forsyth (2005) have shown it is possible to suffer from many of the symptoms of anxiety and yet with mindfulness, move beyond these into those powerful action areas for which coaching and mentoring are famous.

Implications of mindfulness mentoring for the coaching psychology practice

Steven Hayes has argued cogently that if we are to bring mindfulness approaches into our practice, it requires of us a level of personal commitment in our own lives that is not necessary with other techniques such as cognitive behavioural therapy. We are using ourselves as the therapeutic or coaching tool. We are bringing ourselves more fully into the interaction and not simply working as a technician. For example, while it is not essential for an effective mindfulness mentor to have a meditation practice, it can be a very central pillar to the work. At the end of our day, it is this personal mindfulness we bring so powerfully to our work.

I have found it invaluable to have my sessions with people well separated. In retrospect I'm appalled to realize the way that I and so many of us have attempted to work effectively with clients while working back to back. I no longer believe this to be effective or even perhaps professional. The nature of our work is deeply personal even in the more objective goal setting processes of coaching. It makes tremendous demands on us to be fully present to another person. I would suggest spacing of sessions with a half hour gap in between. This allows the clinician time to recover, time to reflect, time to write up notes adequately and time to ground themselves ready for the next person. If we are to use ourselves as an effective instrument, then the instrument needs to be well maintained.

In a similar way, if we are to work mindfully with others we need to ensure the congruence of our lives with the principles that we are teaching. For example, in coaching psychology we're often promoting balanced lifestyles. How present can we be to another if we come into the session tired or preoccupied; in other words, showing the very symptoms that we are there to help others with? Mindfulness becomes a great challenge but also a way of meeting another in a more equal way. In some recent training that I did with George Eifert he spoke of his difficulty in working with another and how important it was to remind himself that inside 'this is just another screwed up human being struggling to do the best they can; just like me'. Being this open with people may not be comfortable or even appropriate for all of us. However, it can ultimately be one of the most satisfying ways to work.

Mindful listening

… … Most of my coaching time is spent tripping over myself. I can hardly wait to explore the coachee's issues before I am rushing in to get them ready to set goals, or to analyse their lifestyle imbalance, do a cognitive checklist or evaluate their own self-care strategies. I am learning to slow down.

Was that good for you?

… … One of the things that has slowed me down is to ask at the beginning of the second session 'What did you get from our first session together?' This is a humbling experience. Those wonderful gems and precious insights that I thought I was sharing are so rarely mentioned. On the other hand a session that I thought was simply me listening and writing down a thorough summary has so often helped the person to hear themselves more deeply and to identify their own themes.

Are you in balance?

… … In Egan's wonderful book *The Skilled Helper* (2002) he argued cogently that effective helping requires a mix of empathy and action. I sometimes wonder if coaching is a response to this perceived imbalance. None of us wants to be entirely and purely understanding: it is too tiring. To be totally surrounded by tea and sympathy sounds lovely but we all strive for a challenge. Coaching is, and should be, ultimately present and future orientated and measured by its results. The main criticism that I hear of coaches and coaching programmes, however, is that they are too task-oriented and superficial. In other words we have not listened effectively enough before moving into the action stage.

If you need a friend

… … I am arguing here for a fuller, deeper kind of listening. My own Australian mentor of many years' experience summarized for me just before his retirement his own changes, 'Nowadays I follow more and lead less'. The emphasis on change can blind us to the obvious needs. Maybe the coachee just wants to be listened to and is not yet ready to change. Maybe in their hectic life this is the only place for them to 'be' and to be held.

   Maybe they lack a sense of sanctuary, are lonely or feel that there is no one there for them.

It is possible to sense all of these needs and to respond to them without going back into counselling.

If it don't fit

… … To go all the way back to Egan again, he suggested that we listen for a person's 'leverage point'. This is a key motivator, theme or concern that is brought into the sessions. When I ask what people got from our first session I am really fishing for this 'leverage point'. I might think that what I am hearing is a serious lifestyle imbalance for example. The coachee's only concern, however, is that their spouse may leave them, as they are so grumpy when they get home. I might be hearing from someone who is 'driven' and in my mind needs to 'chill out'. Their leverage point, however, is how to enjoy their work more. I sometimes think that effective coaching is like one of the gentler forms of the martial arts. We never stand against or push the other person. If they rush at things we simply point out where they might fall over. In the end it is about them standing firmly in the world.

It's up to you

… … Effective coaching does need to draw on known bodies of research and proven skills. I am simply making a plea that our focus on skills and knowledge does not stop us from recognizing the other person's deepest needs. Before I shifted over to coaching I used to do a lot of work with men having sexual performance problems. In one way it was very satisfying and important work. It is an area where there has been plenty of research and hence a client can easily be slotted into a 'programme'. It was the 'programme' that became my downfall in that it became a mechanistic exercise lacking spontaneity and relationship. These qualities – spontaneity and relationship – were of course probably the same things that the clients had missing in their lives!

The answer is 42

… … It is important in coaching that we bring ourselves fully into the relationship; that we are free to be natural and creative including a child-like ignorance. Eric Berne once exclaimed that we are on earth to explore the three big questions: Who am I? What am I doing here? Who the heck are these other people? Coaching is a great way to explore these issues. As a coach when I move away from a coaching formula and walk alongside the other person I gain a sense of wonder. Rather than being overwhelmed by their struggles, I admire their resilience. Rather than attempting to pigeon-hole them, I become genuinely curious about what their next step will be.

Take a bow

… … Being fully present to a coachee is no easy task. It requires a high degree of self-awareness, lifestyle balance, self-care and effective supervision. The rewards are great.

The two bits of feedback that I treasure the most as a coach are: 'You are like a hiking guide' and 'I didn't drive all this way to be in a room by myself'.

Conclusion

I have attempted in this brief chapter to share with you what can happen when we move into a deeper, immediate way of listening and being with a person. In moving fully into the present, we either solve our problems, or have a different perspective on our issues, so that they no longer carry the same weight for us. Coaching assumes that working through future goals with the person is of value. I am suggesting today that this is most effectively done in the context of learning to trust the wisdom of both the body and the mind without having to be purely future driven. What I am suggesting is more than simply a reminder to be client centred. It is a suggestion that we all have a wise mind that we can access by being fully present to ourselves, the other person and the relationship. Finally it is a suggestion that when we allow both of our wise minds to be fully in the relationship, moments of transcendence can take place.

References

Brantley, J. (2003). *Calming your Anxious Mind*. Oakland, CA: New Harbinger.

Egan, G. (2002). *The Skilled Helper*. Belmont, CA: Thomson.

Eifert, G. H. and Forsyth, J. P. (2005). *Acceptance and Commitment Therapy for Anxiety Disorders*. Oakland, CA: New Harbinger.

Groom, J. (2005). Effective listening. *Coaching Psychologist*, **1**, 21–2.

Hayes, S. C. (2005). *Get Out of Your Mind and Into Your Life*. Oakland, CA: New Harbinger.

Joseph, S. (2006). Person centred coaching psychology – a meta theoretical perspective. *International Coaching Psychology Review*, **1**(1), 47–54.

Mathews, A. (1988). *Being Happy – A Handbook to Greater Confidence and Security*. Singapore: Media Masters.

Chapter 8

Offering creative choices in mentoring and coaching

Vivien Whitaker

Introduction

Coaching and mentoring can involve more than dialogue. Different insights can be gained from using creative methods of working together, in addition to talking. When a person chooses coaching or mentoring as a method of self-development, they are often motivated by dissatisfaction and are seeking opportunities to take risks and do things differently. Using creative methods, if a person is not familiar with them, can be a way of initiating risk taking and offering new challenges as part of their process of self-discovery. Engaging with these methods can be a very positive way for a person to expand their current image of themselves and to recognize that they are able to be creative.

Senior executives have worked with creative methods because they haven't found what they were seeking through talking and conventional methods of coaching and mentoring. Creative methods have been successful in assisting them to access deeply held desires and almost forgotten dreams.

This sense of explorative experimentation can increase motivation.

Many people are relatively passive at work – they type, they talk and they move from meeting to meeting. 'Stretch' can be introduced into their 'comfort zone' by offering something outside of their regular pattern of activity, creating new stimulus and variety.

Creative methods tend to open up new possibilities and encourage a more expansive mode of thinking. They can be particularly useful when working with people who have difficulties in hearing, or talking.

This chapter explores:

- An explanation of creativity.
- A rationale for using creative methods.
- A method for clarifying sensory preferences and preferred modes of working.
- Nine creative techniques with supporting case studies.
- Setting creativity in context.
- Recognizing the importance of gaps in the process of creativity.
- Being comfortable with your own creativity.

Creativity

Creativity is a much sought after skill. It involves the ability to do things differently, learn from mistakes, value innovation and initiative and to view issues as problems which have a range of solutions rather than puzzles which have only one right answer.

However, many people, as a result of negative experiences in their past, believe that they are not creative. Twentieth century sculptor, Eric Gill (1996), disagrees and says that:

> Every artist may not be a special kind of person but every person is a special kind of artist.

Art does not have to be about creating something that is aesthetically pleasing. Picasso's (1956) concept of art as research and experiment is important in fashioning an appropriate context. He noted that:

> Paintings are but research and experiment. I never do a painting as a work of art. All of them are researches.

Creative activities can be uncoupled from possible early negative memories by discussing them in terms of 'research and experiment'.

Everyone has the capacity to be creative. However, our creative instincts are frequently squashed by school routines, which penalize daydreaming and oblige people to focus on 'right' answers to problems.

Epstein (2008) claims there are four key competences in becoming more creative:

1. *Capturing* – noting down ideas as they occur to you, without judgement or criticism. For example, spending a few minutes early every

morning just writing about anything that comes to mind. (The brain is still actively developing ideas while we sleep!) The mind's internal censor normally kills promising ideas because they don't fit our existing perspective, but free writing bypasses this censor.

2. *Challenging* – finding tough problems to chew over will promote new approaches and perspectives. These problems need not initially be related to an individual's specific goals – those connections are likely to emerge later.

3. *Broadening* – developing interests in lots of different areas, which need not necessarily be closely connected. The more interesting new knowledge you require, the more connections you perceive with problems that you want to solve. One practical approach is to plan an 'adventure' – a foray into new territory – once a week.

4. *Surrounding* – making the physical and social environments more stimulating. For example, finding interesting places (such as art galleries or museums) to do some quiet thinking; or having conversations with people, who have very different perspectives or jobs to yourself (DiChristina, 2008).

Offering a rationale for using creative methods

These techniques are powerful as they typically:

- Take less time than talking.
- Reveal different aspects than the spoken word.
- Assist in creating an instant overview.

Take less time than talking

Most people at work use the part of their brain that focuses on language, writing and linear thinking. These techniques take us into the creative side of our brain that thinks in pictures, views a situation holistically and explores networks and linkages.

Gladwell (2005) suggests thinking in pictures, rather than words, as our visual recall of images is quicker and easier than our recall of words.

Reveal different aspects than the spoken word

Gigerenzer (2007) argues that once we are skilled at a task, we need to stop thinking in words: that thinking too much about the processes involved can slow down and disrupt performance.

By focusing on images rather than words, we shift our attention away from logic and different information is accessed. Thinking in pictures taps into a different creative part of the brain that recognizes images, uses parallel processing and takes a holistic view of a situation.

Assist in creating an instant overview

When working under pressure, people often focus on an urgent presenting problem, without identifying all the contributing factors.

Drawing or creating a situational model of 'how things are now' can assist in seeing a situation in context, identifying interconnections. The practical laying out of the situation enables an observer to have an overview of the situation rather than being focused on any one dynamic within the issue.

If the problem outlined is one with emotional connotations, this overview can assist a person to look at their own situation more objectively, as they are literally looking at it from a distance. This process enables a person to describe a complex interpersonal situation to their coach or mentor very quickly.

Clarifying sensory preferences and preferred modes of working

Our decisions about which methods to use can be influenced by:

- Aligning the presenting problem with suitable methods.
- Clarifying the sensory preferences and preferred modes of learning of the person we are working with by examining the language they are using.

Shaw and Hawes (1998) suggest the following characterization:

- *Visually oriented learners* use phrases like 'I see what you mean', 'That looks like a good idea'. They respond well to the written word, diagrams and pictures. Methods such as visualization, solution building and drawing can be particularly helpful for visually oriented learners working in a coaching and mentoring relationship.
- *Auditorily oriented learners* use phrases like, 'That rings a bell', 'That sounds like a good idea'. They respond well to the spoken word, scenario creation and discussion. Methods such as analysing using story and metaphor, assessing alternatives and exploring rhythms of working may be particularly useful for auditorily oriented learners working in a coaching and mentoring relationship.

- *Kinaesthetically oriented learners* use phrases like 'I've got the hang of this', 'That feels right to me'. They respond well to movement, hands-on activities and design/creation activities. Methods such as analysing using situational models, working with clay and mask making (Rhodes and Whitaker, 2006), may be particularly useful for kinaesthetically oriented learners working in a coaching and mentoring relationship.

Choice can be offered by matching activity to a person's learning preference, or to the situation that needs to be explored or by deliberately moving someone out of their comfort zone and extending their skills by offering an unfamiliar activity which is not their identified learning preference.

As a coach or mentor, it is important to be aware of your own sensory preferences and modes of working. If you are not, you may find yourself subtly steering your coachee or mentee towards your preferences when the focus needs to be on *their* preferences.

Visual creative techniques

Visualization – expand and contract

Visualization can help us to slow down and focus on a particular issue.

You can assist your mentee or coachee to visualize a key issue in new ways by taking them through the following process:

1. Start by closing your eyes and feeling the pressure of your feet on the floor and of your back on the chair.
2. Become aware of other touch sensations, such as the feel of your spectacles or your watch.
3. Listen to your breathing and maybe your heartbeat. Become aware of the smells around you.
4. Open your eyes and focus on a spot immediately ahead and above you.
5. Without moving your head, increase your awareness of what you can see to the sides – your peripheral vision – but do not be distracted by things you hadn't observed before. Do the same for other points in the room.
6. Enjoy the quiet for a while.
7. Now close your eyes and visualize the issue or situation.

At this point encourage your mentee or coachee to exaggerate or minimize key elements. Ask questions like: 'Suppose that instead of having 1000 people visiting the site every day, we had 10,000 – how would we cope?' 'Instead of charging £1 an hour to park, what would happen if we charged £10?' 'What would we do if we had no acute beds at all?'

When these alternative scenarios have been explored, ask your coachee or mentee to open their eyes and discuss any insights which have arisen.

Although none of these situations may occur, thinking them through in this way could provide useful clues for risk analysis and service improvement (Clutterbuck, 2008).

Solution building

If the situation you are exploring together is unclear, solution building is a way of visualizing and engaging with it:

1. Take a large sheet of paper and draw a blank jigsaw on it. Only the outline of the pieces (20 to 30 is usually enough) is visible.
2. Ask the question: 'What do we know?'
3. For every item you do know, write a note in a piece of the outer edge of the jigsaw, gradually working inwards.
4. Ask also: 'What do we not know?' and write these items in pieces at the centre.
5. Finally, ask: 'What do we not know that we don't know?' and place any items this generates somewhere between. Assume any remaining pieces belong to this category and add colour to emphasize the differences.

In most cases, the 'do knows' will outnumber the other categories substantially, but any combination can and does occur.

Once you have completed the jigsaw, you can begin to discuss how you can change more of the picture to the colour of the 'do knows' (Clutterbuck, 2008).

Drawing

Drawing pictures helps people access creative circuits they may not normally use. Encouraging people to draw using stick figures and speech bubbles, like a cartoon, can assist in enhancing an atmosphere of experimentation and exploration.

One way to start is to ask your mentee or coachee to draw a picture that describes the situation they are in now. This sounds a simple task and it can have very interesting outcomes.

One woman was hesitant to start and asked where she should put herself in the picture. She was asked, 'How would it be if you put yourself in the middle of the picture?' Her response was that she never put herself in the middle, she was always running round after everyone else.

She chose to draw a picture that illustrated her desired situation – putting herself in the centre – and everything in her life started to change.

Identifying over-strengths

Toby Rhodes (Rhodes and Whitaker, 2006), developed the notion of 'over-strengths' – strengths that we have which we either use too much or use in an inappropriate setting. For example a management style which was effective when managing administrative staff may not be appropriate in a different role where someone has been promoted to manage a team of professionals.

Over-strengths can be identified by creating a Strengths Bulls Eye.

Strengths bulls eye

1. Using a strengths bulls eye (see Figure 8.1) on flipchart paper, ask your mentee or coachee to start in the centre brainstorming their strengths and noting them down in the central circle.
2. Then ask them to gain feedback on their strengths from other people they work with, and put this in the second circle.
3. Discuss these findings, recognizing and valuing these strengths and explore how to build on them.

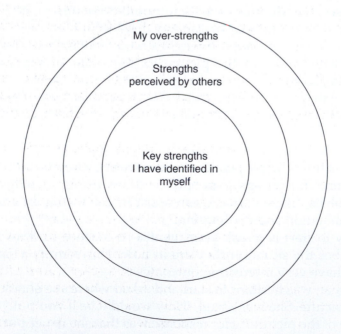

Figure 8.1 Strengths bulls eye.

4. Then ask whether any of the strengths identified could be over-strengths, e.g. over-conscientious – always striving for perfection, over-sensitive – taking professional feedback personally, over-managing – micromanaging competent professionals. Allow time for the person to consider this notion and to note down their over-strengths in the outer column.
5. Explore ways to rebalance over-strengths so they are used less often and more appropriately.
6. Suggest that they put their strengths bulls-eye in a place where they can see it regularly to remind them to build on their strengths and adjust their over-strengths.

Case study   **Drawing over-strengths**

Karen enjoyed identifying her strengths using the strengths bulls eye and was delighted by the feedback she had got from others. She knew she had over-strengths but was having difficulty identifying them. She was encouraged to draw on a large sheet of flipchart paper.

The image that emerged had a large red 'kiss me quick' smile in the centre with two great big hands coming from each side of the smile.

It brought tears to her eyes. This was her over-caring, over-helpful, over-guilty self.

She resolved to let go of guilt from her early religious upbringing, recognize that her views on family life were different from her parents'. She decided to learn to say no more often at work and create more 'me time' to nurture herself.

Auditory creative techniques

Stories are powerful creative tools, because they can touch our deepest emotions. Using metaphor or stories, for example, to illustrate a particular situation can elicit different information than merely describing it. If a person explains their situation at work as feeling 'like I am being crucified', the listener is quickly aware of the seriousness and pain involved in their situation.

Using metaphor, comparing one thing to another, and looking at the commonalities and differences can enrich our understanding of a situation. A metaphor or story can be identified by a coachee or mentee, for example, a battlefield, round the world yacht race or the ugly duckling. Together, the mentor and mentee can explore the issue, in the context of the metaphor. What happened, for example, to the ugly duckling's family? How did the experience affect the way he dealt with ducks and his peer swans after his transformation?

When we do this, we need to be aware of cultural differences in interpretation of metaphor. For example, in British culture comparing a man to a lion is often a positive comparison, implying courage and leadership; in other cultures lions are not perceived positively.

Terminology may also need to be clarified. When working in Istanbul recently I was made aware that they have very few roundabouts and that they referred to them as 'traffic circles'.

Creating new stories – starting from somewhere else

The yokel's comment to the lost driver 'If I were going there, I wouldn't have started from here' has a lot of resonance with real problems people face. History creates a lot of baggage that suppresses creativity – reasons why things can't be done differently.

So, encourage your coachee or mentee to invent a different story about their issue – one with a different starting point, perhaps a 'green field site' or a 'radically different architecture'.

Ask them, if they were in this different story, starting from somewhere else, what would they be doing differently? Once they have listed these differences, encourage them to think creatively about how these approaches might be adapted to overcome some of the constraints they are subject to in their world (Clutterbuck, 2008).

Assessing alternatives

Another way to look at issues as problems which have a range of solutions rather than puzzles with one right answer, is to explore different possibilities through structured verbal brainstorming.

SCAMPER
SCAMPER is a simple menu of creative perspectives to draw upon. It is an acronym for:

Substitute
Combine
Adapt
Maximize/Minimize
Put to other uses
Eliminate (Elaborate)
Reverse (or Rearrange).

Assist your coach or mentee to look at a range of possible solutions to an issue by discussing each of the SCAMPER possibilities with them.

Then switch to a discussion of how to adapt ideas raised to make them work in this context (Clutterbuck, 2008).

Becoming aware of different rhythms

Gabriel Roth (1990) has noticed that there are five basic rhythms of life, which form a wave, and that these are present in everything we do (see Figure 8.2). Knowledge of these rhythms can help us to become more aware of ourselves and the people we work with (Whitaker, 1996).

The Wave of Five Rhythms
1. Flowing Continuous graceful movement – think of a flowing river or a swirling wind. It is purposeful and co-ordinated, yet smooth and strong – focused uninterrupted work
2. Staccato Crisp, building and angular – a faster movement, increasing energy and getting things done – the rhythm of meeting deadlines
3. Chaos High energy, creative, top of the wave – encouraging thinking in random, original patterns – the rhythm of brainstorming, synergistic team work and individual creativity
4. Lyrical Light, expressive, laughter – the rhythm of humour and appreciation – often undervalued and under-used in organizations
5. Moving stillness Reflective, introspective, gentle – the rhythm of completion – 'wash–ups' at the end of projects – reflect on successes, identify what to do differently next time, drawing back to the centre

Figure 8.2   The wave of five rhythms (Whitaker adapted from Roth, 1990).

Research (Whitaker, 1996) has shown that we each tend to have a preferred rhythm/s which can be different from the people we work with. Assisting your coachee or mentee to identify their preferred rhythms and then diagnosing the rhythms of people they work with can provide helpful insights.

Case study   Rhythms

Richard loved chamber music and was fascinated by Gabriel Roth's Wave of Five Rhythms. He spent some time observing his colleagues in the arts organization he worked in.

(Continued)

He could identify with most of the team whose preferred rhythms were staccato and chaos. Then he had an 'Ah-ha' moment. He noticed that their director actively disliked these rhythms and withdrew to his office or to work at home. His colleagues thought that he was 'bunking off'; Richard recognized that the director had a different preferred rhythm – he thought 'moving stillness' and that he could only work at his best away from his colleagues.

When he mentioned this at a team meeting, it opened up a helpful dialogue which improved communication and working together.

Richard also reflected on his own 'wave of rhythms'. He noticed that he went through a wave of rhythms at work and then started a new wave when he went home and often found that he couldn't sleep.

He chose to change his ways so that the pattern of his day followed a single wave, focusing more on lyrical activities in the evening, moving into gentle activity before he went to bed and found that he slept much better and felt much more energized the next day.

Kinaesthetic creative techniques

Letting go using situational models

> Excess baggage *creates* Old Habits *cause* Bad Experiences

Situational modelling (Whitaker, 1998) is an appropriate method to use when we are helping people to surface assumptions and behaviours which hinder their success – what I term 'excess baggage'. It involves creating a kinaesthetic model of a situation which is either presenting challenges or needing further exploration.

Your coachee or mentee can literally 'get to grips' with these difficulties by engaging in this exercise developed by Sue Blow (personal communication).

When a mentee or coachee has issues or memories that they need to let go of, Sue offers them a pile of different sized rocks. She encourages them to select rocks which represent the different presenting issues – the weight of the rocks indicating the current importance of the issue.

Each rock is varnished with a 'wipe clean' surface so that coachees can write their issues on them in a water soluble pen.

The rocks are then put in a rucksack which the mentee or coachee puts on their back.

After feeling the weight of the load, they are encouraged to empty out the rocks and talk about how they could lighten their load by resolving and letting go of some of the issues/rocks. If they want to keep rocks Sue recommends:

> Really dig into why the coachee wants to keep it … because at some level there must be a reluctance to let it go or they would already have done something about it! So, if someone has said "I am a rotten time manager" … what is it about thinking of yourself as "poor at time management" *does* for you? How does this label protect you?

This technique of tracking back the 'old habits' to reveal the 'excess baggage' and letting go of this can prevent 'bad experiences' recurring in the future.

Working with clay

Air dried clay is non-messy and easy to use. It can be used as a three-dimensional way of setting out 'how things are now' and 'how they could be in the future'. It is helpful in shaping images of metaphors of situations, for example creating a sunflower that moves in response to the sun.

It has the advantage that these creations can be easily destroyed, if there is a need to let go of them, or alternatively, they can be allowed to dry and become visual reminders, encouraging moving into the future.

Focusing the senses

One way for a coachee or mentee to surface new ideas is to work with clay blindfold.

1. Set out a board and some clay; a plastic apron can also be helpful as this can get messy.
2. Talk through a relaxation technique, taking the person back to a memory of a place where they felt creative (often back to childhood).
3. Put their blindfold on and let them play with the clay for ten minutes without a fixed idea of what they want to create. Remind them that they are researching and experimenting not trying to create beautiful things.
4. After 10 minutes, take the blindfold off and without any comment or dialogue encourage them to write about their experience with their non-dominant hand (pencils tend to be easier than pens).
5. After 5 minutes, or when they have finished, ask them to share the results.
6. Remember to keep in 'research and experiment' mode as you discuss the experience. It is not your role to judge what they have created.

Being blindfold helps focus the concentration of the senses on the hands and can also reduce our critical/judging response.

Having a mirror on hand can be helpful as sometimes a person's non-dominant hand will do 'reverse writing' – which can only be seen through a mirror. Writing with the non-dominant hand accesses a part of the brain which can surface new information or old ideas we had forgotten.

Mask making

Making and wearing masks assists us to be more aware of the metaphorical 'masks' we put on during our professional life.

Toby Rhodes and I (2006) have found that making masks to represent aspects of ourselves is a very accessible metaphor, through which a coachee or mentee can make both immediate and obvious connections. It also enables deeper insights to be gained, through reflection and feedback.

Using masks in our mentoring practice provides us with a powerful metaphorical tool for two key reasons:

1. We are conditioned to have powerful emotional responses to faces.
2. The masks people make can be transient, malleable or changeable – not only can they be used as metaphors for some aspect of ourselves, but they can be transformed into different metaphors.

The power and potential of masks are great but mask sessions need to be planned carefully and coachees or mentees given choice about using this method. We would only recommend their use to experienced mentors or coaches who have the knowledge to handle dark-side aspects that may emerge.

Advantages
- Accessibility
- Application to real life/work issues
- Flexibility
- Depth
- 'Hands on', practical task
- Enables physical transformation (of mask) as a metaphor for visualizing future behaviour.

Potential pitfalls
- Care needed with process: it is important to structure this experience so that there is an appropriate focus, with reflection and feedback time included.
- Can open a 'can of worms' (care is needed as it's easy to go into deep areas of self very quickly).
- Need resources and private space to be messy in.
- Challenging (especially to those not used to creative processes).
- Can be perceived to be superficial or too deep/scary.

More information on using masks protocols can be gained from Rhodes and Whitaker (2006).

When used as a tool in mentoring, masks can lead learners to a place that just talking does not reach and can help to develop a deeper understanding of themselves and their potential.

Case study   **Mr Happy**

Mark had opted into his organization's mentoring scheme as he had just been promoted to be leader of a team where he was previously a team member. He knew he needed to change his leadership style but hadn't thought through how he could do this.

He enjoyed doing things with his hands so wanted to experiment with mask making.

His first task was to make a mask of his current leadership style. His mask had a big open smiley mouth, rays of sun coming from his eyes, topped with 'just out of bed' rumpled hair. He called it 'Mr Happy' as he maintained a happy 'work-self' at all times, even if he had family problems or was feeling ill.

Rather than create a second mask for how he wanted his leadership style to develop, Mark chose to amend 'Mr Happy'.

Mark called his amended mask 'Mr Approachable'. He still had rays of sun coming from his eyes, but his mouth was more closed and his ears were bigger, signifying that he wanted to say less and listen more. His hair was smoothed down indicating he wanted to improve his time management and become more organized. There was also a tear coming from one eye, showing that he wanted to be more authentic and honest about how he was feeling to encourage his staff to be open and honest with him.

Mark was impressed that he had learned so much about himself in 45 minutes. The rest of the session focused on the practical things he needed to do differently to make the change happen.

At the end of the session, Mark took 'Mr Approachable' and hung him by his desk, to remind himself about how he wanted to lead his new team.

Setting creativity in context

Creativity is within all of us, all of the time. A benefit of using these creative methods is that they can expand the way people use their brains in their day-to-day work as well as in mentoring and coaching sessions.

Whilst acknowledging the skills the mentor or coach needs in order to engage with these methods, being low key and relaxed about introducing these ways of working can be important. To make a big deal about a creativity session and prepare for it in special ways could suggest that we can only access our creativity at certain times or under specific conditions.

Recognizing the importance of gaps in the process of creativity

David Rock (2008) reminds us that our conscious brain is only 4% of our total brain capacity. Solutions and insights can arise between sessions so it can be interesting to start the next session by asking whether there have been any 'Ah-ha' moments since the two of you last met.

Fear of failure can be a significant block to creativity. Replacing fear of failure with anticipation of discovery provides a more positive basis for creative thinking. David Clutterbuck (2008) encourages his coachees and mentees to experiment with creative techniques between sessions. He advises:

- Give yourself permission to be creative, to be silly, to silence the inner voice that tells you how things *should* be. Remind yourself that reality is an illusion our minds create by ignoring most of the information available to them.
- Express belief in the ability of you and your colleagues to be creative.
- Take short creativity breaks of five or ten minutes at ad hoc times.
- Maintain a diary or log of crazy ideas. You'll be amazed at how many of these can be adapted and used in some way, in due course.
- Let go of limits – it's easy to put boundaries on our creative thinking by limiting our expectation of the volume of new ideas we might generate.
- Tap into the hypnagogic state – the point between being awake and being asleep – it is a powerful source of creative ideas. Many people have their best ideas as they wake in the morning. However, highly creative people, such as Salvador Dali and Thomas Edison also used the point just *before* falling asleep. Dali, for example, is reported to have held a spoon loosely in his hand as he relaxed. When he dosed off, the spoon fell onto a metal plate, which woke him and he would sketch the images that had come to him in the semi-conscious state.
- Don't expect instant revelations every time. Some issues require a number of attempts, perhaps using different techniques, with time built in over days or weeks for people's subconscious minds to work on the problem. It's a bit like doing a hard, cryptic cross-word – what stumped you in the evening often appears obvious the next morning. Most really creative, big ideas percolate over time – the eureka moment usually comes after a lot of bouts of thinking round an issue.

Feeling comfortable with your own creativity

If you are planning to use these methods, it is important that you try them out on yourself and feel entirely comfortable with them, before you use them as part of a coaching or mentoring intervention. Peer mentoring or coaching sessions can be a great opportunity to explore your own creativity in more depth and to develop confidence in using these methods.

References

Clutterbuck, D. (2008). *Creativity Toolkit*. Unpublished paper.

DiChristina, M. (2008). Let your creativity soar. *Scientific American Mind*, June/July, 24–32.

Epstein, R. (2008), in DiChristina, M. (2008).

Gigerenzer, G. (2007). *Gut Feelings: The Intelligence of the Unconscious*. London: Penguin.

Gill, E., quoted in Cameron, J. (1996). *Vein of Gold*. New York: Putnam Press.

Gladwell, M. (2005). *Blink: The Power of Thinking Without Thinking*. London: Penguin.

Picasso, P. (1956). *Vogue*, 1 November.

Rhodes, T. and Whitaker, V. (2006). http://www.learnforever.co.uk/articles/ The_ Masks_of_Mentoring. Accessed 14.3.08.

Rock, D. (2008). Keynote speech: European Mentoring & Coaching Council UK Conference.

Roth, G. (1990). *Maps to Ecstasy*. London: Mandala.

Shaw, S. and Hawes, T. (1998). *Effective Teaching and Learning in the Primary Classroom: A Practical Guide to Brain Compatible Learning*. London: Optimal Learning.

Whitaker, V. (1996). The rhythms of organizational life. *Organizations & People*, **3**(1), 23–5.

Whitaker, V. (1998). The holistic manager. In: Lock, D. (ed.), *The Gower Handbook of Management*. Aldershot: Gower.

Chapter 9

Techniques for coaching teams

David Clutterbuck

One of the robust dialogues (debates sometimes, if we're honest) between the authors is over whether there is such a thing as team coaching in the workplace. Certainly, you won't find much in either the academic or practitioner literature on the subject. Although a surprising number of websites claim to offer team coaching, when one of us analysed what was provided from a sample of 30, he found that almost all were actually using the term to describe some form of team building or team facilitation. However, he also found a small number of organizations, which clearly were applying coaching principles to collective learning. The common characteristics of these approaches were that:

- They focused learning around collective, shared goals.
- They involved learning conversations where the sense of direction was always emergent (unlike facilitation, for example, where the facilitator leads the conversation along planned routes).
- They were aimed more at working with and changing team dynamics than simply understanding them; hence the level of engagement between the team and the coach was much higher than would normally be the case in facilitation.
- They saw team coaching as much more than helping the team towards insights into problems, or resolving a single issue; rather, it was about using the resolution of discrete issues to develop the team's competence to tackle similar situations in the future. The outcome of the team coaching process was enhanced collective self-coaching capability.

On the basis that if it looks, sounds and feels like coaching, it probably is coaching, and that there are strong parallels for team coaching in the world of sport (although it can be very dangerous to make direct analogies), it is pragmatic to recognize that team coaching at work is a concept that is here to stay.

Coaching teams is much more complex than coaching individuals, however, for a whole raft of reasons:

- Confidentiality – people may be reluctant to admit in front of colleagues what they would say one to one.
- Pace of thinking and decision making – people work through problems and concepts at different speeds. Going at the pace of the slowest person may frustrate faster, or less reflective thinkers; letting the fast thinkers set the pace will leave colleagues frustrated and feeling railroaded.
- Power differentials: both between the team and its manager and between subgroups and individuals within the team.

Team coaches in the world of employment come in several varieties. The most common are:

- Team leader as coach – first among equals, like the captain in a sports team, who is expected to support the development of colleagues, particularly as a *skills coach*.
- Team manager as coach – like the manager of a football team, on the touchline, not part of the workflow, so able to take a more objective perspective (but also likely to be under different pressures from above), particularly as a *performance coach*.
- Internal team coach – 'in the stands' to continue the sports analogy, typically an HR specialist, who may combine the roles of performance coach and behavioural coaching, with the emphasis on what Hawkins and Smith (2006) would call developmental coaching.
- External team coach – 'not even at the game', an outsider, who has the skills to stimulate deep personal insight and change (what Hawkins and Smith describe as transformational coaching).

Our collection of team coaching techniques includes some from David Clutterbuck's book *Coaching the Team at Work* (2007) and some that have emerged from team coaching skills workshops. We have selected here techniques relating to five issues that provide a basic toolkit for approaching team coaching. These issues are:

- Goals, vision and purpose
- Functional analysis
- Managing interpersonal relationships
- Temporal issues
- The team development plan.

Goals, vision and purpose

Helping teams work out what they are there for is one of the most common team coaching assignments. There are many good reasons why teams are so often befuddled and in disagreement about goals. For example:

- Goals set to provide an anchor point in uncertainty tend rapidly to become irrelevant, yet people are reluctant to let them go, in the absence of obvious alternatives (which may require much deeper and more creative thinking).
- Members of top teams, in particular, find it difficult to separate out their collective responsibilities and aspirations from those relating to their function or department.
- People are simply too busy doing the business to reflect deeply on what and why. Strategic away-days become like annual appraisals – a periodic self-flagellation to be got out of the way as soon as possible. Effective strategic planning, where goals are re-examined and refined, takes place continuously; away-days are then simply opportunities to consolidate what is already in train.
- New project teams tend to be impatient to get on with the task. Studies by Connie Gersick (1988) show that these teams are typically ready to step back and reflect on purpose some way into their life-cycle, rather than at the beginning.
- Many teams are simply teams in name. They have few of the characteristics of a genuine team. Unless the members want to behave like a team, and are prepared to let go of personal priorities, they will not be able to develop shared purpose.

The two first questions any team coach is likely to ask of a new assignment, therefore, are: 'Is this actually a team, or a pretend-team?' and 'How closely aligned are they around the team purpose and goals?' If it isn't a team, the assignment begins with dialogue around whether they want to become one, and the benefits of doing so. If the answer is yes, then establishing a collective and explicit sense of purpose is a good starting point.

The alignment matrix

Overt or covert, conflict about team goals undermines the performance of many teams. We address the three types of team conflict (relationship, task and process) later in this chapter. We deal with the *alignment matrix* here because it is a tool to prevent conflict, specifically in the context of goal management.

	High alignment on what we want	Low alignment on what we want
High alignment on how to achieve our goals	High collective performance, positive conflict	Focus on individual performance
Low alignment on how to achieve our goals	Sub-teams dominate	Disruptive conflict leads to low collective performance

Figure 9.1   The alignment matrix.

As Figure 9.1 shows, high alignment within the team on both what they are trying to achieve and how they aim to achieve it leads to high collective performance. Each of the other alternatives leads to severe underperformance.

The team coach's role is to help the team explore just how much alignment they have and how they are going to deal with any differences or conflict of expectations that emerge.

Case study   Aligning the team's perspectives

The top team of a large public sector organization was about to publish its long-term strategic plan. The coaching question was: 'We have agreed upon the words, but how aligned are we on what they mean?' Working with other stakeholders, the coach was able to identify a series of statements, where there might be differences of interpretation and to express these as pairs of alternatives. In some cases, the difference related to the goal itself; in others to how it was to be pursued. He and the team then examined each pair to determine which interpretation they agreed with. With more than half of the statements, there was little or no disagreement. But in the rest there were strongly held opposite views.

The coach's question 'What is your team process for resolving this kind of disagreement?' pushed the responsibility for resolving the issue back to the team. With relatively little help from the coach, other than to emphasize the need for consensus rather than compromise, they discussed each statement in turn. On only two items was there still a significant gap in interpretation and for these they agreed that the chief executive should make the decision, to which they would collectively agree. The coaching session concluded with a review of how they would ensure in future that they surfaced these kind of disagreements earlier (it had been a lot easier not to rock the boat, but the results of different messages from the directors would have been very damaging) and resolved them, as part of their day-to-day interactions.

The team in question was a high functioning, highly motivated executive group. It's much more common for coaches to be faced with teams that have much less idea of what they are trying to achieve and why.

Functional analysis

Even if a team knows where it is heading, it may have only a vague perception of what it actually does, or should be doing, to take it there. The more varied the tasks and the more strategic the role, the more difficult it can be to tie down team function with precision.

The matrix in Figure 9.2 is one pragmatic way to help the team analyse what it does. Effective teams have both internal and external foci which they manage and where they need to maintain an appropriate balance. They also distinguish between key tasks (what they are there to do) and support or maintenance tasks, which are enablers to the key tasks. The appropriate division of effort and time between key and support tasks will vary with circumstance, but many teams are working suboptimally because they have the balance wrong between these.

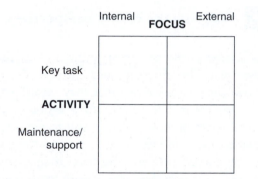

Figure 9.2   Activity diagnosis.

The role of the team coach in this dialogue can be more or less proactive, depending on the team's level of insight into its own processes. It's not unusual to find teams where more than half of the time and effort goes into support tasks. That isn't necessarily a bad thing if, for example, the key tasks involve some kind of emergency response. The coach isn't there to make judgements on the right mix; simply to help the team draw its own insights from the analyses it makes.

Managing interpersonal relationships

Collaboration, in an atmosphere of mutual respect and goodwill, is at the core of all effective teamwork. Psychological safety – the perception of team members that they can raise concerns and be listened to, can admit mistakes without being punished and can be generally open towards colleagues and leaders – is closely associated with both quality and quantity of learning and with performance (Edmondson, 1999). However, the coach's role is about more than helping people get along with each other; it is about helping them develop the capacity to achieve more by being more effective in the way they work together. The scope of coaching intervention therefore includes:

- The norms of behaviour.
- How people communicate within the team and to outsiders.
- How they learn together.
- How they cope with setbacks and disappointments.
- How they recognize and manage conflict.

We have chosen just two areas to explore here, although it is probably the areas in which team coaches have the greatest choice of technique and approach.

Building a positive team attitude

An approach from solutions-focused consultancy is for each subgroup within a team to decide upon a number of things they will do to make things easier for other members of the team, either individually or collectively. They put these into action, but *without informing the rest of the team what the intended changes are*. Each sub-group or individual member also commits to look for and thank or compliment their colleagues for positive changes they become aware of. In practice, the positive actions that get noticed are often much wider than those within the exercise. This reinforces mutual positive regard and encourages yet further positive behavioural and/or process change.

Conflict management

Conflict within a team isn't always negative. It depends on what the conflict is about and on the processes the team uses to bring conflict to the surface and resolve it. In general, the more diverse a team, the greater the potential for conflict, but the higher the potential for creativity. The most productive and effective teams appear to be ones where there is high diversity, but where members have developed robust yet sensitive ways of managing conflict. (Early and Mosakowski, 2000.)

Conflict appears to come in three varieties: relationship conflict (e.g. personality clashes), which is almost always negative in impact; task conflict (how the team task should be done), which may be positive or negative; and process conflict (how duties and resources are allocated), which may also be positive or negative. Key questions for a team coach to ask are:

- What kinds of conflict do we have in this team?
- What are our processes for surfacing conflict?
- What are our processes for ensuring that task and process conflict lead to positive outcomes and greater team cohesion?
- What are our processes for ensuring that relationship conflict is addressed and resolved?

One of the most useful techniques we have built on in our team coaching work is 'fault free conflict management'. This simple, four-step process is particularly relevant to teams where there is substantial conflict and/or where unresolved task or process conflict have given rise to relationship conflict. The four stages are:

1. Reconfirm the positive. The coach helps the team to articulate areas of agreement, using questions such as:
    (i) What do you violently agree upon?
    (ii) Are you prepared to accept that each of you is acting with goodwill?
    (iii) Are we looking for broadly the same outcome?
    (iv) What do you respect the other party for?
    Important in this stage is that no one is allowed to be negative, or accusatory.
2. Fault-free task analysis. Still maintaining the rule of no blame, the coach encourages each team member in turn to explain what they are trying to achieve and why; what's preventing them from achieving it (but not assigning blame to anyone else); the implications for key stakeholders and for achieving the team goals.
3. Fault-free emotional analysis. Up until now, the intention has been to maintain the dialogue at a rational level. But conflict is as much and more about emotion. This is the point at which the coach encourages everyone to talk about how they feel (generally and at the moment) and how they would like to feel. What would enable them to change how they felt? In this way, the emotional content of the conflict is released, yet bounded by the continued avoidance of blame.
4. Solution generation. It's easy at this stage to relapse back into 'you've created a rod for your own back' confrontations. So the coach asks

each member of the team in turn to offer at least one action they can take individually, that will help someone from the other side of the conflict divide with what they are trying to do and how they want to feel, and one thing the team could do collectively.

Ensuring the team sticks to the rules isn't easy, especially if they have become habituated to more negative forms of conversation. Sometimes the coach has to be quite tough in reminding people about the contract they have entered into in this exercise. With persistence, however, the team not only resolves specific conflicts, but absorbs the process and behaviours that will allow it to address future conflict at a much earlier stage.

Temporal issues

There is a whole raft of team issues relating to time – from basic time management, through how/whether people distinguish between personal time and work time, to variations in cultural perspectives on time (do people usually see events as following one after another, or as happening in parallel? – Hampden-Turner and Trompenaars, 1997). Here we have chosen to explore just one: time orientation.

Recognizing a team's time orientation is an important part of understanding its perspectives on the issues it faces. People tend to place more emphasis on one time horizon than others – past, near past, present, near future and distant future – in how they interpret what is happening around them and how they make decisions. Their time orientation may be in sync with that of their organization and/or their environment, or it may not. There may be close alignment between team colleagues on the emphasis of their time orientation, or there may not. If they are closely in sync, there is a danger of groupthink within the team; if they are out of sync, there is likely to be overt or hidden conflict. Being aware of time orientation and managing it appropriately is important in focusing the team's attention where it will add most value to the organization.

People and teams, who have strong preference for the present, tend to be action-oriented and pragmatic. They may dismiss what happened in the past as irrelevant and just history. And they may struggle to look at the bigger picture and longer timescales. People and teams who have a strong preference for future thinking may have great skills at visioning, but be seen by colleagues as impractical and lacking in action. People and teams who are emotionally tied to the past may equally be seen as having closed minds with regard to innovation. Near past and near future domination may be associated with constant crisis management.

The team coach can help by:

- Initiating a dialogue to raise awareness of the team's collective and individual time orientation.
- Focusing attention on those time horizons, which they use least, with the aim of stimulating them to adopt a more balanced, multi-temporal perspective on issues.

Useful questions to help the team consider these issues include:

- When you need to illustrate a point, where do you turn to for examples?
- How often do you respond to a new idea with 'We tried that and it didn't work'?
- List the 10–20 most important issues for you right now, and the 10–20 most urgent. Classify each list according to:
  - Where they originate
  - When would be (have been) the best time to address and resolve them.
- What do you regret and why? What is the likelihood of making the same mistakes again?
- How much of team meetings is spent on the past, near past, present, near future and future?
- How much value do you place on:
  - Experience v. innovation [past v. future]
  - Stability v. change [present v. future]
  - Action v. reflection [near future v. future]
  - Tactics v. strategy [near future v. future]
  - Embedding existing initiatives (good endings) v. launching new initiatives (good beginnings) [present v. near future]
  - Resolving conflict v. preventing conflict [present v. near future].
- How clear is the continuum between past and future?
- How well do you apply lessons of the past to the present?
- How well do you apply visions of the future to achieve change in the present and near future?

Building a team development plan

A team development plan is the link between the business plan and personal development plans. It aligns individual and collective learning for the benefit of the team task and the team members. It helps determine:

- What skills and knowledge the team requires to perform excellently in the working environment now and as it is projected to be in 12 months' (or whatever time frame) time.

- Skills and knowledge all team members therefore need to acquire.
- Skills and knowledge which can be brought in from outside the team.
- Skills and knowledge which are needed by only some members.
- Opportunities for sharing learning, or for being co-coached.

Few teams, in our experience, do more than a perfunctory job of creating the team learning plan. Yet it is an essential element in creating a coaching microclimate. It makes everyone in the team responsible not just for their personal development, but for the development of each of their colleagues, including the team leader. It also helps the coach contextualize task-focused goals, such as 'deliver this project on time and to budget', and to help the team balance those task goals with goals relating to learning and behaviour. The result, in theory at least and more often than not in practice, is that the team becomes more rounded, more resilient and more able to reflect purposefully.

We haven't included any templates for creating the team development plan – each situation is different and we have no evidence that any particular coaching approach is more effective than others in this respect. The key appears to be to make the team aware of the need for and value in having a team development plan and initiating dialogue around how to achieve one. Reported one team coach: 'Once they understood the possibilities in managing their development collectively, they became so engrossed in the idea that they forgot I was there. After a while, I left the table and sat quietly at the back of the room. More than an hour later, with the walls covered with Post-its, they invited me to be a sounding board for what they had decided so far. I asked a few questions, which set them off again. The MD [the team leader] told me later that this was the best team coaching session they'd had. It was also the one where I did least!'

Summary

The ultimate goal of team coaching is to equip the team with the ability to coach itself as much as possible. As with individual coaching, it is important to avoid creating dependency – a very real danger, according to some of the team coaches we consulted in our researches.

Team coaching is not for the inexperienced coach, even if they have facilitation skills. It is very demanding, both in the moment and in the need to have a strong background in coaching, team theory and some understanding of group dynamics. It is a challenging frontier of coaching and one where a large portfolio of techniques and approaches is probably highly advisable!

Suggested further reading

Hackman, J. R. (1990). *Groups that Work (and Those that Don't): Creating Conditions for Effective Teamwork*. San Francisco: Jossey-Bass.

Hackman, J. R. and Wageman, R. (2007). *Senior Teams: What It Takes to Make Them Great*. Boston: Harvard Business School Press.

Katzenbach, J. R. and Smith, D. K. (1999). *The Wisdom of Teams: Creating the High-Performance Organization*. London: HarperBusiness.

Thompson, L. (2000). *Making the Team: A Guide for Managers*. New Jersey: Prentice Hall.

References

Clutterbuck, D. (2007). *Coaching the Team at Work*. London: Nicholas Brealey.

Early, P. C. and Mosakowski, E. (2000). Creating hybrid cultures: an empirical test of transnational team functioning. *Academy of Management Journal*, **43**(1), 26–49.

Edmondson, A. (1999). Psychological safety and learning behavior in work teams. *Administrative Science Quarterly*, **44**, 350–83.

Gersick, C. (1988). Time and transition in work teams: toward a new model of group development. *Academy of Management Journal*, **31**, 9–41.

Hampden-Turner, C. and Trompenaars, F. (1997). *Riding the Waves of Culture: Understanding Diversity in Global Business*. Maidenhead: McGraw-Hill.

Hawkins, P. and Smith, N. (2006). *Coaching, Mentoring and Organizational Consultancy, Supervision and Development*. Maidenhead: McGraw-Hill.

Part 3

Different foci for coach/mentoring techniques

In this part we offer a range of techniques that we have designed and used with individual clients (Chapter 10), with coaches and mentors when we have been training, developing and supervising them (Chapter 11), and when we are developing mentor/coaching relationships (Chapter 12). Chapter 13 offers our conclusions from reflecting on techniques over a five-year period and provides some checklists for developing the use of techniques.

Part 5

Different foci for coach\mentoring techniques

Chapter 10

Client focused techniques

David Clutterbuck and David Megginson

This chapter is the closest in content and intent to our companion volume, *Techniques in Coaching and Mentoring*, being focused on practical approaches a coach or mentor can apply in helping clients address their issues. As before, we have attempted to cluster techniques and approaches broadly around a relatively small number of themes. These are, specifically:

1. Goals – goal-setting, goal pursuit and goal achievement
2. Decision making
3. Understanding the environment
4. Understand self
5. Exploring beliefs and values
6. Managing emotions
7. And finally, a bunch of new additions to our collection of Massively Difficult Questions.

This is hardly an exhaustive list of issues a coach may meet in his or her practice, but it does comprise some of the more common ones and supplements those we described in the companion volume. For many of the techniques we present, we have provided a short case study, which illustrates how it can be applied. Some of these cases are exact accounts of real coach experiences, mostly with the names changed; others are amalgams of two or more cases.

Goals

There is probably more written about goals and goal setting in the coaching literature than about any other aspect of the role. Both the authors have in recent years begun to question some of the assumptions about goals – David Megginson in respect of coaching, David Clutterbuck in respect of mentoring. Our conclusions are stark: some of these assumptions, and particularly those about the need for initial goal specificity, are unevidenced and contrary to what data we have been able to accumulate. In the case of mentoring, on-going quantitative research finds no significant correlation between goal clarity and goal commitment at the beginning of a relationship and either the quality of relationship experience or the outcomes of the relationship for either mentor or mentee. There is, however, correlation between having a broad sense of purpose and *alignment* of purpose and both relationship quality and outcomes for the mentee.

SMART goals (Specific, Measurable, Achievable, Relevant and Time-specific) have become one of the unquestioned bases of modern management. The more precise a goal is, the more easily it will be achieved. Woolliness leads to poor performance and mediocrity. Or at least, that's how the theory goes.

It all started several decades ago with the rise of management by objectives (Drucker, 1954) and goal theory. MBO focused managers' attention on achieving a small number of clearly defined goals, against which performance was measurable. By articulating highly specific goals, with clear timelines, they would be able to exert greater control over the quantity, quality and appropriateness of the work their direct reports performed. Goal theory attempted to put some theoretical underpinning to these ideas. It basically says that motivation and performance are higher when individuals are set and accept specific goals, and receive feedback on their performance. The more demanding the goal, as long as the employee accepts it and views it as achievable, the higher their performance.

The problem is that people are annoyingly incompliant when it comes to conforming to theory. Moreover, the world of work is replete with examples where SMART goals proved in practice to be DIM (Dysfunctional Interventions by Management). Consider the example of the sales team incentivised to sell a premium product by offering bulk discounts. The goal was specific and measurable (80% more sales), achievable (in the sense that customers were amenable), relevant (it was part of their routine job) and time-specific (they were given 5 months to achieve the target). Unfortunately, the capacity of the supplier in China to meet the increased orders was insufficient to meet the demand created, without diverting production from other customers. So customers, whose orders couldn't be fulfilled, became very annoyed. Moreover, sensing that they were now in a seller's market, the Chinese supplier increased prices, turning the premium product into one with much reduced margins. The goal was DIM because it didn't take into account the wider context and because it had no room for adaptability as it worked out.

This kind of goal management is like pointing a bloodhound at a scent. Its nose goes down, its view of the world narrows and it becomes only marginally aware of what happens around it. This may be a great strategy in business, where the goal is short term, task-driven and relatively simple. But personal development goals and many business goals arise in an environment of uncertainty, complexity and liability to change. They also tend to take longer to achieve and have to fit in between the spaces of more urgent, in-the-moment tasks and objectives.

In our studies of goals in coaching and mentoring over the past five years, the authors have independently come to much the same conclusion. Many if not most goals are not clean-cut, rigid and preset. Rather, they are messy, adaptable and *emergent*. Clutterbuck's studies of goals in mentoring (Clutterbuck, 2008) compared three aspects of goals with measures of relationship experience and with outcomes for both mentors and mentees: goal clarity (knowing what they wanted to achieve and why), goal commitment (how determined they were to achieve it) and goal alignment (having a shared sense of purpose for the relationship). Neither goal clarity nor goal commitment – measured in the early stages of the relationship – correlated with relationship quality, relationship satisfaction or relationship commitment. Nor did they relate to any of the outcome measures. However, goal alignment did correlate with both. In other words, tying goals tightly down at the beginning is not a recipe for achievement, but maintaining a sense of direction and purpose is! Success in development is associated with maintaining a balance between the horizon and the immediate surrounding environment.

Although John Whitmore never promoted the GROW model as a rigid structure for coaching conversations, it is often used as such. Hanging on to SMART goals provides a crutch for less confident coaches and mentors. A regular 'fix' of goal-certainty frees them from the anxiety of working with emergence and uncertainty. But at a price. Coachees sometimes report that they feel pressurized into coming up with a goal, to meet the coach's expectations and needs. (For example: 'I didn't want her to feel I was wasting her time.') Or they espouse a goal that is really owned by another stakeholder, such as their boss. In our workshops helping established coaches develop their practice, we find that it is relatively rare for an initial goal to retain its shape and focus beyond the third meeting. Whatever the client and coach thought the goal was, it becomes very different as the relationship progresses.

As David Megginson has found, the value of rigid goals is being questioned in other areas of business and people development, too. For example, Herminia Ibarra's engaging case studies of people's career self-management demonstrate the dangers of too narrow a focus on next career steps (Ibarra, 2003).

So where does this leave us? There seem to be three key lessons, for coaches/mentors and for line managers:

1. Don't become addicted to goals.
2. Let (genuine) goals emerge, but steer the emergence process (i.e. keep your eyes on the horizon, but your hands on the steering wheel).
3. When goals do emerge, make sure they are truly owned by those who have to make them happen.

Don't become addicted to goals

Setting goals isn't always the best solution. If you do it too soon, you risk racing hard in the wrong direction. We have identified three different kinds of stimulus to action, of which goals are but one, as shown in Figure 10.1.

Stimulus	Response	Process
Goal	Score	Keep going until you have a result
Question	Better question	You can stop at any point; pick up again at any time
Itch	Scratch	Decide whether to acknowledge or ignore it

Figure 10.1 Stimulus, response, process.

All three are valuable, but we have become conditioned to think that only goal-setting will take us where we want to go. In practice, a frequent itch (for example, a continuing sense of disquiet about a market trend) will, if you allow it, nudge you in the direction of appropriate choices at a near-unconscious level. Using key questions allows for rapid changes of course in uncertain or evolving environments – compass checks on the route towards a broadly agreed outcome. It doesn't matter if all the questions aren't particularly good ones. As a delegate at a recent research conference commented: 'There's nothing dangerous about asking the wrong question. It's only the right question that has a significant impact.'

Let genuine goals emerge, but steer the emergence process

The following model (see Figure 10.2) is an attempt to capture the pattern of what happens in creating and pursuing goals. It is not yet underpinned by empirical research, but that we hope to initiate by asking a range of coaches to maintain a continuous learning log reflecting on how specific goals evolve in their helping relationships.

Firstly, goals don't just happen out of the blue. There has to be a *stimulus*, which usually has both internal and external components – a combination of what others expect of you and what you expect of yourself.

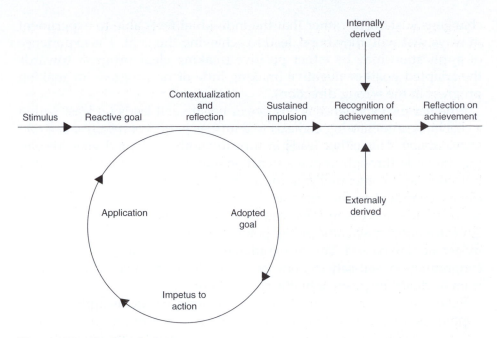

Figure 10.2   Goal evolution.

From the stimulus emerges a *reactive goal* – an instinctive response that gives new purpose to our scanning of the environment. The reactive goal may be relatively ill-defined at this stage. It may also be more motivated by avoiding pain (moving away from something rather than moving towards) and involve some instinctive steps towards achieving the reactive goal.

With time to distance oneself from the stimulus, people can take a calmer, more rational look at the goal. *Reflection and contextualization* allow us to reposition and recast the goal in the light of the bigger picture and other goals, which we may be pursuing. We may also relate the goal more closely to our values. In many if not most cases the goal is substantially amended at this point, as we now see the issue from different perspectives.

From this process of reflection and contextualization, therefore, comes an *adapted goal*, modified to take account of our perception of internal and external realities. The process of adaptation is often very satisfying. People talk about feeling more assured in their judgement and more confident in their ability to achieve the goal. Adapted goals are more likely to be 'moving towards' goals or a mixture of 'moving towards' and 'moving away'.

This new confidence provides an *impetus to action* – motivation to make the goal happen – which in turn leads to changes in behaviour or processes, or *application*. Application does not necessarily mean that the change is sustained; rather that the individual feels able to experiment in ways that will, they hope, lead to achieving the goal. The experience of application may be either positive (making clear progress towards the adapted goal) or negative (making little or no progress, or making progress in the wrong direction).

Whether the experience is positive or negative, it leads (at least within a coaching or mentoring context) to a further period of *reflection and contextualization*. This either leads in turn to another adapted goal (repeating the cycle through impetus to action and application back to further reflection and contextualization); or the learner moves on, being sufficiently confident in the 'rightness' of the goal and the path towards it. Success fuels success in what can be described as a *sustained impulsion*. An extra boost may come at key points from *recognition of achievement* as milestones are passed. This recognition may be internally generated (self-congratulation/self-satisfaction) or externally generated (for example, from feedback by peers or by the coach/mentor.)

Finally, an essential element in consolidating the gains appears to be another period of reflection, this time *reflection on achievement*. The goal, having been accomplished, takes on significance beyond its intrinsic value. It is a symbol of what we can achieve and hence a motivator to pursue other, perhaps more challenging, goals.

Assuming this is a relatively accurate depiction of goal emergence and goal self-management, an implication for coaches, mentors and line managers is that they should adapt and time their helping interventions to the stage that the learner has reached. A critical question might be: Is this a stage where my questions should be opening out their thinking (pointing to the horizon), developing their awareness (understanding the immediate context) or focusing down on specific, short-term goals?

When goals do emerge, make sure they are truly owned by those who have to make them happen

This seems an obvious point to make, particularly in the light of what we have already described. Yet asking the question, 'Whose goal is it?', is an essential part of the process. It can help, if a goal is shared with others, yet it is often not clear to the learner that other people are willing to take co-ownership with them. It's also useful to explore how the goal fits with their instinctive personal values – their inner sense of rightness, because any real or perceived clash here will become an itch that steers them away from the goal.

Visioning the future

This fairly common technique is another way of helping people work out what they want to achieve and how they are going to get there.

By tapping into multiple senses, it frequently stimulates motivation to action.

The three steps in visioning the future are:

1. Creating and 'stepping into' the future as you wish it to be.
2. Working out the milestone actions and events that brought about this future state.
3. Establishing practical ways to start on the journey towards the envisioned future.

Stepping into the future

This involves selecting a desired state and imagining what it will feel like, look like and sound like when you are there. For example, you can close your eyes and imagine yourself arriving at work, going through the main entrance and saying hallo, entering your office, going to a meeting and so on.

The desired state should be something which is important to your client, which is aligned with their personal values and is achievable – even if it will be very stretching.

Having done this generally, expand the exercise to encompass specific changes they want to bring about, i.e. definable achievements. Invite them to imagine the way people talk to them, the certificates on the wall, the books and reports on the shelves. Encourage them to watch themselves making a presentation, coaching a colleague and so on.

Ask them to put a date on this vision of the future. When will it become a reality?

Milestones and events

For each achievement, ask them to describe an action or event that will have brought it about. What will they have done to make this possible? Who else will be involved and how? How does each fit within the timeline from now to the fulfilled vision?

Decide what they are going to do to get started

How can they make each event on the journey more likely to happen than not? What can they do today to improve the probabilities?

Case study	Glenn

Glenn was a senior manager working in a large organization. Glenn had never married and felt that he had given his best years to the organization. The mentoring/coaching conversation began to reveal that Glenn wasn't feeling that he was giving his best at work anymore. Glenn felt that because

(Continued)

he wasn't contributing as much as he should in decision making, he felt that the decisions he was being involved in were no longer high profile decisions. He felt that decisions were being made around him. He felt that he wasn't being consulted as much as he used to be and as a result didn't feel as valued. In fact the further the coaching conversation went on, the more Glenn shared with his mentor/coach that he felt he was being overlooked if opportunities came up.

Further mentoring/coaching conversations started to disclose that Glenn was feeling constrained in his role and was generally just going with the flow around his work and making decisions. He didn't feel he was particularly leading anyone, contributing as much as he possibly could even in day-to-day management of the team, and was quite happy sitting on the fence playing a 'devil's advocate' role. He was aware that members of the management team had dubbed him 'Mr Negative'.

Glenn's mentor/coach decided to use the 'visioning for the future' technique and asked him 'to step into the future and to imagine that he was 5 years in the future and what did the future hold?' Asking Glenn this important question enabled him to select his desired state, and begin to imagine what it felt like and sounded like. He suddenly realized that he was imagining that he was no longer a senior manager working for this organization. It was as though a heavy weight had been lifted from his shoulders. He hadn't thought about a '5 years on perspective' before; no one had ever asked him that question. He was always caught up in the mundane tasks of coming to work and suddenly he could imagine and see what was really important to him.

In that few minutes Glenn had aligned his own personal values and suddenly realized when he put it into a long-term perspective that he wanted to spend more time at home working on his favourite pastime: painting. Glenn could picture himself in his garden room at home painting, physically painting with his brushes, the smell of paint, the pots of paint, designing his own prints, spending more time at home.

For each thought/achievement he described he talked through with his mentor/coach how he was going to bring it about. The mentor/coach asked him to describe how it felt doing those things. What was most noticeable was how Glenn's face lit up when he spoke about his painting and how Glenn's voice became softer to reflect doing things that he enjoyed doing instead of the drudgery that he often felt he was currently involved in.

When the mentor/coach asked him how he was going to achieve this and probed how he was going to turn his 'wish' into a reality, Glenn started thinking about looking at various options and how to approach applying for early retirement.

Looking back to move forward

Most processes for helping people achieve goals involve encouraging them to look forward. Visioning, for example, invites them to imagine themselves in a situation, where the goal has been achieved, and to work backwards to the present. However, an alternative approach, which comes broadly from positive psychology, is to look backwards.

Looking backwards often works because it raises the learner's awareness of the progress they have already made towards their goal. Even if no results are visible, a great deal of progress may have been achieved in terms of, say, developing the right mental attitude, gathering resources and developing an understanding of the barriers and how these might be overcome.

The starting point for this technique is usually a timeline, which can be expressed as a line on a sheet of paper, a strip of tape on the floor, or any other device, that indicates a sense of distance. The middle of the timeline is marked as the present and some form of marker (for example, a coin or bottle) indicates the point on the timeline where the conversation is focused at the moment.

Starting in the present, the coach might ask:

- What, if anything, makes this goal unique in your experience?
- What other goals can you compare it with, which you have already achieved, in whole or part?
- Why have you chosen this goal to work on now?

Moving to the past, the coach might ask:

- When did you first become consciously aware of this goal as meaningful to you?
- How long do you think it was unconsciously lurking ready to come into awareness?
- What have you already done, in terms of thinking and preparing, to progress towards this goal?
- What knowledge and skills do you already have, which will help you achieve it?
- What experience have you acquired, which will be useful?
- What resources have you identified, which might help you?
- What barriers have you partly or wholly removed?
- What lessons have you learned/could you learn from your experience achieving similar goals in the past?
- What personal strengths have you drawn on in the past, which will be useful in pursuing this present goal?

Moving back to the present, the coach might ask:

- What does your experience of pursuing previous goals tell you about the issues you need to be aware of in pursuing this one?
- What will you do better, in terms of managing the goal, than you have in the past?
- When and how will you look back at your progress?
- Compared to when we started this conversation, how far along the timeline to this goal do you think you are now? (Physically moving the marker may be strongly motivating at this point!)

Case study   Samantha

People who have a tendency to be visual can sometimes specify precisely what they are feeling more easily with pictures than by using spoken words. Working with Samantha's drawing it was obvious to the mentor/coach that there were some areas that she could ask questions around and obvious to the mentor/coach that there were some areas which would require some sensitivity.

Using the 'looking back to move forward' technique the mentor/coach tried to distinguish significant life events which may have affected Samantha's career lifeline. It is interesting from both the mentor/coach and mentee/coachee's perspective to look at the obvious turning points and to explore what decisions were made at those times, what resources were made available to the mentee/coachee, what influenced decisions and what learning there may be now from reflecting on these events.

By asking someone to reflect on their past it may trigger off their dwelling on their past not the present! Therefore the mentor/coach must always leave enough time for adequate debriefing.

The mentor/coach asked Samantha to pause for a few minutes and reflect on the lifeline and pictures that she had drawn. The mentor/coach asked Samantha, 'What do you notice about the line or the drawing?' Samantha had drawn cloud shapes in thick black marker pen at different points on her timeline. The mentor/coach explored with Samantha what the clouds represented. It transpired that Samantha used the black clouds to symbolize what she described as her 'bad times' that she had experienced both in her personal life and in her working life. For example, she had placed a black cloud where she had left school and the mentor/coach started to unravel that Samantha felt because she hadn't got the grades at school that she had hoped for, she didn't pursue a career in law. Samantha symbolized this as one of her bad times. Samantha had opted out of university and drifted from one job to another and was now working as a customer service manager in an IT organization.

(Continued)

The mentor/coach explored with Samantha the positives from drifting 'from one job to another' (being careful to use Samantha's own words). Looking more positively at the situation helped Samantha draw on the good times that she had experienced, the friends she had made, the good lessons that she had learned.

Further mentor/coach questions uncovered that another of Samantha's black clouds represented a difficult time in her personal life: the death of her sister.

The mentor/coach then started to explore the pattern or theme that was occurring after each black cloud: it was transpiring that Samantha would work even harder to ensure she achieved something such as a further qualification.

The mentor/coach looked at the low points with Samantha and they explored what she might have done differently, what might have helped her?

The mentor/coach also explored the high points on Samantha's drawing which were illustrated by 'smiley faces' and which illustrated Samantha's inner strengths and determination to succeed. Again they were able to investigate the external conditions that had helped.

This 'looking back to move forward technique' is a way of accessing strengths, resources and values. It provides a creative way of looking at career development. It also provides a useful structure/model to build into a mentor/coaching session.

Building a sense of purpose

A number of coaching approaches, including basic life coaching and ontological coaching, aim to help people work out what they want from their lives and why, then how they will get what they want. The concept of a life purpose statement, expounded by Teri-E Belf (Belf, 2002), or a personal mission statement is one way of beginning this journey.

A useful set of questions is summarized in the acronym LIST – Life purpose, Importance, Sharing/support, Time. The coach selects from these or similar questions to stimulate the client's thinking.

L = Life purpose
- Whether you believe in an external agency or not, what is the reason you are alive?
- What do you want to be remembered for?
- What kind of difference do you want to make?
- Who is your ideal self?
- What would make you feel fulfilled?

- When you listen to the still, small voice at your centre, what does it tell you?
- What is the metaphor for your life purpose?

I = Importance

- Why does this matter to you?
- How much of this do you need to do/how like this do you need to be to feel fulfilled?
- How big a hole in your life will there be if you don't make any progress towards achieving your life purpose?
- How important does it have to be, to make you change your day-to-day priorities?

S = Share/Support

- Who shares your life purpose?
- Who would you like to share it?
- Where can you find others who will share it?
- How could you work with them to achieve more than you could alone?
- Who else do you talk to about your life purpose?

T = Time

- How much of your time and energy do you currently spend on activities that support your life purpose, compared with time spent on other things?
- When are you going to start investing seriously in achieving your life purpose?
- If you have started, are you making enough progress and what can you do to make faster progress?

Sub-techniques in working with life purpose include: Meaningful moments, Digging for holes and Making the right difference.

Meaningful moments

Meaningful moments involves recollecting occasions that carry special meaning in terms of self-fulfilment and being aligned with our positive sense of identity. What aspects of these events do we want to reproduce in the present or future? The coach or mentor can also stimulate thinking using questions such as:

- When have you felt fully at peace with yourself?
- When have you felt that your talents have been used to their full?

- When have you contributed most?
- When did you feel you made a real difference?
- When did you feel you were who you aspire to be?
- When have you felt most alive?

It's important to recognize here that meaningful moments are defined solely by how the client perceives them.

Case study   **Ray**

This is one of the shortest case studies in the book. It shows the power of the massively difficult question. Ray was CEO of a retail company, part of a larger retail group. He explained to a newly appointed coach that he didn't really have any problems, just a vague sense of unease that he was in the wrong job. He was seen as a rising star and he had a good, highly effective team working for him. He just had an itch …

The question that unlocked the issue was 'When have you felt most alive?' It turned out that Ray was an enthusiastic walker and climber. If he were to have any regrets about his working life, it would be that he had spent too much time indoors. Could he combine his career and his interests? After a few months, it turned out that he could. He became CEO of a struggling sports goods company, where his enthusiasm gradually turned it round. The new job was harder and much more stressful, he subsequently told the coach, but he could identify with the product and he felt a much greater degree of alignment between his work and non-work lives.

Digging for holes

It's common for people to talk about feelings of emptiness, especially when they have experienced a severe loss, or are suffering from despair. But it can be hard for them to describe the feelings with sufficient accuracy to deal with them. The coaching question here is: 'Where's the hole?' – if there is something missing, surely there must be a hole to define where it was? Clients sometimes point to their hearts ('I can't feel sympathy for anyone'), or in their heads ('I feel stupid') or their whole body ('I'm just numb'), or their legs ('I feel cut off at the knees'); or, using the analogy of a lake or sea, they say the hole has filled itself in – which allows the coach to suggest that maybe they could move on right away.

Sometimes the coach can step beyond the body metaphor and use a wider metaphor about mind and brain. What has been taken away? What has withered away? What is simply bruised? Then it is a relatively easy step onwards to talk about how to fill the hole, what will help the swelling of bruised parts go down (embrocation for the ego!) and so on.

Visualizing what is missing in this way enables the client to build boundaries around what they are lacking in their lives and to be more rational in considering what strategies they can adopt to fill the holes and become a more complete person.

Case study   Vanessa: Part 1

Vanessa was an extremely successful hairdresser and was managing four very busy hair salons in the city. She had been married for a number of years and loved her husband dearly. They didn't have any family/children. When her mentor/coach questioned why they didn't have any children Vanessa realized that she felt there had never been a 'right time' to have children. There had always been something going on in her business career that she felt meant that she had to be in the salon.

Vanessa was very much a people person, loved being around people, but she confided in her mentor/coach that when she went home she felt so lonely, empty. The mentor/coach conversation started to unpick that Vanessa felt she rattled around in their big empty house. Vanessa wished that at some point in her younger days she had taken time to have children but now had come to terms with the decision that Vanessa and her husband had both made and that it was now too late in her life to think about starting a family.

With further questioning, Vanessa thought that she might talk about adoption or fostering with her husband but still wasn't sure whether this was right for them. She felt that she had made the decision not to have a family in return for having a successful business.

Using the 'digging for holes' technique helped Vanessa to explore her emptiness and helped her to be more rational in considering what strategies she and her husband could adopt to fill the emptiness to help her become more of a complete person.

Making the right difference

Most people want to make a difference, if not in their work, to their families or to society. Sometimes, it's just not possible to achieve the chosen difference. In which case, part of the coach's or mentor's role is to help them identify a different, but equally or more compelling difference they can aspire to making. Useful questions in this regard include:

- What talents do you have, that could most benefit others?
- When you have made a difference before, what ideal were you living up to?
- What part does other people's opinion and responses have in determining how self-fulfilled you feel?
- What would give you the strongest boost about how good you feel about yourself, for the least change?
- What kind of a difference would those you respect/love like you to make?
- Could a lot of small contributions be worth as much or more than one or two big ones?

Case study   Vanessa: Part 2

Following on from the 'digging for holes' technique the mentor/coach started to explore the 'making the right difference' technique with Vanessa in considering what strategies that she might want to adopt to fill the emptiness to help her become more complete.

Vanessa had many talents in cutting and in styling and in running businesses. Vanessa suggested that other business entrepreneurs may want to hear and benefit from listening to how she had approached opening her salons, hurdles that she had overcome and some of the pitfalls that she had fallen into along the way.

Vanessa started to question whose opinion she was seeking and started to realize that perhaps she was living up to other people's business expectations (the bank/the accountant/competitors/the staff) and ideas of what other people see as success rather than looking at what she had really achieved in her life. She loved her husband dearly and it started to unfold for Vanessa that perhaps she hadn't asked her husband if he was happy and if this is what he wanted.

The mentor/coach conversation started to unpick moments and occasions when things had not gone so well in Vanessa's business. The mentor/coach questioned from the perspective of how this made her feel when she was driving home, approaching the house and in the house. It transpired that Vanessa said that her husband was always there to pick her up when she was feeling low or if there was a business crisis.

The more moments and occasions that the mentor/coach explored with Vanessa the more she started to realize how much she depended on her

(Continued)

husband being there, coming to bail her out and that she saw him as her 'rock'. Vanessa just hadn't realized.

Interestingly Vanessa was really looking forward to going home that evening and the drive home and her house just seemed all the more inviting and not half as empty as it had appeared before ...

Decision making

People generally think of decision making as a predominantly rational process. They assume that they gather all the relevant facts, consider the options, then select the most rational way forward. In reality, they filter the facts to give greater weight to biases and prejudices, make values and judgements about the various options, and rationalize their instinctive reactions.

Flawed decision making appears in many guises. For example, people usually underestimate how long a task will take; they place more value on information from an in-group than an out-group; and they are consistently more positive than an independent observer about the goodwill, competence and performance of their own team or organization, compared with rivals.

The coach or mentor's role is often to help people revisit decisions, unpicking the process and the assumptions they have made; or to be more aware of their assumptions and biases in decisions still to be made. In doing so, they reinforce the quality of the learner's thinking both specifically and generally.

Useful questions in doing this include:

- What assumptions did you make in reaching this decision?
- Who might have been able to offer a different set of assumptions? How valid might these have been? (The technique 'separate selves' from the companion volume can be powerful here.)
- What did you *want* the answer to have been?
- How did you assess the evidence? (What weight did you give to various sources and why?)
- What outcomes might you expect from the opposite decision?

Sometimes it helps for the coach/mentor and the learner to develop together the counter-argument to the decision taken. This frequently results in modification of the decision, or of the rationale behind it.

The coach/mentor can also help the learner clarify the critical roles in decision making. According to Paul Rogers and Marcia Blenko (2006), these are:

- Recommend – making proposals, gathering data and making appropriate analyses.
- Agree – have the power of veto over the decision, but are not the final decision makers.
- Input – people who are consulted, because they are impacted by the decision and/or will have to implement it.
- Decide – the person who carries the can, has the authority to resolve disagreements and impose a decision if required.
- Perform – those responsible for implementing the decision.
- Distinguishing between these roles helps the learner develop pragmatic strategies for influencing decisions and how they are implemented.

Our own preferred model of decision making has six critical steps:

- Purpose: why do we need to make a decision about this and why now?
- Awareness: How well do we understand this issue and its context? What assumptions are we making that might limit the options we consider?
- Definition: How precise can we be in describing the issue? Is it really one issue or several interlinked ones? (One of the reasons SMART goals often don't deliver is that they are not grounded in equally specific problem definition.)
- Creative thinking: What options can we generate? What didn't work before, but might work now? What if we did the opposite to what we've always done?
- Choosing between alternatives: How can we be sure that we are applying the same weightings in valuing alternatives? What biases should we be aware of in how we select?
- Implementing: Do we have the resources and energy to implement? Who needs to be engaged in thinking about implementation? How will we ensure they understand the decision emotionally as well as rationally? Who has what role in implementation? Is there a robust link between the macro-decision (usually by executives) and the micro-decisions (making it work, usually by people much lower down)?

In the context of coaching and mentoring, we find this framework useful in the sounding board role. It provides a structured approach to address specific decisions or decision making in general.

Some useful additional techniques to aid decision making, which we explore now, are:

- For, against, interesting, instinct
- Conjoint analysis
- Procrastinate later
- Turning problems into opportunities
- Antecedents, behaviours, consequences.

For, against, interesting, instinct

This simple process (Figure 10.3) helps ensure that you see an idea or proposal from several perspectives and don't jump to decisions. It stimulates a breadth of dialogue and creativity.

For	Against	Interesting	Instinct

Figure 10.3   For, against, interesting, instinct.

- *'For'* refers to the potential benefits of the idea
- *'Against'* refers to the possible downsides
- *'Interesting'* is an opportunity to capture aspects of the idea, that don't necessarily belong to 'for' or 'against'
- *'Instinct'* captures how you feel about the idea and the issues generated in the other columns.

The art is to generate as many points as possible to go under each of these headings. Once all the thoughts have been combined, they provide a rich resource for an informed dialogue.

> **Case study**   **Using for, against, interesting, instinct**
>
> This example comes from team coaching, working with the top team of a medium-sized enterprise. The issue – whether or not to acquire a partial competitor – had split the team in two, with the CEO and marketing director strongly for and the finance director equally strongly against. The issue wasn't one specifically on the coaching agenda, but the coach and the CEO recognized that failure to resolve it was preventing the team tackling the developmental issues that coaching was intended to address.
>
> *(Continued)*

The coach began by giving the team some direct feedback. In her observation, the more each side insisted they were being rational and the other side was being emotional, the more entrenched and polarized their views were becoming. Did they accept that this might be the case? After some discussion, everyone agreed that it could be. Did they accept that emotional judgements could be important, both in linking decisions to values and in ensuring commitment to subsequent decisions? Yes. Did they therefore accept that the other perspective might have both emotional and rational validity, even if they consider their arguments were stronger than the other party's? Yes. Were they now ready to bring together their analyses of the opportunity, taking the perspective that the decision was still wide open?

The team listed all the for, against and interesting items, without at this stage assigning any weight to them. Then the coach asked them to split into two groups: one composed of people who still felt drawn to the 'for' decision and one who still felt drawn to 'against'. Each group was asked to go into a separate room and identify as many counter-arguments as they could to their position. Three people, who were undecided, were formed into a third group and asked to discuss: 'What have we not considered (fully or at all)?' When they came back together again, this third group presented their thoughts first and the other two groups were offered a chance for further reflection on either their initial position or the counter-arguments they had been asked for.

The ensuing dialogue was notable for the very different tone compared to the original conversation. Both sides commented that the issue was more complex than they had allowed themselves to recognize. In particular, both the potential benefits and the potential risks of the acquisition had become much clearer. Against a background of cautions from the coach not to seek compromise, but to aim for a solution that they could all believe in, they found ways to reduce the risks. These included telling the seller that they did not want one division, which they perceived would eat up management time and had been a source of the competitor's difficulties; and setting a ceiling on how much they would pay. Surprisingly quickly, the seller agreed to these terms – the unwanted division was where his real interests and enthusiasm lay and the deal gave him the opportunity to concentrate on this area, while still acquiring a retirement nest egg.

The experience demonstrated to the team that robust argument – something they all professed to value – was only effective within a robust framework of decision making.

Conjoint analysis

The purpose of this technique is to help people prioritize between different goals, or different options generally. It is a useful alternative to

	Salary	Location	Supportive colleagues	Work–life balance	Benefits package	Training
Location	*Salary*					
Supportive colleagues	*Salary*	*Location*				
Work–life balance	*Salary*	*Work–life balance*	*Supportive colleagues*			
Benefits package	*Salary*	*Location*	*Supportive colleagues*	*Work–life balance*		
Training	*Salary*	*Location*	*Supportive colleagues*	*Work–life balance*	*Training*	
Job stretch	*Job stretch*	*Job stretch*	*Job stretch*	*Job stretch*	*Job stretch*	*Job stretch*

Figure 10.4   Conjoint analysis matrix: an example.

the 'change balloon' approach we presented in the companion volume. The process is as follows:

1. List all the options, in whatever order they occur, to the learner. For example, what they want in their next job or in a new house; or where they can concentrate their developmental effort for the coming 12 months.
2. Take some additional time to reflect if there are further options or choices to add.
3. Create a matrix as in Figure 10.4. Note, salary is not included in the vertical column because as the first item on the list it gets compared with all the others in the first vertical column.
4. Ask the learner to compare items 1 and 2 and to choose between them (e.g. Which is most important to you? Which do you value the most?). Write the choice in the relevant box.
5. Compare each item one with all other items, in turn, and record which item was chosen in each comparison, ensuring all items have been compared only once with each other.
6. Add up the scores for each item. The number of ticks indicates the relative ranking.
7. If appropriate repeat the exercise, using a different criterion of selection (e.g. if the first selection was by what the learner values, the second may be by what they think another stakeholder would value).
8. Finally, verify with the learner:
   (i)   Does this make your choices clearer?
   (ii) How do the results match your instincts?
   (iii) Do you feel motivated to act upon these insights?

In this example, the client has identified seven things she would ideally want in a new job. By comparing each against the other, we get a picture of their relative importance to her. Adding the number of times each is the first preference, we find that the order of importance is: job stretch (6), salary (5), location, supportive colleagues and work-life balance (3) training (1) and benefits package (0).

Case study   **Victor**

Victor was an account manager with a major career decision to make. His home circumstances had changed substantially with the birth of his first child and he felt the need to earn more money. He was also eager to move up the management ladder – for someone who had just worked to live, he now had the bit between his teeth in terms of career. He'd demonstrated skill and commitment in a series of projects and roles at a non-managerial level, to the point where he was an automatic choice for troubleshooting territories in difficulty. As a result, he had come to the notice of senior management, one of whom now offered him a new role, with a large increase in both salary and responsibilities – but also some significant risks attached.

Victor's mentor, a senior manager in another division, helped him enumerate the risks and opportunities. The list of risks and downsides included:

- The new role had a high potential for failure.
- The company did not have a good reputation for rewarding 'good attempts'.
- Predicted changes in legislation might make it much harder to reach targets.
- This was his first step into management, so he had a lot to learn in a short time.
- There were a number of difficult characters to deal with, who could influence his results, but over whom he had no control.
- The job involved a lot more travel and hence time away from his wife and new baby.

The opportunities and pluses included:

- The rise in salary and job grade, with attractive bonuses if he hit his targets.
- Promises of support from several sponsors in the senior team and the opportunity to work more closely with them – and hence build alliances.
- The new role, being cross-functional, would give him a much wider understanding of the organization and hence be a stepping stone to the next layer of management.
- The challenge excited him.

(Continued)

Most of this Victor had already worked out in his own mind. It all seemed finely balanced. So the mentor combined the list and, using conjoint analysis, helped Victor compare how important to him each of the factors was against the rest. The results showed that the opportunity factors outweighed the risk factors more often than vice versa. Finally, the mentor asked the classic question, 'How does this result fit with your intuitive, gut feeling?' Victor took the job.

Procrastinate later

Procrastination can easily become a habit. One way to begin to break the habit is to ask the question: 'When would be the best time to procrastinate about this?' This approach helps to remove the blame or guilt about avoiding an issue and recognizes that sometimes, putting off a decision or action is an appropriate response. Without the interference of these negative emotions, the learner can consider whether there are some actions they can take in the short term, or allocate thinking/decision-making time to a specific point in the future.

Case study   Gerald

Gerald was CEO of the UK subsidiary of a large Japanese multinational. He had been in the role for four years and had performed well. He already knew that his next appointment would be in twelve months' time and would be a transfer to the United States, where he would become second in command of the company's North American business. He also knew that he was in danger of leaving behind a relatively weak management team. His finance director was particularly inexperienced; Kemal, his head of sales and marketing was due to retire only a few months after he moved on and there was no obvious internal successor. Yet, he had already sat on this problem for nearly a year, without taking any decisive action.

When the coach asked 'When would be the best time to procrastinate about this?' Gerald was forced to admit to himself that he had been procrastinating for a year already. Exploring his motivations for not taking action, he explained that he knew he would face opposition from Kemal, who was championing his own deputy, in whom Gerald had little confidence. Kemal had considerable influence with the United States and could, if he chose, undermine Gerald's promotion there. Gerald was experiencing internal conflict between what was good for himself and what was good for the division.

(Continued)

The coach helped Gerald distinguish between procrastination, in terms of not planning a solution, and procrastination, in terms of not taking action. A crash plan to bring along the new finance director, which included putting him on the board of another group company with a very experienced finance director, who could be a strong role model, could be implemented straight away. With regard to the sales and marketing position, he could continue to procrastinate about the actual appointment, as long as he developed a strategy to ensure an appointment would be made before he left. He used this time to clarify with his own bosses who his successor as CEO might be, and spent time with each of the two possibles explaining the situation and seeking their advice as to good internal candidates for the sales and marketing role. Hence, when Gerald's successor was announced, she had already primed her own candidate for the sales and marketing role and was able to bring that person in with her.

One of the lessons from this example, was that *planned* procrastination can be a viable approach.

Turning problems into opportunities

Even the worst disasters may have silver linings. The Black Death, which killed millions, brought to an end the slavery of serfdom. The Great Fire of London cleared the City of the Black Death and gave rise to a flurry of outstanding architecture. Helping people find the opportunities inherent in their problems is a core skill for coaches and mentors.

There are several ways to do so. One is for the coach or mentor to offer alternative perspectives. For example, Alex has never got on well with a particular female colleague, who he sees as huffy and unfriendly. He feels she looks down on him, because he takes a light view of things and uses a lot of humour, which she seems to take as frivolity. Matters came to a head, when he was mimicking her behaviour at a meeting, only to realize that she was standing immediately behind him. Knowing that she had the ear of senior managers, Alex was very concerned about his future with the company. The conversation with the coach went something like this:

> Coach: Has this relationship been getting steadily worse anyway?
> Alex: I guess it has. But I've been avoiding her so it doesn't deteriorate even faster.
> Coach: Is a poor relationship between you damaging in any way – for you, for the team, for the company?
> Alex: For all of those, but it's not my fault.
> Coach: Blame isn't the point here. It's how you manage the situation. What's stopped you addressing this issue before?

Alex: I'm afraid of putting my foot in it again and making things worse.

Coach: Could the relationship be much worse now?

Alex: Not really.

Coach: Then you've nothing to lose by addressing the issue now? Maybe this is the trigger to make you do what you should have done long ago and have an open discussion with her about how you work together?

Alex: It's true, I've nothing to lose, but I'm scared stiff of going near her.

Coach: OK, so how do we overcome this fear?

A second approach is to focus on the question '*What does this change?*' Sub-questions might, for example, be:

- What can you now do that you couldn't do before?
- What can you now not do that you could do before?
- What do you want now that you didn't want (as strongly) before?
- What can you let go of/stop doing that will free up time and energy for other things?
- What has become clearer as a result of this?
- What decisions/actions has this pushed higher up your agenda?
- What matters less to you now?

A third approach encourages the client to focus upon the learning to extract from the situation and to use this to stimulate positive reflection and action, as illustrated in Figure 10.5.

Useful questions in the learning box include:

- Did you see this coming?
- If you did, what prevented you taking avoiding action?
- If you didn't, what prevented you from seeing it?
- Is this a repeated pattern?
- What would you *like* to learn from this?
- What will you learn from this?

What can/should I learn from this?	What change do I want to bring about in the circumstances?	What change in behaviour does that require in me?
For the immediate situation? For the future?	Now? In the future?	Now? In the future?

Figure 10.5   Learning, circumstances and behaviour.

- What benefits will flow if you demonstrate to others that you have learned from this?
- What strengths did you demonstrate in this situation?

Useful questions in the change in circumstances box include:

- What fallout do you need to manage/ameliorate?
- How can you prevent longer term negative consequences?
- How motivated are you to prevent this recurring?
- How can you use the situation to advantage (your own or the organization's)?
- Is this an opportunity to tackle a number of related issues you (or others) have been avoiding?

Useful questions in the change in behaviour box include:

- What learning and performance goals should you set yourself as a result of this?
- What could you do more of to bring the change in circumstances about?
- What could you do less of?
- What opportunities can you find to practise these different behaviours?

Finally, the *worst case scenario* helps to put things into a larger perspective. Here, the coach or mentor encourages the client to imagine what could have happened to make the situation even worse. For example:

> Mentor: So you've lost a valued client. But how would you be feeling now if they had also told some of your other, bigger clients why they were leaving?
> Mentee: A lot worse, of course!

The absence of these negatives starts the journey into positive territory.

> Mentor: Can you put right the systems and people problems that made them leave?
> Mentee: We're already doing that.
> Mentor: Perhaps they've done you a good turn, in the long run, then? Haven't you prevented the same thing happening to the bigger customers?

(In this example, as a result of the change in perception about the issue, the mentee went back to the lost customer, thanked them for making him aware of the problems and asked if he could keep them informed about progress in overcoming it. A year later, the customer returned.)

Gerald Egan, author of *The Skilled Helper* (1994), suggests the following questions to stimulate opportunity finding:

- What are my unused skills/resources?
- What are my natural talents?
- How could I use some of these?
- What opportunities do I let go by?
- What ambitions remain unfulfilled?
- What could I accomplish if I put my mind to it?
- What could I become good at if I tried?
- What opportunities should I be developing?
- Which role models could I be emulating?

Antecedents, Behaviours, Consequences

ABC analysis is the name given to a long-established approach to achieving specific behavioural change. It is based on the premise that every behaviour has a cause or causes (the antecedent) and one or more consequences. Changes of behaviour can only occur when this pattern is broken and this requires the client to become aware of each of the three stages. A manager, who bullies, for example, may be unconscious that he does so – he may simply see his behaviour as being positively assertive. He may be partially aware that he comes on strongly when he perceives the other person to be weak, but he may rationalise that into managing poor performance. And he may feel comfortable in the belief that he is respected for being firm but fair, when in reality he is perceived as weak and arbitrary. With knowledge comes the potential to bring about behavioural change, by addressing all three elements of the chain of cause and effect.

Case study   **Peter**

Peter is a manager in his early thirties in a retail company. He had joined as a graduate recruit and worked his way through the ranks to take over the largest store in his region. He was seen as bright and capable and was delighted to be offered a move to a staff position at headquarters. Not only was it a significant promotion, but it provided a stepping stone into senior management.

Four months into the new role, it was all going wrong. The job required him to gain the cooperation of a range of people, most more senior than

(Continued)

himself. Up until now, his boyish good humour, combined with the authority of his job roles, had enabled him to develop a track record of getting things done with minimum fuss. Indeed, he had been brought to headquarters in part because of his reputation as an effective trouble-shooter.

Peter asked his boss, his mentor and a couple of other people he trusted for feedback. The recurring theme that emerged from these conversations was that he was seen by some people as too 'flippant'. This feedback took the wind out of his sails. He had always seen his sense of humour as a strength. Had he simply entered an environment of humourless people, or were his assumptions wrong about how he interacted with other people? Peter's boss suggested that he have three or four coaching sessions with a member of the HR team, who had been trained to be an executive coach and was also a psychologist.

The coach could have started at any point on the antecedent, behaviour, consequences continuum, but he chose not to begin with behaviour, the area that Peter was most focused on, because Peter was too confused in his thinking about it. Instead, he explored first the consequences – how other people reacted to his behaviour. They worked through several examples of conversations which had not gone well and tried to establish patterns in what the other people had said, their body language and what might have been going on in their minds. A key question was: 'What qualities do you think they were looking for you to demonstrate?'

Next, the coach steered the conversation towards antecedents. How had Peter used humour effectively in the past? Had there been occasions when it had 'gone wrong' then? How had he learned to place so much value on humour as a way of getting things done? The coach explained how behaviours, which work in some situations, can become our dominant response to all similar situations, but that they may not be universally appropriate. He also explained that using humour is a common avoidance mechanism.

As they reflected on the various situations Peter had described, he realized that he instinctively turned to humour in situations of stress, either within himself, or observed in other people. He also realized that a potential consequence of that strategy was that the other person would misinterpret his attempt to lighten the mood.

From here it was a short hop to thinking about alternative behaviours he could use in stress situations – about widening his portfolio of responses and exercising conscious choice about which he would employ. The coach stimulated him to think of other strengths he could draw upon. One of the most obvious was his ability to empathize. Could he achieve more by saying less, encouraging the other person to talk and expressing understanding of their dilemmas? When Peter put these new behaviours into practice, he found that relationships improved significantly and that gradually he could reintroduce humour, but in a more spontaneous way. (NB: It may or may not have helped, but the coach recognized a lot of himself in this case!)

Understanding the environment

It's very rare that a client brings an issue in that can be isolated from the environment in which they live or work. Part of the task of the coach/mentor is to help the client recognize the context in which the issue rests and the influence elements of the environment may have on hindering or facilitating resolution of dilemmas. Equally important is for the coach/mentor to ensure they have sufficient contextual understanding of the client's situation, before taking the learning conversation into solution mode. It's a common error in inexperienced coaches, even if they come to coaching or mentoring from another helping discipline, to want to offer solutions, or to come to conclusions ('I know what's wrong with you …') at far too early a stage in the dialogue. Useful questions we sometimes employ to test where we are in the conversation are:

- If we were approaching this issue completely naively, what would we want to know about it, before we started thinking about decisions?
- What part of the context here have we avoided or skipped over as unimportant?

In this section, we examine some approaches that help the coach/mentor raise contextual awareness for the benefit of both the client and themselves.

Opening up the topic

Mind-mapping is most frequently used for capturing thoughts in a meeting or workshop. But it can also be used to explore complex issues. The coach/mentor can help the client at each stage of the process:

- Defining the issue: what should go at the centre of the mind-map? Sometimes this is the hardest part. Helpful questions to capture the concept include:
  - Is this a dilemma (i.e. about choosing between two or more difficult options)?
  - Is it a case of knowing what needs to be done, but not wanting to do it?
  - Is it about knowing what needs to be done, but not knowing how?
  - Is it about not knowing either what needs to be done or how to do it?
- Defining the strands of relevant concepts. Again, the coach/mentor can help to categorize these. One possible stimulus is:
  - People – who?
  - Processes – how?
  - Resources – what? How much?
  - Objectives/outcomes – what?

- Stimulating the client's creativity in expanding the branches of the mindmap. Useful questions include:
  - What's the last thing you would want here?
  - How will you know if …?
  - What is that like? What does it remind you of?
  - Can you represent that thought as a picture or symbol, rather than as a word?

Case study — Mind-mapping uncomfortable messages

An HR director was having sleepless nights thinking about how to communicate to employees some unpleasant messages about plant closure and job losses. With his coach, he wrote at the centre of a mind-map the words 'closing down'. Then the two of them recorded all the of words and concepts that came to them in five minutes, using the closest lines on the map for key concepts and the branches for ideas associated with the concepts. They were then able to cluster these into four kinds of message:

- Those the company wanted the employees to hear and accept.
- Those the company didn't want to the employees to hear or believe.
- Those the employees wanted to hear.
- Those the employees didn't want to hear.

From this came a clear strategy for structuring the communications and managing the dialogue with employees before, during and after the formal announcement.

Responsibility mapping

Responsibility mapping (Figure 10.6) is a simple process for helping people think through how much choice they have about what they take responsibility for and how they feel about the responsibilities they have. It's a useful tool in stimulating insight into how comfortable the learner is with their responsibilities and the demands upon them.

The matrices can be adapted to circumstance and are intended to allow the learner to rate their responsibilities from a variety of perspectives. Having analysed each perspective, the coach or mentor leads them through a discussion of the implications, with questions such as:

- How well do you fulfil the responsibilities you have now? How do you know?
- How well defined are those responsibilities? Would it help to make them clearer? If so, how can you influence that?

What do you want to/need to... → What are you... ↓	Take full responsibility for?	Take some responsibility for?	Take no responsibility for?
Completely responsible for			
Partially responsible for			
Not responsible for			

How much does this impact on you? → How much responsibility for it do you carry? ↓	A lot	Somewhat	None at all
Full			
Partial			
None			

Figure 10.6   Responsibilities, taken and given; Impact map.

- To what extent are these responsibilities imposed on you or willingly accepted?
- How can you exert greater control over the responsibilities you want to keep/gain?
- What responsibilities can you/do you want to let go? What ones do you want to acquire?
- Who do you want to transfer some responsibilities to? How can you make that happen?
- How would you feel if you could change your responsibility map in these ways?

Case study   Elaine

Elaine was finance director of a business that had seen better times. Acquired as a thriving independent concern six years before, it had changed hands twice since. Underinvestment and uncertainty had combined to undermine its sense of direction. Although all of her original colleagues had left, Elaine still felt loyal to the business. At some indefinable point, that loyalty had turned into a sense of personal responsibility for the business and its diminishing employees. Although she was responsible for the accuracy of the finances and for financial strategy, she also felt personally responsible

(Continued)

for the collective performance of her top team colleagues, some of whom she perceived as not pulling their weight. In particular, she saw the new managing director as a short-term thinker, who was too weak to stand up to his bosses in the holding company. She admitted to her coach that she was feeling greatly stressed and had considered taking early retirement.

The coach used the responsibility matrices to help Elaine clarify those responsibilities that belonged to the role of finance director, and those that she had assumed, because she was conscientious. They also categorized responsibilities in terms of what she could control, what she could influence and those over which she had little control or influence. Elaine saw that she could focus the majority of her energy on the things that were within her direct responsibility and which she could control or influence; for everything else, she would set aside a maximum of 10% of her time and energy. Letting go was hard, but whenever she found herself feeling stressed, she was able to use the responsibility map to put her emotions in context.

Being more focused ('bounded responsibility' as the coach described it) enabled Elaine to work out with the coach how she and the managing director could clarify their expectations of each other; and what she could do to support him. The result was that she increasingly became the spokesperson to group management on difficult issues – a role she enjoyed immensely. Previously unknown in the group, she began to build alliances. Slightly more than a year later, she chaired a steering group to merge her company with another, recently acquired subsidiary. When she was offered the opportunity to take on a more senior finance role at group headquarters, she told the coach that she had no hesitation in accepting – she now felt she had fulfilled all her responsibilities to the original company.

Unpicking issues

A simple and much-used process for helping a client work out what is going wrong in a problem situation is to compare and contrast with a similar situation where things went well. The coach or mentor asks the client to visualize both instances, preferably starting with the positive case, and draws out key components, such as:

- Who was involved?
- How well prepared were you?
- What were the certainties and uncertainties?
- What happened that you did/didn't expect?
- How did you feel at each key stage?
- How did you know how well things had worked out?

Focusing on the differences allows the client to develop an understanding of the issues and an agenda for change.

Case study   Simon

Simon admitted his fear of public speaking was irrational. Yet the thought of standing up to present in front of an audience was enough to raise his pulse rate and instil a sense of panic. At work, he'd avoided making presentations as much as possible, but now he had to be a best man at a friend's wedding.

The coach asked him to recall an occasion when he had felt relaxed and comfortable making a presentation to a small group of people. What was the size of this group?

Next the coach asked him to focus on the conditions or circumstances of this event. With help, Simon described himself as being confident in his knowledge of the subject, amongst a group of supportive friends, to whom he had nothing to prove, and interacting closely with them. In particular, there were lots of nods, smiles, some laughter and an evident interest in what he had to say.

'Let's imagine, then, that there are only four of you at this wedding dinner. You know them all well and like them. How would you feel about making your speech in this environment?' Gradually the coach coaxed him to role play what he would say and how he would feel and behave.

'Let's add a couple more people … Who would you feel most comfortable about inviting in? … How would the speech go then?'

'And maybe a couple more?' …

Gradually, they increased the numbers to around 15. Simon volunteered that he could get people, who he felt less instinctively comfortable with, to nod in agreement early on, by asking them if they agreed with something fairly obvious and light-hearted. ('He's grown up a lot now … well maybe a bit?'). He could also increase his confidence by learning his speech, practising until he could recite it without notes.

Was Simon willing to double the number to 30? And again to 60? Gradually Simon recognized how he would apply the approaches, which he was now relatively comfortable with in small groups, to ever larger groups. He and the coach also practised what he would do if something happened in the middle of his speech, which sent him back into his habitual panic state. He practised the panic control measure Stop, Breathe, Think, Act, returning in his mind to the occasion when he felt relaxed presenting to a small group, and extending the scope of his confidence up again through increasing audience numbers.

In due course, Simon learned through exposure to other public speaking duties that he could hold a conversation with the audience, to speak with, rather than at, them. As a result, his confidence increased to the extent that it was no longer obvious to observers that this was not a natural skill for him.

Different realities

This is a technique to open up blind spots for discussion. One of the authors has the privilege to work frequently with people on the autistic spectrum, who quite literally see the world differently. The remarkable abilities of the idiot savant, who can draw in precise detail any building he observes, come about because the filters, which tell most people's minds what to notice and what to ignore, simply don't work in his case. To him, everything he sees is of equal importance. A lesson from this is that reality is no more than a particular perspective we choose to adopt at a particular time. Existential coaching and the reframing techniques of NLP (neuro-linguistic programming) are based to a large extent on enabling clients to countenance and explore different realties.

When faced with a client, whose fixed views may hinder achievement of their goals, coaches and mentors can help them to:

- Accept that other people may have different perceptions of reality and that these may be as valid as their own; or (if the issue is not one involving other people) that their existing perception of reality is simply one of many that they could choose to adopt.
- Understand different realities and the consequences of seeing the world differently.
- Choose realities, which will help them towards their aspirations and goals.

For example, a European expatriate manager working in an African country had very fixed views about the indigenous employees and their attitudes towards work. It was only in coaching that he began to question whether his view of reality might actually be creating some of the poor performance amongst his direct reports. Experimenting with different realities allowed him to try out different expectations and behaviours, which resulted in improved performance from these employees. The more open he became to seeing the world through the direct reports' eyes, the more cooperative they became.

A useful cascade of questions is:

- What do you see in this situation?
- What do others see?
- How would you describe the difference?
- What filters are you applying when you see this situation? What might you be avoiding noticing?
- What filters do you think they are they applying? What might they be avoiding noticing?
- What benefits are there for you in holding this view on reality?

- What benefits are there for them in holding this view on reality?
- What would be the benefits to you of a different view on reality?
- What would be the benefits to them of a different view on reality?
- What would be the benefits to the organization if you and they shared a common view on reality?
- What dialogue would help you and them to adapt your perception of reality?

Achieving influence

A common issue for executives is the need as they become more senior to achieve through influence rather than command. For many people, this is a very difficult transition, not least because it requires them to become much more contextually aware. For the coach or mentor, the challenge is to help them both perceive influence differently and to develop the skills to exert influence in constructive and effective ways. These influencing skills are sometimes referred to as 'environmental management'.

Case study   Philip

Philip was used to getting his own way. He'd risen through the ranks from graduate engineer, to supervisor, to manager and senior manager. Then he was promoted to a staff role, where few people reported to him, but where it was vitally important to the business that the cross-functional projects he initiated were successful. However, all the resources he needed – money, people, equipment and so on – were under the control of other people; and they had problems of their own.

His frustration at not getting his own way – at being seen to fail, for the first time in his career – was eating away at him. He described himself to his coach as feeling impotent; he described his peers, who were not helping him, as selfish.

The coach began by asking him what he thought were the aims and first principles of influence. Philip replied that he thought influence was about making things happen and that influencing skills were primarily about manipulating people and situations until they complied with what you wanted. It was that lack of compliance that Philip so resented.

Next the coach asked him to describe what was happening when he tried to influence others. Philip talked about how he first explained what he was trying to do, sold them the benefits and asked for their help. When that didn't work, he had tried explaining to them the difficulties he was facing, and how it made the whole team look bad if he wasn't able to deliver – but

(Continued)

again, little actual cooperation emerged, although his colleagues always made sympathetic noises.

Then the coach offered a different definition of influence – creating the conditions where people feel motivated and empowered to do what is needed and/or right. In this definition, the role of the influencer is not to control or cajole, but to understand and enable. As Philip talked this alternative perspective through, he realized that he had viewed influencing through only one set of eyes – his own. He had seen his objectives and motivations, his sense of the barriers to overcome, his ways of doing things and the impact that other people had on him and on his job. What he had neglected was their objectives and motivations, their ways of doing things, how they saw him and the impact he had on them.

Working with the coach, Philip set out to understand. He sat with each of the key people he needed to influence and didn't mention what he wanted them to do. When they queried this, he replied that he had realized he couldn't make progress with his project until he understood in a lot greater depth what the implications were for other people and functions. When he had spoken with all of them, he wrote a short paper summarizing what he had learned, then began a second series of meetings, this time aimed at exploring how he could make it easier for them to give practical support to his project. It soon became clear that in some cases, he and the colleague both needed to influence people at more senior levels and together they applied the same strategy of building understanding and enabling with these persons. (In one case, for example, the more senior manager simply wanted better information upon which to base resource allocation decisions.)

Over a couple of months, Philip gradually obtained the willing collaboration of all of his key colleagues. When asked by the coach what he had learned, he replied that influencing was 'not about the stick or the carrot, but about taking off the blinkers'.

Some questions to explore influencing

- How often do you get frustrated that other people operate with different priorities to your own?
- Can you describe a situation when people have been happy to go along with your ideas? And one where they weren't? What was the difference?
- What are the pluses and minuses of manipulating other people to do what you want them to?
- What could you do to create the environment where people are pulling you along, rather than being dragged by you?
- If you were in your colleagues' shoes, what would influence you to follow this path?

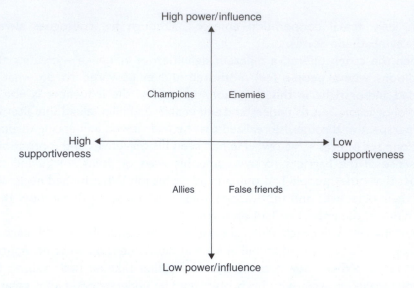

Figure 10.7   The support matrix.

● Given the choice between acquiescence, compliance or commitment, which would you choose?

The support matrix

This is a simple tool to help coachees/mentees think through how they will ensure they have the support they need to implement change, without becoming a casualty of the process. Organizations have a remarkable propensity to retaliate against those who initiate significant and discomforting change. Success often comes at a cost to the change agents.

The matrix's two dimensions are power/influence (low to high) and supportiveness (low to high), as in Figure 10.7.

Ask the coachee/mentee to think who would fit into each box. Enemies may have one or both of positional power (by virtue of the hierarchical authority they hold) and referent power (the ability to influence by bad mouthing or providing ammunition for more senior level).

They may identify a number of 'unknowns' – people, whose attitude and orientation towards the change and the change agents is not clear to the client. A useful question here is:

● What could you do to bring this person into one of the four quadrants?

Champions are people at a more senior level, who provide active support. Useful questions include:

- What can you do to make them support you even more?
- What risks lie in using the relationship with champions to drive the change process? (Where might resentment build up?)

Allies, sometimes called friends, provide practical ground support and encouragement. Useful questions include:

- What support do you need from them?
- How can they influence champions for you?
- How can they protect you from false friends?

Enemies are open about their opposition. Useful questions include:

- How much is their opposition directed towards the change or the agents of change?
- What would move them to another quadrant?
- How will you do that? Can champions help?
- What are the risks of building better relationships with enemies?

False friends make pretence of support but either fail to deliver support or actively undermine the change process and those associated with it.

- How can you make the risks of opposition greater for them?
- How could they be shifted to allies?

General questions, applicable to all four groups, include:

- What is this person's primary motivation?
- What other, less obvious motivations might they have?
- Who influences them and how?
- How courageous are they?
- In what circumstances would you trust them?
- How might your personal perception of them prevent you from using them effectively to support the change?

Understanding self

It's doubtful whether anyone ever gets really close to understanding themselves, no matter how many psychometric tests they take. The best we can hope to achieve is to understand ourselves a lot better and, in the context of coaching/mentoring, to understand ourselves in ways relevant to achieving our personal and work goals. A task of the coach/ mentor is therefore to stimulate *purposeful self-awareness*.

The toolbox for doing this is vast. At the simplest level, asking the right question at the right moment (the massively difficult question) can produce reflection that results in self-insight. At more complex levels, a cognitive behavioural coach might recognize dysfunctional patterns of thinking and behaviour and guide the client towards seeing them for themselves. The techniques we present here are derived from a wide spectrum of coaching and mentoring conceptual models.

Changing the script

This approach – one of the oldest and most powerful in our toolbox – is based on the observation that people's conversations tend to follow habitual paths, in terms of what is said, how they say it and what they feel. Married couples often describe 'falling into the groove' of old arguments. The same phrases recur and, more often than not, the same outcomes result.

Becoming aware of this script is the first step in changing negative outcomes. If you can predict what is going to happen, you have at least some chance of preventing it.

In the workplace, it is also common for important conversations to become habituated into a negative, dysfunctional pattern. Where this appears to be occurring, the coach/mentor can help the client relive the most recent occurrence and capture the 'script'. Usually, three columns are needed, one each for:

● What the client said
● What the other person said
● What the client felt.

It may occasionally be useful to include also what the client thinks the other person felt (though this becomes very subjective) and/or what each person did (for example, go very quiet, walk away or flare up).

Having captured one example, the coach/mentor encourages the client to capture the script next time it is played out, as well. This gives a record, which they can compare to the first script. Almost inevitably, the two scripts will be very similar.

Armed with this knowledge, the coach/mentor invites the client to select a point in the script, where they would like to make a change. Where they choose is of less importance than their intention to make a change. The pair then discusses how that relatively small change can be achieved and the client agrees to try this the next time the script is in danger of being replayed. As they become confident in changing one element of the script to be more positive, they can move on to another, until the whole conversation is different.

Case study   Alison

Alison was a team leader, who had been appointed from the ranks. She was very nervous about her responsibilities and took them seriously. However, she found it very difficult to confront her former team-mates when their performance or behaviour was inappropriate. For example, she felt constrained from pulling them up if they took too long a lunch hour. Instead, she stored up her anger until, after a number of provocations, she would erupt like a volcano. This tended to occur in front of the whole team and on one occasion, in front of a customer. She and her boss had discussed the problem and she was in no doubt that her future in management depended on getting to grips with it.

Her mentor helped her capture the script on two occasions. As expected, there was a lot of similarity in the sequence of events, words used and outcomes. 'Which bit do you want to change first?'

She could have chosen to start at the beginning – her inability to deal with poor behaviour at source – but she felt this was too hard, because it required substantial changes in her own behaviour. Instead she chose to alter the ending. With the mentor she developed a strategy that involved recognizing the feelings that would lead to an explosion. She realized that she adopted a defensive, tight posture and that her tone of voice gradually increased until she was shouting.

The alternative script, which she practised in front of a mirror, was to change her posture (shoulders back, head up), adopt a controlled tone and say: 'I'm very angry, but I'm not going to deal with this now. I want to see you in my office in 30 minutes.' This gave her time to compose herself, and the direct report time to reflect on their own behaviour. They were then able to have a more rational, appropriate discussion behind closed doors.

Once she had mastered this process, she gradually worked backwards towards the beginning, making small changes in the script until she was able to develop tactics for confronting poor behaviour as it occurred. Each step gave her more confidence in tackling the next.

The mindset for learning

There is increasing evidence that habits of mind learnt at a very young age have a major influence on people's ability and motivation to learn; and that these habits can be changed (Dweck, 2006; Blackwell et al., 2007).

Psychologist Carol Dweck's experiments with children identify two mindsets, which affect how they approach problems. People with *fixed mindsets* assume consciously or unconsciously that there are some things they are good at and some they are not good at, and that their ability is effectively set in stone. They therefore tend to avoid challenges, which take them into their areas of perceived weakness, or where there is a risk of failure. People with *growth mindsets* see themselves as having potential in a wide range of areas. They relish the opportunity to stretch their ability, regardless of whether the subject is one where they are 'naturally' talented. Failure to them is just a step on a learning journey.

Children with fixed mindsets, who get poor scores on a test, tend to study that topic less and even to consider cheating. Their performance deteriorates. By contrast, children with growth mindsets are motivated to try harder. Tests measuring electrical activity in the brains of children showed that both fixed and growth mindset participants became more mentally vigilant as they waited a short time to find out whether their answer to questions was right or wrong. However, only the growth mindset children remained vigilant while they waited to see what the correct answer was. The latter were significantly more motivated by learning.

An important conclusion from Dweck's work is that praising children for their talent and intelligence is likely to push them towards a fixed mindset. Praising them for their effort and perseverance tends to reinforce a growth mindset.

How does this have relevance to coaching and mentoring? It's no secret that managers can get a long way on bluff and avoidance – but that for most such people, the wheels eventually fall off the wagon as they take on jobs which leave less space to hide. Whether a manager has a predominantly fixed or growth mindset will likely have a substantial impact on how they face up to (or avoid) situations which are complex, involve high degrees of uncertainty, or simply stretch them beyond their comfort zone. If a manager seems to be resistant to the coaching process, making little progress in tackling their issues, then mindset is one area the coach might usefully explore.

How to broach the topic will depend a lot on circumstance and the particular skills of the coach/mentor. But there will normally be a lot of clues in the client's speech, if you are alert to them and encourage them to talk about relevant subjects. For example:

● Tell me about how you define talent in the people around you? … *Leading to* … How do you describe yourself in terms of talent?
● Tell me about a time when you were faced with an apparently insoluble problem. How did you tackle it?

- How do you decide when to stick with a problem until it's solved and when to decide there's no point in putting in more time or effort?
- How important is it to you to be right?
- What excites you about taking on new responsibilities?

If the pattern of responses indicates that the client tends towards a fixed mentality, then the coach/mentor can help them become aware both that this is the case and what the implications are for tackling the issues which the coaching/mentoring relationship is intended to address. Sharing the concept of the two mindsets provides a language which they can use to explore or prevent impasses, by asking questions such as:

- If we were having this conversation from a growth mindset, what would we be saying differently?
- Which mindset do you want to apply here? (Do you feel that you have the power to choose your mindset?)

The evidence on change in adult learning performance as a result of discussing mindset is relatively thin. But Dweck's work with children indicates that it can be transformational.

Entrepreneurial preferences

The concept of the entrepreneur (or within an organization, the intrapreneur) has much in common with leadership. Both are hard to define. Both have in recent years come to be seen as important parts of the competency mix for managers, even in sectors of public service, where finding creative ways around the rules was discouraged.

One of the most common developmental issues at senior levels is that the organization wants a client to become more entrepreneurial. But what does that mean? And how do you facilitate someone in developing skills which may be innate and/or personality-based?

We have found it useful to break down the entrepreneurial process in such a way that the coach or mentor can help a client identify where they have instinctive capabilities and preferences, and where they need support from other people who have different strengths. In other words, how can they establish a cooperative grouping, which will deliver the required entrepreneurial or intrapreneurial behaviours?

It seems from the literature on entrepreneurism that there are a number of capabilities required, each representing a different stage of the process. These include:

Opportunity recognition, which has two parts
- *Having innovative ideas*. In the main, these are not blue-sky, off-the-wall, but extrapolative thinking – for example, seeing new applications for

existing technologies, or seeing the potential for putting together two or more existing ideas or processes.

- *Adapting ideas* – moving from the theoretical to the practical. Here, the entrepreneur uses creativity and experience to find ways to turn the idea into a saleable product, a reproducible process and so on.

Coalition-building, which involves

- *Networking* – finding and bringing together people who will provide advice and help develop the concept.
- *Alliance-building* – the politics of gaining support from people, who will cooperate in making the project work.

Development, which involves

- *Product development* – the detail of making the product or process market-ready. Conceptual thinkers often have lots of ideas, but lack the patience and focus to carry them through. Product development may also include figuring out how to make money from the innovation.
- *Route to market* – developing a clear understanding of who will buy the product and why; of how to reach them; and of the psychology of the sale.

Resourcing, which involves acquiring

- *Funding* – the financial wherewithal.
- *Permission* – in an intrapreneurial context, the sign-off from key resource holders in the organization.
- *Expertise* – in the form of people and other stores of know-how.

Risk-management

- It's common to confuse the audacity and creativity of innovation with taking great risks. In reality, successful entrepreneurs tend to be relatively risk-averse. The risks they take are considered and calculated rather than instinct or reckless. Once a decision is taken, however, they are typically impatient to see it implemented.

Action-orientation, consisting of:

- Championing the changes – taking ownership for them, promoting them at every opportunity.
- Inspiring others to action – instilling a sense of urgency in others.
- 'Stickability' – working through setbacks with determination.
- Chasing change – ensuring that support is maintained, that barriers to making it happen are overcome.

There are very good frameworks of decision making (www.Kennedy BusinessSolutions.com), which follow a similar pattern and to some extent, the qualities of a good decision maker are similar to those of an effective entrepreneur. Similarly, decision making consists of a series of processes, in each of which the client may be relatively strong or weak.

How the coach or mentor can help

The immediate need of the client will usually be to work out what is lacking in their entrepreneurial/intrapreneurial inclinations. The coach can help by discussing each stage of the entrepreneurial process and how the client approaches them. Some useful questions at each stage are:

Opportunity recognition

- Do you often wake up with original ideas?
- Do you frequently see potential new business opportunities?
- Do you habitually see possibilities where other people see problems?
- Do you easily combine ideas to produce a new approach or perspective?
- When and how have you been an active participant in coming up with innovative ways forward?
- Do you see ways in which half-thought-through ideas could be turned into something more practical?
- Have you ever found ways to capitalize on ideas that didn't work before, so that they will work in a different context?
- Do you find you can borrow from other areas of expertise to make an idea more workable?
- Do other people use you as a sounding board for their ideas?

Coalition building

- Do you find it easy to identify people who might be useful to you?
- Do you usually know where to find a source of advice or help for the business issues you encounter?
- Do you actively construct and maintain networks?
- Do other people want to be networked with you?
- Do you find it easy to identify what's in it for other people to collaborate with you?
- Do you enjoy the politics of keeping people 'on side'?
- Do other people see you as a source of influence or opinion former?
- Do you often act as the bridge between groups with different interests?

Development

- Do you frequently work through and test the logic of proposed innovations?
- Do you enjoy working at an idea until it feels completely 'right'?

- Are you good at following through the implications of ideas until you have mapped out all the details?
- Are you adept at 'packaging' a concept or product so that it is professionally presented?
- Can you visualize clearly who will buy a new product and why?
- Do you systematically investigate and define the intended market?
- Do you have the skill to distinguish between what you would like to believe about the market and what the evidence says?
- Do you instinctively work your networks to find people who will be intermediaries to the market?

Resourcing

- Can you usually find a 'crock of gold' for something worthwhile?
- Can you persuade people, who hold the purse strings, to back your judgement?
- Are you good at getting things done on an inadequate budget?
- Do you find it easier to ask for a lot of money than for a little?
- Do you often work on the principle of seeking forgiveness rather than permission when you know something needs to be done?
- Do you often maintain support for a project by tackling it through small increments which appear less of a risk or threat?
- Do you have a good mental picture of the skills and experience of the people around you?
- Do you usually know where to turn for specific expertise, directly, or through your networks?
- Do you frequently make a mental or physical note of a resource that might prove useful in the future?
- Are you good at persuading other people to give you access to resources they control?

Risk management

- How would you describe your attitude towards taking risks?
- Do you have a good understanding of and skill in using risk management processes?
- Are you often taken by surprise by failures which you had not imagined?
- Can you easily describe and quantify for your own and other people's benefits the risks of failure and the risks of success?

Action-orientation

- Do you take visible ownership for projects or ideas you want to succeed?
- Do you take every opportunity to talk about them to relevant other people?

- Are you prepared to risk your own reputation by championing the project or idea?
- Do people typically see you as a leader or follower of change?
- Do you demonstrate a strong belief in ideas you espouse?
- Are you perhaps a little obsessive about them?
- Do you communicate a sense of urgency about the project or idea?
- Do you listen to and work with other people's concerns about the implications of change?
- Do you get easily discouraged if nobody seems interested?
- Do you get easily distracted by the next new idea?
- How do you sustain your own enthusiasm as the project progresses?
- How do you decide when enough is enough?
- What strategies and processes do you use to sustain other people's enthusiasm?
- Can you easily predict when projects or people are likely to 'go off the boil' and take preventative action?
- Do you monitor progress closely without getting bogged down in detail?
- Do people keep you informed of progress or do you have to go find out?

Of course, there are other questions, which could equally throw light on these topics and the questions listed here are not intended to be a quantifiable diagnostic tool. The aim is to help the client recognize why they sometimes fail to turn good ideas into good outcomes and to develop practical ways for them to be more effective – and to be seen to be more effective – in the future.

At the same time, it is important to recognize that even the most successful entrepreneurs fail frequently; they gain their reputation because they are able to accept failures, move on and try again with something slightly different. It is often the *volume* of ideas taken through to action stage that distinguishes a true entrepreneur from an aspirant. So, having clarified with the client where their natural entrepreneurial inclinations are strongest, the coach can help with questions such as:

- How can you make sure there are more ideas to consider, even if you don't create them yourself? (How can you encourage people to bring you more ideas?)
- What can you do to question established ways of doing things?
- What could you do to improve your networking skills?
- How can you identify and attract the right coalition partners?
- Who will flesh out the idea, if you don't?
- What expertise do you need to tap into, to ensure there really is a market and that it is prepared for this idea?

- What's your strategy for getting the money to make this happen?
- What's your strategy for making it less threatening?
- What will your ideal team for this project look like?
- How will you establish and manage the risks?
- What behaviours would you expect from a change champion?
- How will you capture and sustain your own and other people's enthusiasm?
- How will you get over the inevitable setbacks?

The 5 whys

Received wisdom says that coaches and mentors avoid why questions, because they tend to close down conversations, rather than open them up and because they can imply judgement on the part of the coach/mentor. This absolutist position is increasingly challenged by experienced coaches and mentors, who find that a well-placed *why* can give a sudden hard edge to an otherwise soft conversation – a short, sharp shock. Like a powerful medicine, *why* needs to be used expertly and sparingly. However, there is also a school of thought that says a structured, planned use of why questions can be effective in digging more deeply into a client's motivations.

The 5 whys is a simple technique for assessing motivations and making decisions. It begins with the question *Why do I want to do this?* And keeps asking why until a much more comprehensive picture emerges. A typical cascade might be:

- Why do I want to take a degree? To be more qualified in my role.
- Why do I want to be more qualified in my role? To earn more money.
- Why do I want/need to earn more money? To pay the mortgage.
- Why do I need to pay a mortgage (why not rent)? Because I want the security of owning my own home.
- Why do I need security? Answer?

The cascade of whys almost invariably leads the discussion to a deeper level of reflection that encompasses values and self-identity.

Temporal orientation

People differ considerably in their temporal orientation. Cross-cultural comparisons, for example, show wide variations about how people think about time; these are reflected in both language and behaviour. The sharp division in Western thinking between past, present and future is not reflected in all cultures.

Within the Anglo-Saxon culture, however, it is generally the case that people tend to have a preference as to whether they position issues in the past, the present or the future. People who have a past orientation, tend to have a preference for routine and what is known. They take as their reference point what has happened before, rather than what is happening now or may happen in the future. They are often good at establishing historical analogies, which can be very helpful, for example, in avoiding repeating past mistakes. However, they may also tend to miss current and future opportunities, to be reluctant to experiment and to question the present validity of solutions and processes that used to work.

People with a predominantly present orientation, at the extreme, live for the moment. They take the view that 'what is done, is done' and are eager to move on to the next problem or opportunity. While this is highly beneficial in terms of getting things done, they tend to miss opportunities to reflect upon and learn from experience. They may be, for example, always busy but not necessarily delivering the goods or improving performance.

People with a strong future orientation are either visionaries (when effective) or dreamers (when not effective). They may lack the sense of urgency inherent in present-oriented colleagues, but they are often very good at working steadily towards a long-term goal, using what happens in the present to create conditions under which that goal may come about.

In practice, both managers and the organizations in which they work need to have a balance between all three temporal orientations. The advantages of a strong orientation in one can very easily be undermined by a lack of attention or lack of capability in the others. The coach or mentor can help:

- Raise awareness of what the temporal orientation is.
- Examine the implications of the temporal orientation.
- Capitalize on individual variations in temporal orientation between team members.
- Develop tools and processes to ensure that the team achieves the balance of temporal orientation that will most effectively help it meet its goals.

Case study   **Sarah**

Sarah is an HR director, who was struggling to cope with her new team, which had been formed from the HR departments of two companies which had recently merged. The merger had resulted in redundancy for colleagues in both departments, including both the previous heads of HR, and Sarah

(Continued)

had been brought in subsequently to upgrade the role of HR in the new organization. This was the first time the team had been led by a director. 'I've never met such a negative crowd', she told her coach in exasperation. 'Everything I suggest, they find a reason for not doing. It didn't work before, we haven't got the resources, we find it better to do it the old way ... They just seem resistant to thinking about the future.'

> 'Who does think about the future?' asked the coach.
> 'Me! And that's it. It's as if they think that's my job only and not theirs at all.'
> 'What forces might be focusing their minds on the present, or on the past?'
> 'The merger hasn't helped. There's a lot of survivor syndrome there, I know. And they are all overworked, because we are trying to do more with a smaller team. But surely they know we can't stand still?'
> 'What might they be trying to protect or preserve?'
> 'It was pretty cosy in the old structure. I think some of them would like to go back to that ... I guess, too, that there's something about maintaining a level of certainty about what we do and how we do it. But I can't give them that, because our environment has changed and we have to change too.'
> 'How do you think they view your emphasis on the future?'
> 'They keep using words like "unrealistic visions" – but they don't offer any alternatives.'
> 'What changes in your behaviour and language might bring them to dialogue about this?'

The coaching conversation brought Sarah to a realization that she might be able to engage the team, if she made more effort to recognize and legitimize their time orientation, with the aim of encouraging them to recognize and participate in hers. With the coach's help she devised a strategy in which she hoped to enable them to view the future through the lens of the present.

In the next team meeting, she initiated a discussion around what members valued from the past and wanted to preserve in the present and future. She also encouraged them to discuss what they would like to leave behind from the past. Then she moved to the present. 'What strengths do we have that we don't want to lose? And what strengths do we not have – yet?' The positive language infected the meeting sufficiently for one of the most recalcitrant members to make the comment: 'We have to stop worrying about throwing the baby out with the bathwater. We just need to work out how to take the baby out before we pull the plug on all that dirty water.'

(Continued)

Acknowledging the team's temporal orientation gave them the psychological safety to accept that she needed their support in focusing on the future. A practical suggestion from one of the team was that they could henceforth divide their meeting agendas into three, equal parts:

- Past-oriented – feedback from surveys and happy sheets, reports on work done, plus opportunities to learn from each other's varied experience.
- Present – sorting out immediate problems, allocating work and making short-term improvements in processes.
- Future – where are we going and why?

Another team member built on the idea by suggesting that the order these three parts appeared on the agenda should be rotated, meeting by meeting. A few months later, the team decided there still wasn't enough time to talk about future issues and suggested they should have quarterly strategic meetings in addition to their normal team meetings.

Exploring beliefs and values

Most psychologically based approaches to coaching and mentoring place a great deal of emphasis on helping clients recognize and understand the conscious and unconscious 'rules' that govern their thinking and hence their behaviour. Cognitive behavioural coaching, in particular, aims to change behaviour by making those rules explicit and offering alternative rules to live by. The sometimes heated debate about whether coaches should be psychologists is too complex to review here, but suffice to say that a basic understanding of how to help people change beliefs – especially self-limiting beliefs – is essential to most coaching roles. In this section, we present some approaches relating to raising awareness of personal beliefs and values, with a view to initiating change.

Changing belief sets

This technique aims to help people understand and question their beliefs. It has strong parallels to 'different realities' above. Like so many techniques in coaching and mentoring, it is basically a logical sequence of questions.

1. What is your belief about XYZ? Can you be precise about it?
2. How consistent is this belief? In all circumstances? Most? Some?

3. Where and how do you apply this belief in practice? For example, in how you judge your own actions and motives? Those of other people? Can you give me some examples of how you have acted out this belief?
4. Where do you think this belief comes from? (Your personal experience? Your parents? Society in general? etc.)
5. What's the benefit of this belief to you?
   (i) Mentally
   (ii) Physically
   (iii) Materially
   (iv) Spiritually.
6. What's the benefit of this belief to others?
   (i) Mentally
   (ii) Physically
   (iii) Materially
   (iv) Spiritually.
7. How might this belief work to your disadvantage?
   (i) Mentally
   (ii) Physically
   (iii) Materially
   (iv) Spiritually.
8. What would be the value to you of a different belief?
   (i) Mentally
   (ii) Physically
   (iii) Materially
   (iv) Spiritually.
9. What would be the value to others if you had a different belief (e.g. about them)?
   (i) Mentally
   (ii) Physically
   (iii) Materially
   (iv) Spiritually.
10. What's preventing you accepting and living out this alternative belief?
11. What would you like to do about that?

Cognitive dissonance

When an executive is forced by circumstance to act against an essential belief, he or she often rationalizes the conflict by creating a third, new belief. For example, 'I know this isn't good for the environment, but I'm creating jobs' or 'everyone else is doing this; what we are doing makes only a tiny contribution to the problem'. Similarly, people tend to avoid personal responsibility for failures by rationalizing that 'I didn't really want that job anyway'.

For the coach or mentor, an important skill is to recognize this phenomenon (sometimes called cognitive dissonance), to help the client recognize what s/he is doing, then to help them address the issue in a more self-aware, self-honest manner.

The most obvious signs of cognitive dissonance are when the client appears to be acting in a way or taking an attitude that is contrary to beliefs or values you expect or know them to hold.

When the coach suspects that this may be the case, s/he needs to refocus the client on their values and attempt to identify a different and preferably better way of resolving the conflict. Useful techniques include:

- Helping them visualize a situation in which there would be no conflict of values or beliefs. For example, 'Suppose you had got that job. What would you be doing and saying differently now?'
- Quantify: 'How big a real or potential environmental impact would there have to be for you to come to a different decision?'
- Help identify the emotional mix. 'How comfortable do you feel with this decision on a scale of 1 to 10?' 'What fears do you have about this?'
- Follow the chain of reasoning:
  - If you hadn't had to worry about people losing their jobs, what would you have decided?
  - When and where did you become aware of potential conflict of values?
  - What pressures did you feel that influenced your thinking and decisions?
  - If you could have passed the responsibility for the decision to someone else to have decided for you, what would you have wanted them to say?
  - When you look back on the decision in X months'/years' time, do you think you will see it as short term or long term? Avoiding the issues or confronting them?
  - Does the decision you have made enhance or demean your ideal self?

The diversity awareness ladder

Research into human behaviour, when we are faced with someone who we perceive to be different to ourselves, reveals consistent patterns. The greater the perceived difference, the more likely we are to ascribe to the other person malevolent intent, inappropriate values and even lower intelligence. In groups, the effect is often magnified – witness the behaviour and attitudes of some football fans towards rival teams. The biggest barrier to diversity in the workplace is people's inability to recognize and manage this instinctive and dysfunctional reaction to difference.

Mentoring and coaching provide a safe environment, in which people can explore the assumptions they make about other people and develop the confidence to engage with them and others from the unknown group – be the difference one of race, gender, sexual preference, disability, personality, or whatever – in normal, productive conversation and collaboration. It's not surprising that there's a growing literature around diverse and cross-cultural coaching/mentoring (for example, Clutterbuck and Ragins, 2002; Rosinski, 2003; St Claire, 2005; Passmore, 2009).

To develop that level of confidence and conversational ability, mentor and mentee typically need to work through a number of transitions in their relationship. How many transitions depends on where each of them starts on the diversity awareness ladder (see Figure 10.8). Clearly, each may be at a different point, so it's important to try to establish

Stage	The inner conversation	The outer conversation
1. Fear	What do I fear from this person? What do I fear learning about myself? What might I be avoiding admitting to myself?	What do we have in common? What concerns do you have about me and my intentions?
2. Wariness	What if I say the wrong thing? Is their expectation of me negative and/or stereotyped? How open and honest can I be with them?	How can we be more open with each other? How can we recognize and manage behaviours that make each other feel uncomfortable/unvalued?
3. Tolerance	What judgements am I making about this person and on what basis? What boundaries am I seeking/applying in dealing with this person?	How can we exist/work together without friction? How can we take blame out of our conversations?
4. Acceptance	Can I accept this person for who they are? Can I accept and work with the validity of their perspective, even if it's different from mine?	What values do you hold? How do you apply them? How can we make our collaboration active and purposeful?
5. Appreciation	What can I learn from this person? How could knowing them make me a better/more accomplished person?	What can we learn from each other? How will we learn from each other?

Figure 10.8   The diversity awareness ladder.

where the other person is and begin the learning dialogue at the lowest (i.e. earliest) point.

The five stages of awareness are:

Fear – characterized by low self-awareness and low awareness of others. At its extreme, the fear stage becomes bigotry – the deliberate avoidance of examining one's own beliefs and perspectives, for fear of undermining them. Having the inner conversation is essential in moving people on, allowing them to confront and understand their fears. The outer conversation is a stepping stone to doing so, but equally the inner conversation may stimulate more productive outer conversations.

Wariness – when the individual is sufficiently self-aware and aware of others to recognize that their fears are irrational, but lacks the confidence to be truly open with people who they perceive as different. At this stage, for example, managers are often reluctant to give clear and open feedback to black or opposite gender direct reports, because they are overly concerned not to offend, or worried that they will be accused of bias. This isn't helpful for the team or the direct report.

Tolerance – people who express *tolerance* of other groups often can't let go of their own feelings of superiority. Tolerance involves no attempt to understand issues and events from the other person's perspective. It assumes that the tolerant person is right and the other person is misguided, sinful, or in some other way less worthy.

Acceptance – involves an understanding that the other person's perspectives are valid, well-intentioned and reasonable, in their own context. Acceptance creates the possibility of working together in a truly collegiate manner, with differences put aside as simply part of the wallpaper.

Appreciation – takes the relationship and the conversation into the realms of mutual learning. The very fact of difference becomes a valuable opportunity to explore new perspectives and ideas, to test assumptions and to create a new, more powerful sense of reality. Difference becomes a driver of change, self-awareness and the creation of a wider, healthier and inclusive community.

Interestingly, these levels of diversity awareness have great similarity with the stages of adult development (Kegan, 1982). The more mature an individual is in their approach to learning, the more likely they are to be at or near the appreciation stage.

The ladder of diversity awareness is useful in several respects. Firstly, it provides a language by which individuals and learning facilitators can create the kind of conversations that help people explore their perceptions and make transitions to a higher level of diversity awareness.

Secondly, it helps mentors and mentees set goals for developing their diversity maturity. It is quite possible for someone to be at level four or even five with one or two 'groups of difference', with which they are familiar, yet back at level one or two for others, with which they are much less familiar. (For example, Western managers may be relaxed in dealing with people of a different gender or with people from a black and minority ethnic background generally, yet have a relatively high degree of Islamophobia.) Thirdly, the ladder provides a practical basis for assessing the level of diversity maturity across a population within an organization.

Making use of the diversity awareness ladder

How, as a coach or mentor, or simply as a line manager, can you get the most out of the dialogue using this model? Here are some simple but effective approaches.

Invite the client to either:

- Close their eyes and think of a stranger they have recently met, who is from a different racial background, culture or sexual preference.
- Identify a situation, where they have felt uncomfortable or unsure how to react in the presence of someone from a different racial background, culture or sexual preference.

Then ask them to choose between the following sets of words and phrases, according to which most closely describes how they felt (there is no option for neither nor 'somewhere in-between' – they must opt for one over the other):

- Relaxed or tense
- Like or dislike
- Trust or distrust
- Cold or warm
- Valued or discounted
- Respected or disrespected
- Open or defensive
- Reassured or threatened
- Welcoming or reserved
- Empathetic or uninvolved
- Intrigued or dismissive.

Repeat the exercise for how they think the other person felt.

Talk through with them what this might tell them about where they are on the diversity awareness ladder, if their reactions to people from that background were always similar. It's easy for people to convince themselves that their reactions are just based on the other person's particular personality and behaviour, rather than generalized to a whole group. That position becomes increasingly untenable when they are invited to consider several examples and a pattern emerges.

It's hard for anyone to move up the diversity ladder until they:

1. Acknowledge where they are now.
2. Perceive the personal and wider benefits of a change in how they react and behave.
3. Begin to have the kind of conversation that helps them explore and become comfortable with the next rung up.

Like all scales of maturing of human thinking, this takes time. A coach or mentor can be very valuable in this context, because they can assist the learner with all three of these requirements for change. Common ways of doing so include:

● Asking questions that stimulate insight.
● Giving feedback that helps the learner recognize their current reality and question any self-deceptions that, for example, allow them to convince themselves that they are not 'really' biased.
● Demonstrating values and behaviours at the next layer of awareness (more than one rung above and the learner may struggle to understand what is being asked of them).
● Talking through tactics to help the learner engage in conversation with people different to themselves.
● Providing support in working through setbacks.

Exploring values

The coach or mentor initiates a discussion around a variety of themes about which the client is likely to hold strong values, starting with those closest to the client and working outwards. Key questions include:

● What causes you to have strong positive and negative experiences about …
● What's most important to you about …

The progression can be seen as a step-by-step expansion through four worlds.

The inner world
● What you feel you need to live up to.
● Who you feel you are.
● What raises/lowers your self-respect.

- What you feel you have achieved in life.
- What you feel you still have to achieve.
- What gives you a purpose in life?

The world of close others

- Who do you most care about and why?
- What is it about these relationships that you value?
- What things (as opposed to people) do you value?
- What makes you feel good/bad about these people?

The outer world

- Who you work for/with.
- Where you live.

The distant world

- What values do you hold about the environment? Foreign aid? Economic migration?

You can then use these insights by the individual to help them apply their values more consciously to issues they are facing.

The values matrix

This approach comes from one of the authors' work in mentoring programmes that support diversity objectives (Clutterbuck and Ragins, 2002). It provides a straightforward method for exploring values and it works particularly well across barriers of racial, cultural or gender difference. It works better when focused on specific situations or issues than on abstract or theoretical ones.

Self-image in Figure 10.9 concerns how the individual sees themselves, both as they are and as the person they strive to be. This is important for

	Image	**Responsibility**
Self	Who you are currently Who you aspire to be What makes you feel good/bad about yourself What you are at best	Your responsibility towards other people What to want to give
Others	How you want others to perceive you Who you want to impress, have impact on	Your expectations of other people's responsibility towards you What you want to receive from others

Figure 10.9   The values matrix.

putting goals into context and often provides numerous points of similarity and hence empathy with the coach or mentor. Not surprisingly, there may be large gaps between their actual and desired personae.

Other-image concerns how the person wants to be seen by other people, and how they think they are seen by those people. Useful subsidiary issues here are who these people are, i.e. whose opinion of them is particularly influential. Again, there may be considerable gaps between how they want to be seen and how they think they are seen.

Self-responsibility concerns who the person feels responsibilities toward and the nature of those responsibilities. A recurrent issue here is the degree of willingness the client feels towards this responsibility: is it a privilege or an obligation?

Other-responsibility concerns the client's expectations of other people. What is 'right' in the way other people should behave towards them? People who are inner directed (i.e. feel that they can control and are responsible for what happens to them) will tend to have very different values from people, who are outer-directed (i.e. feel that the responsibility for their circumstances lies elsewhere).

Exploring the four quadrants of the matrix can give the coach/mentor valuable insights into what makes the client tick and hence what drives their response to situations they encounter. Understanding where they have significant differences of value to the coach/mentor's own is important in building rapport. Sharing those differences may be the first steps in helping the client examine their values and perhaps changing them (although, of course, the coach must beware of imposing his or her own values!)

Emotions

Most coaches and mentors have encountered 'emotion-avoidant' clients – people, who try not to express emotion themselves, who become uncomfortable at displays of emotion by others, and who seem to have a belief that emotions are a weakness that has to be controlled. In some cases, these are damaged personalities, who need professional therapeutic help, but many cold fish can also be helped by coaching. The coach in this instance needs to respect their perspective and to manage their own levels of emotional radiation and personal disclosure, gradually weaning the client towards greater emotional openness and awareness.

In this section, we present two approaches, which we have developed to facilitate rational discussion about emotional themes. The drama triangle outlined in Chapter 11 is also useful for exploring when emotions in the relationship go awry.

Emotional mapping

Emotional mapping is particularly useful in helping a client work through the mix of emotions they are feeling about an issue. It's rare for a strong emotional reaction to consist of just one emotion, but people tend only to be aware of the most powerful emotions that possess them. Identifying other component emotions can:

- Help the client see the issue, which has given rise to the emotional response, from different perspectives.
- Identify contradictory emotions – and hence encourage a greater depth of analysis and insight.
- Permit the examination of each emotion individually, so that the client can determine how they want to deal with it. (Rather than tackle the bundle of emotions together, which is likely to be less effective.)

The simplest way to use the emotional map is to ask the client to underline all the emotions they are feeling. Sometimes this may involve only two or three cascades; at other times, a really difficult emotional situation may involve ten or more different cascades. Ask them also if they are experiencing other emotions, which aren't on the map. Add these.

Before proceeding to any form of structured analysis, ask the client to reflect upon their responses. What learning can they extract from an analysis of Figure 10.10 immediately? A typical reaction is that they had not realized how complex their feelings were and/or that they had some of the marked feelings at all.

Ask them which feelings they'd like to explore first. Then help them to examine those feelings one by one, with questions such as:

- What does the word 'despised' (or whichever word the client has chosen) mean to you?
- What makes you feel like that?
- What inner need drives that feeling?
- Is this a 'good'/appropriate feeling?
- How long, if at all, do you want to hang on to this feeling?
- If you'd like to change the feeling, what would you like to change it to? (Typically, but not always, this will be another word or phrase from the same cascade.)
- What would be the likely consequences of such a change?
- What could you do to make that change happen?

Positive emotions often form part of a general negative mix of feelings. Helping the client focus on these positives may energize them sufficiently to accept and deal with stronger negative feelings.

Calm Placid Content Relaxed Laid back Angry Furious	Bored Uninterested Disinterested Curious Intrigued Stimulated Inspired/radiant	Friendless Deserted Alone Welcome Included Supported Engaged	Distressed Miserable Sad Numb Pleased Happy Joyous	Cynical Suspicious/wary Unconcerned Open Confiding Trusting	Hating Disliking Ignoring Neutral Liking Caring Loving
Drained Tired/weary Idle Interested Energized	All at sea Unsure of myself In control Masterful	Despised Ignored Respected Valued Proud	Aimless Confused Purposeful Decisive	Overwhelmed Frustrated Keeping the lid on In control In the flow	Frivolous Whimsical Thoughtful Serious
Cowed Compliant Assertive Rebellious	Contemptuous Disrespectful Respectful Admiring	Terrified Afraid Threatened Secure Confident	Inferior Equal Superior	Transparent Open Reserved Mysterious	Self-contemptuous Self-pitying Realistic Good about myself Arrogant
Vengeful Judgemental Accepting Forgiving	Trapped Constrained Manipulated Empowered Liberated	Ignorant Uninformed Informed Knowledgeable	Disappointed Unimpressed Impressed Delighted	Betrayed Let down Supported Strongly supported	Sick Not at my best Not bad Healthy
Ugly Plain Pleasant Attractive	Discouraged Unmotivated Encouraged Determined	Resentful Unappreciative Appreciative Grateful	Self-sacrificing Generous Self-interested Selfish	Stupid Uninspired Clever Inspired	Hopeful Unconcerned Worried Despairing

Figure 10.10   An emotional map.

Tackling component emotions one by one is similar to tackling the components of a rational puzzle. If the big picture is too complex to tackle at once, breaking it down into manageable elements is a practical way of 'eating the elephant'. However, it is important to retain the bigger emotional picture in mind. The solutions identified for each component emotion must be capable of integration into a coherent way forward, which the client can understand and commit to.

Maintaining the boundaries

It's important for the coach or mentor to recognize when the client may need professional therapeutic help to deal with particular emotions or mixes of emotions. A rule of thumb here is to consider counselling if:

- The emotion is at the extreme of one of the cascades, or flips between two extremes, *and*
- The emotion is a permanent or semi-permanent feature of the client's predominant mood.

If in doubt, discuss with a qualified colleague, preferably in the context of supervision of practice.

Case study   **Emotional mapping – our experience**

One of us was helped by the other to use the emotional map to take a retrospective look at a period a few years before, when his university had been going through major structural change, which had caused considerable stress for many of the staff. As is so often the case, he recognized and recalled a number of different emotions which the situation had aroused in him. But at least one was a surprise, because it was not an emotion he would normally associate with himself – feeling self-interested. His learning from this was that his resentment of the behaviour of some managers at the time had had deeper and more lasting impacts than he had realized. Having surfaced this 'unfinished business', he was able to deal with it and finally put it to rest.

Making the client happier

Research into happiness suggests that, on average, three factors affect people's level of happiness (Sheldon and Lyubomirsky, 2006). Genetic predisposition is the largest factor, accounting for 50% of our base level of happiness. The individual's current circumstances (how well off they are, where they live and so on) account for only 10% of overall variation in happiness. The remaining 40% is determined by how the person sets and pursues goals, how optimistically they view their world and how physically active they are. In other words, what you do is more important than the circumstances in which you find yourself.

The implications for coaching and mentoring are profound. Helping the individual look beyond the specific, immediate problems, and to focus on things they can do something about, will give them a greater feeling of well-being. And the more active they can be, the more likely they are to change the circumstances that reduce their sense of happiness. Spending too much time commiserating with the coachee or mentee may actually make things worse!

Useful questions for a coach or mentor to ask include:

- How can you put your current concerns into context within the bigger picture?
- What are you doing in the rest of your life that compensates or could compensate for the problems you are experiencing in this area?
- How could you improve your *physical* well-being to increase your capacity to cope?
- What would be the right balance of pessimism/optimism for you at this time?
- What goals could you set that would make you feel better about yourself and your circumstances?

None of this is going to change the coachee's or mentee's natural disposition; but reflecting on the dynamics of their happiness quotient may stimulate a more positive approach to doing something about it.

For the coach/mentor, who wants to delve deeper into this aspect of their practice, there is a growing school of coaching, often described as positive psychology coaching, or PPC (Boniwell, 2008; Kauffman and Boniwell, 2009). This is built around the assumption that well-being is critical to personal and professional achievement and fulfilment; and that focusing on the whole person, and in particular on their strengths and positive behaviours, is more productive than trying to analyse and resolve their problems.

And finally, more Massively Difficult Questions

Massively Difficult Questions are questions that stimulate reflection, often at many levels, producing insights that may be the stepping stone to transformation of individuals, teams or organizations. We presented a long list of these in our first volume of techniques. In that list as in the one here, note the predominance of 'How' and 'What' questions over 'Why' questions. There were three 'Why' questions in the companion volume and there are none here. Our experience is that 'Why' questions take you into the past and lead to conversations where the coach/mentor can be seen to be suspecting the motives of the client. Here are some of the new questions we have gathered in workshops and conversations since:

1. Are you ready to make and commit to a decision now?
2. Choose a point between now and, say, 12 months hence. What are your options at that specific point?
3. Do you have the courage to tackle this issue/pursue this course of action?
4. How could you find peace with your current situation?
5. How do you reward yourself?
6. How easily do you get bored?
7. How important to you is it to like yourself?
8. How much [money, time, recognition, etc.] do you need to be happy?
9. How much worse does it have to get before you *have* to do something?
10. How ready are you for change?
11. How sure are you that the other person knows your intentions?
12. How would X describe you at your best?
13. If at the end of the day, I felt I had become a better person, what would have happened to me?
14. If the worst happened, what would the silver lining be?
15. If you are stuck, where precisely are you stuck and how?
16. If you can't, you're not in control; if you don't, you are. Which describes your situation and which do you want it to be?
17. If you had made my day, what would you have done?
18. If you knew you couldn't possibly fail, what would you do differently?
19. If you looked in the mirror now, what would you observe about yourself?
20. In what ways do you want to be different?
21. Looking back to now from a year ahead, what will you wish you'd have done now?
22. To what extent do you think your perceptions and expectations of X may be contributing to the problems in your relationship with them?
23. What are the risks of success?
24. What are the three things you have to be really good at in your role? Which are you least confident about?
25. What are you addicted to?
26. What are you doing that gets in the way of what you want to achieve?
27. What are you growing out of?
28. What are you like at your best?
29. What are you not noticing/choosing not to notice?
30. What are you ready to commit to?
31. What assumptions or beliefs do you hold that limit you?
32. What baggage are you/we bringing to this conversation?

33. What could you do that was neither X nor Y?
34. What could you do today that would make you like yourself more?
35. What decisions did you avoid this week?
36. What did you do that you can no longer continue to do in the same way?
37. What did you do today that helped your direct reports perform?
38. What did you do today that got in the way of their performance?
39. What do you already know that you will only realize you knew in a year's time?
40. What do you avoid admitting to yourself?
41. What do you notice now that you weren't aware of before?
42. What do you say to yourself silently that you could say out loud now?
43. What do you think you should be growing out of?
44. What do you *want* to believe about this?
45. What does the gap between success and failure look like?
46. What don't you know you do know? (What will you realize in a year's time you knew today?)
47. What don't you know you don't know?
48. What has changed that might cause you to question long-held assumptions?
49. What have you done recently that you should give yourself a pat on the back for?
50. What have you done today to help make a dream a reality?
51. What have you not noticed that is important?
52. What insights would you like to bring to our next session?
53. What is it about you that made you notice that behaviour in someone else?
54. What is your contract with yourself?
55. What is your general sense of direction? Are you going towards what you want to achieve or being blown off course? If the latter, what by?
56. What is your personal unique selling point?
57. What other goals do you have that are conflicting/supporting/compatible?
58. What other goals do you have that might/will take higher priority than this one?
59. What questions should you ask yourself before our next meeting to make good use of our next coaching/mentoring session?
60. What questions would you least/most like to be asked about your role? Your organization?
61. What really matters for you?
62. What will you start doing now to make that (goal) happen?
63. What would have to change for you to rule in solutions that you've ruled out?

64. What would help you generate the right question for this situation?
65. What would other people feel least comfortable about telling you?
66. What would you expect your hero to do in this situation?
67. What would you like to believe about yourself?
68. What would you want *not* to be afraid of?
69. What's in the best interests of … the team, the customer, the future, our children?
70. What's stopping you doing that?
71. What's the biggest lie you have told to someone else recently?
72. What's the biggest lie you have told yourself recently?
73. What's the dialogue you really need to have but haven't had so far?
74. What's the most useful thing you could do right now? That others could do right now?
75. What's the question you would least like to be asked about your work?
76. What's the question you would least like to be asked right now?
77. What's the real issue for you in all this?
78. What's your best (most useful) mistake recently?
79. When did you last feel content with yourself?
80. When do you get the best out of others?
81. When would be the best time to procrastinate about this?
82. Where do you get your energy from (in life and/or work)?
83. Who are you trying to avoid being like?
84. Who are you trying to please?
85. Who believes in you? Who do you want to believe in you and why?
86. Who do you know who handles this differently? What do they do?
87. Who does your inner voice remind you of?
88. Why do *you* care?
89. Will it take you nearer to where you want to go?
90. Will this make you feel better or worse about yourself?
91. Will this make you like yourself more or less?
92. Would you choose the status quo alternative if it wasn't the status quo?

Notice that there is only one 'Why' question in this list, nine 'How' questions and even more 'What' questions. What issues does this raise for you about coaching and mentoring? (There's another 'What' question.) And finally, to round the number up to 100, here are some MDQs for reviewing the relationship:

93. Have we become too cosy?
94. Do we challenge each other enough?
95. Are we taking enough risks in our conversations?
96. Are we sufficiently clear about the changes we want to see in our circumstances?

97. Are we sufficiently clear about the changes we want to see in our abilities?
98. Are we sufficiently clear about the changes we want to see in our behaviours?
99. How have we improved the quality of the relationship in terms of:
    Rapport
    Process.
100. How honest have we been in our reviews of the relationship?

References

Belf, T. E. (2002). *Coaching with Spirit*. San Francisco: Jossey-Bass/Pfeiffer.

Blackwell, L., Trzesniewski, K., Dweck, C. (2007). Implicit theories of intelligence predict achievement across an adolescent transition: a longitudinal study and an intervention. *Child Development*, **78**(1), 246–63.

Boniwell, I. (2008). *Positive Psychology in a Nutshell*. London: PWBC.

Clutterbuck, D. (2008). A Longitudinal Study of the Effectiveness of Developmental Mentoring. Doctoral thesis submitted to the University of London.

Clutterbuck, D. and Ragins, B. R. (2002). *Mentoring and Diversity: An International Perspective*. Oxford: Butterworth-Heinemann.

Drucker, P. F. (1954). *The Practice of Management*. Oxford: Heinemann.

Dweck, C. (2006). *Mindset: The New Psychology of Success*. New York: Random House.

Egan, G. (1994). *The Skilled Helper: A Problem Management Approach to Helping*. Pacific Grove, CA: Brooks and Cole.

Ibarra, H. (2003). *Working Identity: Unconventional Strategies for Reinventing Your Career*. Cambridge, MA: Harvard Business Press.

Ibarra, H. and Lineback, K. (2005). What's your story? *Harvard Business Review*, **83**(1), 64–71.

Kauffman, C. and Boniwell, I. (2009). Positive psychology coaching. In: Clutterbuck, D., Cox, E. and Bachkirova, T. (eds), *Sage Handbook of Coaching*. London: Sage.

Kegan, R. (1982). *The Evolving Self*. Cambridge, MA: Harvard University Press.

Kennedy. www.KennedyBusinessSolutions.com

Passmore, J. (ed.) (2009). *Diversity-in-coaching*. London: Kogan Page.

Rogers, P. and Blenko, M. (2006). Who has the D?: How clear decision roles enhance organizational performance. *Harvard Business Review*, **84**(1), 53–61.

Rosinski, P. (2003). *Coaching Across Cultures*. London: Nicholas Brealey.

Sheldon, K. M. and Lyubomirsky, S. (2006). Achieving sustainable gains in happiness: change your actions, not just your circumstances. *Journal of Happiness Studies*, **7**(1), 55–86.

St Claire, B. A. (2005). *Carrying Cultural Baggage: The Contribution of Socio-cultural Anthropology to Cross-cultural Coaching*. Oxford: Oxford Brookes University.

Chapter 11

Coach/mentor focused techniques

David Clutterbuck and David Megginson

This chapter takes the perspective of the coach and their professional development. There is a (hopefully short-lived) vogue for people to call themselves 'master-coaches' – yet the essence of mastery is that it is always on the horizon. The more we learn about coaching and mentoring, the greater our recognition of the gap between the professional we are and the professional we could be. The techniques and approaches presented here represent some of the most common and significant issues we have encountered in coach/mentor development.

The motivation to coach

Why do people coach? For some people it is a calling; for others, it simply 'snuck up and took over my life'; for yet others, it is an obligation placed upon them in their role as a line manager. Truls Engstrøm's (Engstrøm, 1997) studies of informal mentoring in Scandinavia suggest that some motivations are less desirable than others. In particular, altruistic motivations ('I want to put something back' or 'I want to prevent them making the same mistakes as I did') are not closely associated with positive, effective relationships. Altruism can easily lead to the mentor talking at the mentee, making assumptions about what is best for them – it is, in some ways, an unconscious form of self-gratification. Mentors who care too much can be dangerous. In many cases, they conceal a deeper, even more dangerous motivation – the sublimation of their own problems by seeking to help solve other people's. As a result, they see the client's issues through the filter of their own, leading to misdirection and subtle control of the vulnerable client.

A motivation much more clearly associated with positive mentoring is enlightened self-interest, especially as expressed through the mentor's desire to learn. In general, we find that the most effective coaches and mentors tend to place personal learning – being challenged, having access to different perspectives, tackling different kinds of problems than those they experience in their own life and work – at the top of what they seek and receive from their involvement in developmental relationships. Internal manager mentors also say that they are able to practise different developmental approaches on people outside their reporting line, with whom they feel they can be more adventurous.

Within the individual mentoring or coaching relationship, one of the questions an effective practitioner may find helpful in grounding their practice is *'For whose benefit am I asking this question?'* It's very easy to convince oneself you are acting from a fully altruistic and disinterested perspective, when the opposite is the case.

One way of taking this inner conversation deeper – and of structuring discussion around this theme during supervision – is to examine your 'responding state'. By this we mean the underlying attitudes and motives that shape your responses to the client and what they say. There appear to be three broad states, which people operate under in their dialogue with others. These are:

- *Protect*. The instinct to preserve a more vulnerable individual from harm is deeply ingrained in us. If the protect instinct predominates, however, it leads to dependency and a tendency to dismiss the experience and perspective of the other individual. A useful question is: *'What am I attempting to shield them from?'*
- *Exploit*. The predatory instinct also runs deep. It may reveal itself, for example, in sexual lust, or in using others to bolster our own position or ego. A useful question is: *'What kind of gratification am I seeking or receiving from this relationship?'*
- *Equate*. Here the instincts are in balance. The client is seen as an equal in status, experience. Whereas in Protecting, the coach does things *for* the client and in Exploiting *to* the client, in Equating, he or she does things *with* the client. There are no hidden agendas and processes can be observed, critiqued and amended by both parties together. Equating can be overdone if the coach/mentor foregoes leading initiatives that might usefully shape the conversation. Alternatively the coach/mentor might insist on a fair share of the influence on the shape of the conversation when the client wants and needs to take control. A useful question here is: *'Is there a sense of calm about the interaction between us?'*

An examination of motives after each mentoring or coaching session makes sense as part of reflective learning and as an integral part of all practice review processes. In our experience, however, it is one of the areas many coaches (and some supervisors) avoid, because the insights produced have a tendency to dent our self-images! It helps to remember that even the most apparently altruistic behaviours have one or more selfish motives at a greater depth; and that bringing more of this trail to the surface will make us more effective in using our instincts to help the client.

Case study   Anna

Anna brought to supervision the case of a client, who has reached a very senior role in a public sector organization, but who has difficulties expressing emotions and dealing with emotion in others. Working in a high stress environment, he was nonetheless regarded by people in levels below as a good leader – he demonstrated a high degree of integrity, was compassionate in his deeds, if not his words, and had a very positive and clear sense of where he wanted the organization to go. Recognizing his problems with some aspects of emotional intelligence, he had appointed a deputy, who had the qualities he did not – someone, who had warmth and an easy manner presenting difficult matters to a heavily unionized workforce.

Anna was appointed as his coach as part of a broader leadership programme aimed at all senior people of his grade. Another part of the programme involved a competency assessment, as a result of which he was given a somewhat ham-fisted warning by central human resources that he would have to work on building his emotional intelligence.

As Anna described this situation, the supervisor explained some of the hallmarks of someone with high-grade Asperger's syndrome. Anna thought this was a very close match and this conclusion initiated a discussion around the legality of requiring someone with this disability to change the way their brain was wired – even if that were possible.

As the session continued, Anna became visibly angrier and angrier, to the point where the supervisor suggested they pause and examine this emotion. What kind of anger was it? Where was it directed? How useful was it? And finally, whose anger was it? This last question stopped the conversation in its tracks (a moment of disconnect – see Chapter 12) as Anna reflected on it. After a while, she breathed out deeply, visibly releasing the anger and said: 'It's mine, isn't it? He's not angry at all. He's just used to this kind of ignorant stupidity from HR and takes it in his stride!'

(Continued)

Further conversation revealed that, by seeing the client as vulnerable, she had allowed herself to assume a protective mode towards him. (A protective or nurturing parent in Transactional Analysis speak.) By over-empathizing, she had begun to project her own emotions onto him. With this understanding, she was able to step back and consider how to bring the relationship back into equate mode, helping the client widen his portfolio of coping strategies and develop tactics for educating HR.

The mindset for coaching

It may seem an obvious thing to say, but coaching and mentoring sessions are likely to go a lot better if the participants begin with an appropriate mindset – if they are both prepared and ready for dialogue. Peter Hawkins, who has pioneered supervision in coaching (Hawkins and Smith, 2006), points out that the coaching session starts from the moment the client and coach meet – the informal greetings and preparation can be very informative about the client's state of mind. Equally, however, the coach or mentor needs to pay attention to their own state of mind and this attentiveness may need to start well before the session. Useful questions to ask oneself include:

- Am I truly ready for coaching? (Am I relaxed, focused and able to focus fully on their issues?)
- What personal baggage am I in danger of importing into this conversation?
- What do I already know about this client, which may prevent me being as helpful as I'd like?
- What does my body tell me about my own mental state?

With practice, such reflection becomes automatic and brief. If the coach feels unready, then he or she can use relaxation techniques to change their mindframe before the client arrives.

There is a growing recognition that back-to-back coaching sessions are not good for the coach, and thus not good for the client. In Chapter 7 John Groom makes this point forcibly.

As an aside, it can sometimes happen that the coach/mentor is jolted out of their helping mindframe by something that happens in the learning conversation. This happened recently to one of the authors, in a supervision session. An admission by the coach supervisee about their fears elicited such a strong empathetic response in the supervisor that he asked for a short reflective pause. After a couple of minutes, he explained to the coach that this was an issue so relevant to his own circumstances that he had needed to make sure that he separated the coach's issues from his own. This encouraged the coach to dig deeper into her own feelings about the situation she was describing. The supervisor subsequently took his own issue to his own supervision group (great fleas have lesser fleas etc.).

Achieving equilibrium

This isn't so much a technique as another mindframe. For both the coach and the coachee, achieving a sense of personal equilibrium is a great asset in making the most of the learning conversation. A mental state of high alertness, combined with relaxation, stimulates awareness of both self and each other, better listening behaviours and positive attentiveness. The problem is that most people are rarely, if ever, in true equilibrium. A practical way of achieving at least a broad sense of equilibrium is to take time to reflect on where you are on nine areas of balance:

- *Doing v. being* – the core of our model of mentoring in *The Situational Mentor* (Clutterbuck and Lane, 2004). Doing refers to our behaviours and actions; being to our sense of identity and awareness of self. Key to establishing equilibrium here is to take time occasionally to slow down, both mentally and physically, until you are calm enough to take stock of everything within and around you.
- *Me space v. them space* – allowing both action time and thinking time for oneself, rather than allowing all our attention to be taken up with things we do for or on behalf of others.
- *Past, present and future* – is your mental attention appropriately distributed between these temporal perspectives?
- *Balanced v. unbalanced body* – very few people have perfect posture. How we sit, stand and move has a strong impact on how we feel and vice versa. Checking for positive posture is a useful habit for any activity, from sports competition to a coaching conversation.
- *Participating v. observing* – we all have a natural inclination to either get stuck in or watch from the sidelines. Effective coaching – from the perspective of both the coach and the coachee – requires a conscious moderation to avoid going too far to either extreme. Part of this is the balance between talking and reflecting quietly.
- *Knowing v. innocence* – some knowledge is important in shaping the conversation, but both coach and coachee need also to cultivate a degree of naivety, from which spring penetrating questions and honest responses.

- *Accepting v. judging* – it's common for pundits to say that coaches should never make judgements about people and situations. That's delusional, of course; unconsciously, we are all making judgements all the time. Raising our awareness of where we may be prone to make judgements and whether those are justifiable on the evidence, promotes openness in the coaching conversation.
- *Support v. challenge* – coaches/mentors can usefully attend to how they balance their support and challenge. An appropriate point on the scale will differ from client to client and from time to time with any one client. For example, one of us worked with a robust and confident manager who normally relished lots of challenge, but in one session shortly after his father had died he sought and was given much more support than was usually the case.
- *Concrete v. abstract* – some clients focus on immediate issues or defined projects and find abstractions difficult. However, if they are to generalize their learning they will need to make broader sense of their immediate learning. By contrast, others like to deal in abstractions, and the coach/mentor's role is to help them focus on grounding their learning, for example by answering the questions: *What? So what? Now what?*

Reflecting on these balances – by both coach and coachee – creates a set of positive expectations of the conversation. It also helps to ensure that both coach and the coachee are able to slip quickly and effortlessly into flow.

Case study   **Too fast to think?**

One of the authors was working on their mentoring skills with top managers in a UK bank. At lunch on the first day of the course, the head of management development in the bank came to the facilitators and said that things were going well, but that some participants felt that the course was going a bit slowly. When the participants assembled after lunch, David said, 'I hear that some of you think that things are going a bit slowly. I'm really worried about that, because if it is only a bit slow, then we're going far too fast. We'll aim to slow down a lot more this afternoon.'

Empathetic curiosity

A common issue for discussion in coaching and mentoring programmes targeted at diversity management – but equally valid whenever partners in a learning alliance have significant differences in gender, age, culture, race, disability and so on – is how central to the mentoring dialogue should this difference be? On the one hand, we have numerous examples of coachees/mentees who have felt patronized when the coach/mentor has studiously ignored referring, for example, to their colour or disability; on the other, it can be equally disruptive of rapport for the mentor to make intrusive enquiries. Building a relationship around a perceived disadvantage can be as disempowering as not mentioning it at all!

Previous experience can make coachees/mentees very sensitive about well-meant but clumsy inquiries into the aspect of difference. Here is a conversation that happened to a colleague:

> Question: How long have you been in a wheelchair?
> Answer: Yes, I do have sex, thank you.

The expectation of being patronized can make the coachee/mentee highly defensive. So how can the mentor overcome this instinctive response, and move on to a position where the difference or disadvantage is appropriately positioned as either within or outside the legitimate context of the mentoring dialogue?

Empathetic curiosity is a technique for demonstrating interest in the other as a person, while being sensitive to their concerns and emotions. The essential process is as follows:

Initial questions the coach/mentor should ask of himself/herself
- What is my motivation in asking this question?
- How will it help me: (a) feel comfortable in the relationship?; (b) frame appropriate questions?; (c) understand issues from their perspective?
- What preconceptions do I have about people in their situation? How deeply have I questioned their validity?

Initial questions to ask of the coachee/mentee
- What do I need to know about you and your circumstances to be of real help?
- What do you like to be valued for? What makes you feel devalued?
- I'm very aware that people can sometimes be *too* helpful. What can I do to be just helpful enough?
- How can you help me avoid being patronizing? What do I need to learn?

Subsequent questions for the coach/mentor to ask of himself/herself
- How clear am I about how the coachee/mentee feels?
- Have we identified where and how the difference currently prevents them achieving their ambitions?
- How honest are we being to each other?
- Are we making the most of the potential to learn from the differences between us?

Subsequent questions to the mentee
- What do you want to change in your circumstances?
- What can you change and what can't you change?
- How relevant is [difference] to that?
- Can we start the changes here, in this relationship?

Figure 11.1 gives what are, of course, only sample questions. But they illustrate a progression.

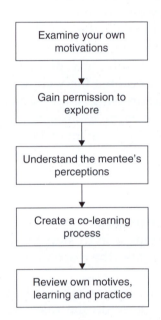

Figure 11.1   Empathetic curiosity.

The drama triangle

The drama triangle is a useful framework when empathetic curiosity breaks down. This commonly used coaching tool is derived from Transactional Analysis and is attributed to Steven Karpman (for a discussion of its origin see Karpman, 2006). It is most often used to identify and explore dysfunctions in relationships at work or home.

In the triangle, there are three roles people play towards others:

1. Persecutor – someone who either attacks aggressively, or simply disturbs the equilibrium by innovating or asking awkward questions.
2. Victim – someone who feels the persecutor is targeting them, or who is affected by changes the persecutor initiates (for example, a new boss, who wants to introduce different ways of doing things).

3. Rescuer – a white knight or protector; or someone who tries to restore the equilibrium. (Sponsorship mentors can easily fall into the rescuer role – the title protégé suggests being there for the learner to lean on.)

The characters in the drama triangle can be specific (a particular person) or general (a financial situation, or an illness). Roles are also not static – people move from one to another rapidly, repeating old behaviours. Once trapped into a drama triangle, it can be hard to extricate oneself, because the other players are still playing the game. These power games can be very destructive.

In coaching, it is common for the coach to become either the persecutor ('Why do you keep asking me these difficult questions?') or the rescuer ('You are going to solve my problems, aren't you?'). It's less common for the coach to become the victim, but it still happens ('This client is wilfully not addressing their issues, or implementing the changes we discuss. It makes me feel useless.').

Sometimes, the drama triangle may be appropriate as a healthy response to a temporary situation. But getting locked into a drama triangle is rarely, if ever, healthy. To break out of a drama triangle, the coach can:

1. Recognize that you are in one.
2. Consider how important it is to stop the drama. Are you and the other parties willing to take the discomfort of 'outing' it? What is the payoff for doing so?
3. Step back mentally and analyse what is happening. Who is playing what role? When and how do the roles change? What benefits do they derive from behaving in this way? How can we become emotionally detached from the game?
4. Explain to the other players what you think is going on and the implications this has for your relationship (and, in a team, for the team task).
5. Invite them to join you in analysing the 'game'. What do we agree and disagree on? How do we want this relationship to function?
6. Work with them in committing to a more adult relationship, in which none of the drama triangle roles are played; and in which it is acceptable and welcome to query whether a colleague is slipping back into a dramatic role.

Seven coaching/mentoring conversations

There probably is a coaching or mentoring textbook out there that doesn't make the assumption that a session with a client is about one conversation, but we haven't found one, although books on coaching supervision do mention a range of conversations. Hawkins and Smith (2006) talk about seven relationships, however these differ from the framework described here. In our view, the coaching conversation is actually seven conversations:

1. My dialogue with myself before the session.
2. The client's inner dialogue before the session.
3. My inner dialogue during the conversation.
4. The spoken dialogue.
5. The client's inner dialogue during the conversation.
6. My reflection after the conversation.
7. The client's reflection after the conversation.

Most coach training focuses on the middle of these – the spoken dialogue. Yet the effectiveness of the spoken dialogue depends heavily on the other six conversations. Building our competence in each of the conversations is essential in mastering the coaching role.

The coach's preparatory inner dialogue

The purpose of this dialogue is to ensure that the coach is mentally prepared for the coaching conversation. The quality of the conversation is dependent, to a significant extent, on the quality of thinking both coach and coachee put into their preparation – although spontaneity of dialogue still plays a major role, too! Useful questions include:

- How have I helped so far?
- What are my motivations in this relationship?
- What is the 'big picture' for this client?
- Do I really understand what drives them?
- What is this client avoiding?
- What am I avoiding?
- How do I feel about this relationship?
- Am I looking forward to this meeting? (If not, what's the issue and what should I be doing about it?)
- What are my responsibilities in this relationship?
- Who else is present and in what ways?

The client's preparatory inner dialogue

Preparation by the coachee is equally important and can be equally demanding. At least an hour's quality reflective space is typically required to prepare for an intensive coaching session. Questions coachees can ask of themselves before the meeting include:

- What has happened to me since our last meeting? How have I changed?
- What issues have been resolved and what new issues have arisen?
- What's the relationship between these issues and my overall goals?
- What thinking have I already done around these issues?
- How do I want my coach to help?
- What information can I provide to help the coach understand the issue?
- Do I really want to resolve this issue? What are my motivations for introducing it *now*?
- How do I feel about this relationship?
- Am I looking forward to this meeting? (If not, what's the issue and what should I be doing about it?)
- What are my responsibilities in this relationship?

The coach's inner dialogue during the spoken conversation

This inner dialogue takes place in parallel with the process of listening and asking questions. Sometimes called 'reflection-in-action' (Schön, 1991), it requires us to both participate fully in the conversation and observe it as dispassionately as possible. In some ways, it's like the running commentary advanced drivers use, when they talk themselves through how they observe the road ahead of them. Useful questions include:

- What is the quality of my listening? (Am I fully focused on the client?)
- What am I observing/hearing? What am I missing?
- Is my intuition turned on?
- What assumptions am I making? How might these be acting as a filter on my listening and my understanding?
- Am I spending too much attention on crafting the next question? (Is this affecting my ability to be 'in the moment'?)
- How am I helping?
- What is the client not saying?
- What is the quality of the client's thinking?
- How am I feeling in the moment? If I feel uncomfortable, what is making me so?
- How is the client feeling at this moment?

The spoken conversation

This is the part that attracts the most attention. It's also the easiest conversation and therefore highly beguiling. Inexperienced or inexpert coaches frequently are aware only of this conversation, and oblivious to the inner conversations going on simultaneously in themselves and the client (if they have an inner conversation at all!). Effective coaches maintain awareness of all three, while instinctively reviewing the dynamics of the spoken conversation, asking themselves questions such as:

● Is there consonance between what is said and our body language?
● Is there a logical pattern of development to the conversation?
● Are we exploring issues from multiple perspectives?
● Who is doing most of the talking/coming up with most of the ideas?/asking most of the questions?
● Is the pace sufficiently varied (e.g. is there space for both quiet reflection and rapid building on ideas)?
● Are we both engaged in the conversation?
● Are we exploring issues in sufficient depth?

The coachee's inner dialogue during the spoken conversation

The coachee can contribute more to the learning dialogue, if he or she is also process-aware. The management of the conversation and its direction become a shared activity. It's a further step, however, to becoming aware of the inner conversation. The coach can help build that awareness by interrupting the flow of the spoken conversation at appropriate times to raise the coachee's internal awareness, helping them to reflect upon questions, such as:

● How open and honest am I being with myself and with my coach?
● Am I saying what I want to say?
● What assumptions or filters am I applying in answering the coach's questions?
● How am I feeling about the conversation? If I feel uncomfortable, what is making me so?
● How is my coach feeling at this moment?
● What are the opportunities for learning in this conversation?
● How am I helping the coach understand my issues?

In due course, some coachees learn how to carry on the inner conversation without prompting from the coach.

The coach's inner conversation after the session

'Reflection-on-action' is also a critical part of the coach's continuous improvement and personal growth. While the meeting is still fresh in his or her memory, the coach should review the five antecedent conversations, asking, for example:

- How did I help? What insights did we create together? What did I do to enhance the quality of the coachee's thinking?
- Was I appropriately directive/non-directive?
- Where did I struggle?
- Did we create a 'bias for action'?
- What insightful questions did I ask which might be useful in other learning conversations?
- What questions did I withhold and why?
- Was I sufficiently challenging? Did I receive sufficient challenge in return?
- Did I give the coachee sufficient time to think?
- What did I learn?
- What patterns can I discern from this and previous conversations with this client?
- What would I do differently another time?
- Am I still looking forward to the next meeting?
- What can I usefully discuss with my supervisor?

The coachee's inner conversation after the session

The coachee's post-meeting reflection is vital in terms of translating good thoughts into practical action. The thinking process can be helped through questions such as:

- What did I learn?
- How am I going to put that learning into practice?
- What do I need to think about more deeply?
- What do I want to explore with other people?
- Was I sufficiently open and honest?
- What could I have done to extract more value from the conversation?
- What could I have done to make it more enjoyable for myself and/or my coach?
- What changed expectations do I now have of myself? How do these align with other people's expectations of me?
- Am I still looking forward to the next meeting?

Each of these conversations requires an appropriate space and sufficient time (at least half an hour in most cases) for reflection. The quality of reflection at each stage can also be improved through:

- Initial mental relaxation exercises to establish an appropriate mental state.

- Doing something completely different and enjoyable beforehand, to stimulate creativity.
- Considering what psychological contract we have with ourselves about coaching in general and this relationship in particular.
- Being as open as one can to discovery – about the context, other people and oneself.

For the coach, it can also be valuable to summarize reflection by thinking what your supervisor might say, were they listening in. What elements of each of the seven conversations would be helpful in giving the supervisor greater insight into the dynamics of the issues and how you approached them? Other useful questions include:

- What am I aware of, but have not yet recognized or acknowledged?
- What is the coachee aware of, but has not yet recognized or acknowledged?
- What is the quality of the learning that is taking place? How have I contributed to that?
- How can my reflection-on-practice and reflection-in-action improve my performance as a coach?

The seven conversations provide a useful framework for planning a coaching intervention. They can also be valuable in helping the client understand how they can make the most of the learning dialogues in which they engage.

A systems approach to coaching and mentoring

Any coach or mentor, who has been through an advanced level of training in the role, should be fully aware of the dangers of accepting presented issues at face value. One experienced executive coach recently told me that it was a rarity for any of his clients' presented issues to be what they really needed to work on. Almost invariably, the presented issue was a clue to deeper or broader issues, which the client had not identified or had been deliberately or unconsciously avoiding.

At the same time, however, it is important that the coach or mentor should not place himself or herself in the role of amateur psychologist. Having enough knowledge to recognize indicators of psychological conditions that require specialist help is critical in recognizing and respecting the boundaries of competence. But stepping over those boundaries is both dangerous (for both parties) and irresponsible.

Does that mean that all professional coaches and mentors should be psychotherapists? It is difficult to sustain such a position, especially with regard to mentoring, where critical parts of the relationship are empathy and mutual respect, based on the mentor's practical experience in the world the mentee wants to learn about. In a sounding board role, clinical detachment is a hindrance to the learning dialogue.

So how can the non-therapist coach or mentor ensure that they manage this delicate balance, adding real value to the client's thinking, assisting them in making behavioural change, yet remaining within the bounds of their psychological competence? The answer appears to lie in the development of an entirely different competence – systems thinking.

Thinking systematically is commonplace among coaches and mentors. It is, for most experienced managers, relatively easy to acquire the skill of listening to what someone says and following the logic step by step, until conclusions emerge that are either tenable or untenable. Socrates, the Greek philosopher, demonstrated the technique admirably more than 2000 years ago, although we have only other people's accounts of his dialogues.

Thinking systematically about emotions is a less common skill. Here the coach or mentor follows the stream of emotions in a similar manner, attempting to help the client explore where and how emotions originate and how helpful or unhelpful those emotions are in terms of what they want to achieve.

However, thinking systematically is not the same as systems thinking. Systems thinking is about taking a holistic approach that views the individual and his or her environment as interconnected and complex. Instead of focusing on problem/solution, it attempts first to understand the context in which an issue is grounded. It explores the impact or influence parts of this larger picture have upon each other – what may make a change in one factor more or less effective, and what unexpected outcomes may occur.

The coach or mentor using a systems-thinking approach may help the client 'map' the context of a presented issue by capturing on paper a range of factors associated with it. Some of these factors may be obvious; others may only be revealed in the flow of the learning dialogue. Headings to explore may include: goals, ambitions, values, people, fears, skills, resources, self-esteem, beliefs and so on. Approaching from the presented issue, the coach might ask *'Who are all the people, who have an influence on this issue and how you react to it?'* Approaching from a broader perspective, the coach might ask, *'Who are the people who matter to you?' 'Whose opinion of you influences how you think and/or behave?' 'Who can make a difference to your ability to achieve what you want at work? In your non-work life?'*

Each of these people may, if the occasion demands it, be linked to other factors in the system. For example: 'What are your fears with regards to this person?' 'How does this person affect the resources available to you?' 'Or What values are you applying to your judgement

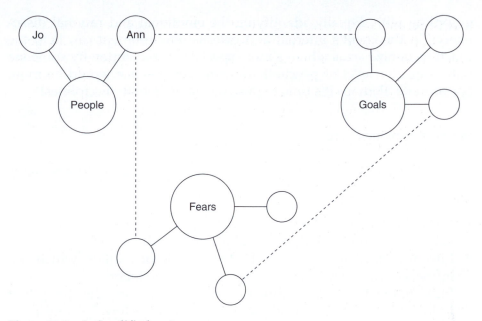

Figure 11.2 A simplified systems map.

about this person?' 'New factors can be added continuously, as they emerge from the dialogue' (see Figure 11.2).

The systemic (as opposed to systematic) approach also reveals critical discontinuities. *'For example, why do you hold these values about this situation, but different values about another?'* It also helps both coach and client to avoid simplistic analyses and solutions. One of us coached a chief executive who had decided to work around a difficult character in a partner organization. Having drawn the map she recognized that she needed to work through the individual concerned and this strategy had powerfully positive results.

Of course, not every situation requires drawing a detailed map. The advantage of doing so, however, is that systems don't have to become very complex to exceed the capacity most of us have for retaining the full picture in our heads. For anything beyond, say, three factors with an average of three sub-elements, we are likely to miss potentially important linkages. Equally, however, an over-concentration on the detail of a complex system can cause coach and coachee to lose sight of the big picture – it is important to be able to dip in and out selectively and the coach's intuition may play a strong part in determining where to drill down and where to seek broader patterns.

Taking a systems perspective may also be the route to bring the therapist and non-therapist together. Exploring the organization, its culture and demands can inform and enrich the therapeutic process, by grounding it more firmly in the complexity of the world the client is grappling with. Equally, identifying the emotional and rational dissonances in the client's internal and external environment can help the coach recognize areas where a more specialist intervention by someone with a greater level of psychotherapeutic competence would be more appropriate. Perhaps it's time to raise the game in both disciplines!

Systems thinking exercise

From what you know of a particular coachee/mentee, build a systems map of their situation, as follows:

1. Write their name and a short description of their issue (20 words or so) in the centre of a large sheet of paper (size A0 or A1).
2. Link the individual with all the key people or entities, which can influence what they do, or can be influenced by them.
3. Indicate the direction of influence (using arrows) and the strength of influence (using width of arrow and numbers 1 = low, 5 = high).
4. Draw in the pattern of influences between these different people/entities in the same way, using a different colour.
5. Consider the coachee's/mentee's current issues in the light of this systems map.
   (i) What does it tell you about what tactics might succeed or fail?
   (ii) What critical judgements will the coachee/mentee have to make to achieve their goals?
   (iii) Are their goals realistic within the existing network of influence? If not, how can they change the network/system?

> ## Case study   Alex
>
> Alex, a chief executive, was not clear which relationships in his partner organizations he needed to focus upon. As preparation for their next meeting, his coach invited him to draw a complex map with the size of circles indicating importance and closeness to his circle in the middle symbolizing closeness of the relationship. Alex decided instead to just list them as the issues were clear to him without these refinements. At the next meeting they worked through the five most important relationships and Alex made plans for improving these key partnerships.

This short case study reminds us that sometimes less is more in developing techniques and one criterion for a good technique is that it is no more complex than is needed to address the issues that the client wants to address.

Tolerating ambiguity

What proportion of the time when you are coaching are you unclear about what the client needs to do to resolve the issue they are exploring. One of us reckons that it is about 90% of the time. Is he worried about this? Not at all. He is more worried about the 10% of the time where he thinks he knows the answer. It is then that he runs the risk of second guessing the client and asking what David Rock at the 2008 EMCC UK annual conference described as 'queggestions'. These are suggestions disguised as questions. A favourite example is: '*Have you thought about trying ...?*' How can you monitor your rate of queggestion asking? Do you practice coaching with a colleague while another observes you? Could you get feedback on your queggestion rate from some of the people you coach/mentor?

What if the problem appears insoluble?

As Alexander the Great demonstrated when he cut the Gordian knot, every problem has at least one solution. We see problems as insoluble when:

● We don't like the solutions we are aware of, and/or
● We are limited by the boundaries of our imagination.

The key to tackling insoluble problems is to start with our imagination. Useful approaches include:

● Asking: 'If you did have a solution, what would it look like?'
● Choosing different characters from history, films or literature, how would each of them tackle this problem? What can you learn from their approaches?
● Another useful question is: 'What solutions have you been avoiding?' Sometimes we just don't want to admit that a solution is readily available, because it means facing up to other issues, which we don't want to acknowledge.
● Breaking the issue into chunks and exploring potential solutions to each. Do solutions for some or all of the parts suggest a solution for the whole?
● Exploring the opposites. Draw a process map of the problem. What would happen if you tackled every step in completely the opposite way to what you do now?
● Redefine the problem as a series of opportunities. What's the silver lining in each aspect of this situation?

If we still don't like any of the solutions on offer, then we have several choices:

- Keep looking for an alternative. Does this problem have to be solved now? Is there a valid argument for allowing a solution to develop of its own accord? One of the most common outcomes of a learning conversation is that the learner's mind becomes open to a wider range of different solutions. As a result, they tend to notice possibilities which would otherwise have passed their attention by.
- Accept the least worst solution. Ranking various solutions against each other (for example, using the Change Balloon technique on pages 44–45 of the companion volume, *Techniques in Coaching and Mentoring*) identifies the solution with least downsides. Is the learner prepared to accept this as a means of moving on and dealing with other, more important issues?
- Accept that we will just have to live with the problem.
- How could the coachee/mentee move out of the situation?
- What changes would the coachee have to make to themselves, their attitudes or behaviour or assumptions to get a new perspective on the situation?

Many of the techniques of solutions focused coaching are useful in this context and Berg and Szabó (2005) outline clearly a range of these.

Case study   Control, influence, accept

This is another perspective on a case we have already explored, in the context of supervision. The client is a young man in a high pressure job in a multinational company. His family, who were all living in another country, were uniformly high achieving and he, as a result, saw his self-esteem and life meaning in terms of his success in the fast-moving world of his profession. His self-image was based on the internalized expectations of his parents and siblings and on the successful colleagues, with whom he worked.

Energy and intellect had coped with all life's problems so far, but he felt a driven need to perform and excel, with the evidence of success being constant career progress and an income he could boast about. Then in a dramatic shock, he became seriously ill. With support from his boss, he kept going, albeit with reduced performance and recovered – only for the illness to recur less than a year later. Then his employer got into difficulties and laid off large numbers of employees, including him. With his illness, he could not get another job without lying to potential employers. Suddenly, his whole world – everything that gave it and himself meaning – had come crashing down.

He did, however, have a coach as part of an educational course he had been taking. Mindful of the need not to cross boundaries into therapy, the coach helped him to map out all the important things in his life he still had control over – for example, engaging the help of his friends, how productively he spent the sudden free time he had been given, and what attitudes he chose to take towards his illness. Then she helped him think about things he couldn't control, but could influence – for example, what he ate and his overall life, which might help fight off the illness a second time. Clarifying these issues gave him sufficient anchor points to feel less panicked and more able to consider the third category of issues – those he could not control or influence. Here he again had a choice – to fear them or accept them. The coach and a specialist counsellor worked together, with the coach concentrating on practical support in coping through crisis and the counsellor focusing on the emotional and psychological aspects.

Who can I work with?

Every coach or mentor has boundaries in respect of who they can work with. Some of these boundaries relate to the difference in our experience or culture – it is generally easier to build empathy and rapport with someone with whom we share important life experiences. So, for example, convicted prisoners often find it helpful to be coached or mentored by someone who has themselves been in gaol, but has subsequently 'gone straight'.

Equally, some boundaries are needed because the coach/mentor is too similar or too drawn to the client. When a relationship demands a high level of personal disclosure, the level of intimacy may need careful management, if the coach/mentor is not to over-identify with the client, for example.

Figure 11.3 illustrates some aspects of the boundary dilemma. The place, where the coach/mentor can operate most effectively and most comfortably is in the middle, where three elements of an effective helping relationship defined by Carl Rogers (Rogers, 1961) come together. These are:

- Genuineness (congruence)
- Respect (unconditional positive regard)
- Empathy.

Too much respect (awe) does not lead to a healthy relationship. Nor does too little respect (disrespect). Similarly, it is difficult (though not

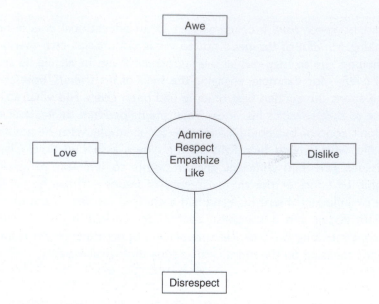

Figure 11.3   Boundaries of the coaching/mentoring relationship.

impossible) to coach someone you don't like. And liking them too much can blind you to characteristics or behaviours which they would benefit from addressing in the learning conversation.

The opportunity for the coach or mentor is to experiment with these boundaries and with specific clients to see how far they can expand their central circle. They can, for example, learn to accept and work with people who they might otherwise avoid as clients because they disliked them, by searching out and finding things they *can* like about them. The coach/mentor can similarly learn to change their own responses to authority and power, to enlarge their comfort zone with respect to people who currently overawe them.

In short, recognizing and challenging boundaries is an important part of continuous development for a coach or mentor. One of the case studies below addresses this issue specifically. One the authors tested his own boundaries by taking on an assignment in the justice system, which meant that he would have opportunities for dialogue with a variety of prisoners. He moved most of his boundaries in this context well beyond their previous point, but found a new boundary when it came to prisoners who had abducted and murdered children. At this point, it became difficult for him to apply any of the Rogerian principles. While this is an extreme example, we do take the view that most people – coaches and mentors included – tend to seek clients who are like themselves. We commend the developmental opportunities inherent in seeking clients who are different.

Case study   Jenny

Jenny, an experienced coach, brought to supervision an apparently routine case of working with a director. At one point she voiced a concern that she would not be the right person to continue coaching this client once he became a chief executive, as was expected in a few months' time. The supervisor encouraged her to explore this concern, but she switched back to talking about the client's perspective about his job opportunity. The conversation lost much of its energy. After a while, the supervisor shared the feeling that she had walked to the edge of a cliff, shuddered and walked away. The image clearly resonated with her. What was she walking away from?

After some discussion, it emerged that she had substantial doubts about her self-efficacy in coaching CEOs, having never been a CEO herself. Would she be able to extend the necessary empathy, not knowing what it felt like to be in the top job? Turning the issue round – why would she not be able to help? – and giving her space to look at the issue through the client's eyes allowed her to come to the conclusion that this was a great opportunity to learn how to coach CEOs, with a client who was already well-disposed towards her.

Case study   Raj

Raj is a devout, though not orthodox Sikh. He was therefore placed in a dilemma when he was asked to mentor a new colleague, because this colleague was gay – something the Sikh religion takes a strongly negative view of. His duty as a manager was in conflict with the teachings of his religion. After reflection, he decided to take on the role as a learning experience. He reported back: 'I thought I knew where my boundaries were, but now I don't'. He found that it was relatively easy to park this aspect of the other person's life and concentrate on issues where they had a common interest – the mentee's work and career.

Twenty-five questions to prepare for supervision

Supervision – and the quality of supervision – has gradually risen up the agenda of all the professional bodies in coaching. There are still a lot of questions about how much supervision coaches and mentors operating at different levels and frequencies need, and whether informal peer supervision is an adequate substitute for formal group or individual supervision. But supervision, particularly for executive coaches and mentors, is definitely here to stay.

For the most part, publications specifically on coaching and mentoring supervision have focused on the role of the supervisor (Hawkins and Smith, 2006; Hay, 2007). We expect to see increasing emphasis on being an effective supervisee. Approaches, such as the seven conversations above, are proving very useful in helping coaches analyse their coaching conversations and identify issues and concerns they want to bring to supervision. As is so often the case, however, the very basics of being an effective supervisee rest in asking massively difficult questions about the coaching process, and about oneself as a coach. Here are some of the questions we've gathered which coaches and mentors have beneficially applied in their pre-supervision reflection:

1. What has changed for you and your client since the previous supervision session?
2. What is the psychological contract between you and your client? Between you and your supervisor?
3. How do you feel generally about yourself as a coach?
4. When did you feel 'moments of disconnect' in the coaching conversation?
5. What questions worked well? Less well?
6. What questions did you not ask and why?
7. What is happening within your client's system (the people and circumstances they interact with)?
8. What is your reaction to the client's situation?
9. Where do you feel least confident?
10. What fears or other baggage did you bring into the coaching/mentoring conversation?
11. How do you want to grow as a coach?
12. What is your ideal of a coach? How do you compare yourself to this ideal?
13. What have you done recently to make you a better coach/mentor?
14. What do you want from this supervision session? From supervision in general?
15. What do you not want from supervision?
16. To what extent did you help by just being there?
17. What patterns do you notice in the client?
18. What patterns do you notice in your reactions to the client?
19. What themes have emerged with more than one client recently? Is this coincidence, or does it reflect something in your own life?
20. Who else is in the room in the coaching conversation?
21. What is the question the client is looking for?
22. In what ways might you be colluding with the client?

23. What stage has this relationship reached in its evolution?
24. What challenge can you offer the supervisor?
25. What stage has my relationship with the supervisor reached? (Is it time to move on?)

As with massively difficult questions in general, we shall continue to build our data base of MDQs for supervision, as readers and workshop participants add to the pot.

Summary

One of the results of the increasing professionalization of coaching and mentoring is that continuous professional development (CPD) is a *sine qua non*. But to be most effective, especially within an eclectic model of coaching/mentoring, there have to be some clarity of purpose and sufficient, well-founded models that enable practitioners to recognize what CPD looks like in this relatively young field. The approaches described in this chapter provide some of the building blocks. Further exploration of issues around CPD can be found in Megginson and Whitaker (2006).

References

Berg, I. K. and Szabø, P. (2005). *Brief Coaching for Lasting Solutions*. New York: Norton.

Clutterbuck, D. and Lane, G. (2004). *The Situational Mentor: An International Review of Competences and Capabilities*. Aldershot: Gower.

Engstrøm, T. (1997). Personality Factors' Impact on Success in the Mentor–Protégé Relationship. MSc thesis to Norwegian School of Hotel Management, Oslo.

Hawkins, P. and Smith, N. (2006). *Coaching, Mentoring and Organizational Consultancy, Supervision and Development*. Maidenhead: Open University Press/McGraw-Hill.

Hay, J. (2007). *Reflective Practice and Supervision for Coaches*. Maidenhead: McGraw-Hill.

Karpman, S. (2006). Lost in translation: Neo-Bernean or Neo-Freudian? *Transactional Analysis Journal* **36**(4), 284–302.

Megginson, D. and Whitaker, V. (2006). *Continuing Professional Development*. London: Chartered Institute of Personnel and Development.

Rogers, C. (1961). *A Therapist's View of Psychotherapy: On Becoming a Person*. London: Constable.

Schön, D. (1991). *The Reflective Practitioner: How Professionals Think in Action*. Aldershot: Ashgate.

Chapter 12

Process focused techniques

David Clutterbuck and David Megginson

This chapter focuses on the coaching or mentoring relationship – on how the coach or mentor can ensure that the relationship is purposeful, ethical and effective. It's very easy to confuse models of the coaching/mentoring conversation (like GROW) with the learning relationship, which is wider, more complex and which evolves over time.

One of the interesting differences between the teaching of mentoring and coaching is that the former typically places much more emphasis on the relationship. Indeed, while mentoring research very quickly focused on relationship evolution, there has still not been any significant empirical attempt to plot the stages of a coaching relationship. In sponsorship mentoring, Kram (1985) described from her interviews with mentors and protégés four phases of the relationship. Clutterbuck (1992) built on these to establish phases of developmental mentoring, as follows:

- *Initiation* – getting to know each other; building rapport and agreeing the 'contract'. Hale (2000) has shown that an exchange of values is important here.
- *Goal-setting* – establishing a general or specific purpose for the relationship. As we have discussed in the previous chapter, the goals emerge gradually rather than form the basis of the relationship. As mentees learn more about themselves and their environment, the broad sense of purpose is honed down to specific themes and aspirations.
- *Progress-making*. The learning process becomes much more two-way and day-to-day issues are more clearly linked in the mentoring dialogue with the relationship purpose.

- *Winding up.* In our study of relationship endings (Clutterbuck and Megginson, 2004), we found that relationships regarded by participants as strongly beneficial were associated with a planned and well-managed disengagement from the formal process. Negatively perceived relationships were associated with a gradual drifting away.
- *Moving on.* Having more or less achieved its original purpose, the relationship evolves into a more ad hoc, informal relationship, in which either party may use the other as a sounding board from time to time.

Given that executive coaching relationships tend to be over shorter time periods than mentoring relationships, superimposing this five-phase model over coaching simply doesn't work. One of us has suggested elsewhere (Clutterbuck, 2009) a three-phase model, consisting of:

- A short *contractual* phase, often before the formal start of the relationship, which can be seen as amalgamating the initiation and goal-setting phases of mentoring. Within this phase, relationships are also defined with other stakeholders, such as the client's boss, if appropriate. Overspecifying goals at this point can be highly dysfunctional.
- A *transactional* phase, in which the coach helps the client explore specific issues, relating to the goals initially agreed. (Again, the coach needs to be alert to the danger of focusing too much on initially stated goals at the expense of allowing new, more relevant goals to emerge.)
- A *review* phase. Here coach and coachee assess the outcomes of the relationship bringing in, where appropriate, the views and observations of other stakeholders, such as the coachee's direct reports and boss.

Of course, phase models are only generally descriptive of what happens in a relationship (Bullis and Bach, 1989). In practice, the transitions between phases become blurred, changes in circumstance may force the dyad to return to goal-setting, or even to rapport-building (initiation) in mentoring, or to recontract in coaching. It may seem obvious, but knowing where you are in the lifecycle of the relationship is likely to be important in determining the appropriateness of the coach/mentor response. Yet when, for example, we ask coaches what point they have reached in their relationship, they tend to respond in terms of the number of meetings left. We feel that this leads to an impoverished perspective on the coaching process. Effective coaches, we suggest, are fully aware of the nuances of how the relationship is progressing; they reflect routinely on where it has reached; and they make a point of reviewing the relationship regularly with the client. This is where our first topic, *'Questions for reviewing the relationship'* comes in.

Questions for reviewing the relationship

Whether these are massively difficult questions depends, we suspect, on the context. However, we have found them to stimulate a high quality of feedback from the client and reflection by the coach/mentor.

- Have we become too cosy? Do we challenge each other enough?
- Are we taking enough risks in our conversations?
- Do we really look forward to the coaching/mentoring sessions?
- Are there topics we have avoided?
- Are we sufficiently clear about the changes we want to see in the client's:
  - Circumstances?
  - Abilities?
  - Behaviours?
- Do we feel we are genuinely making progress? What evidence do we have for that?
- What stage of the relationship are we in?
- What is the next stage, and what do we have to do to get there?
- How have we improved the quality of the relationship in terms of:
  - Rapport?
  - Process?
- How does this relationship compare to the ideal?
- How honest have we been in our previous reviews of the relationship?

There is no set pattern for how and when to review that covers all applications of coaching and mentoring. A very general template, however, might be to conduct a short, 'soft' review at the end of each session ('Did we accomplish what we intended?' 'Do you have specific items you want to reflect more deeply on before our next meeting?' '(How) have I helped?'), then a more formal review every third session. Some executive coaches say that their relationship reviews form the basis of their supervision, surfacing issues that they had not otherwise been able to articulate.

Preparing the coachee to be coached

It's easy to assume that a coaching client is ready for coaching, but as every experienced coach knows, that isn't always the case. Some clients are there reluctantly, because they have been sent – so they may even arrive with an adversarial attitude towards the coach. Others may recognize the value of coaching in general terms, but have no clear idea of what specifically they want it to do for them. Yet others may simply not be in an appropriate mental state for coaching – they may be in the midst of a severe psychological trauma or burnout (Casserley and Megginson, 2008) or they may be so wrapped up in the urgency of doing that they are unable to step into the calmer world of reflection and being.

A lot can be deduced from simply observing the client as the introductions take place. Does their body language indicate that they are relaxed and open, or tense and suspicious? Does their verbal language suggest openness and reaching out to you, or reserved aloofness? Eagerness to learn or fear of being found out?

Experienced coaches often put a distinct 'readiness for coaching' spin on the initial getting to know you conversation with the client. Here are some of the questions we use ourselves or have observed other coaches using to this end.

- What do you expect coaching to do for you?
- Who else has an agenda for you to address through coaching? What do they want you to do or achieve? What do you think/feel about this?
- What fears or concerns do you have about the coaching process?
- What previous experience have you had of being coached? What was positive and negative about it?
- What is your energy level for coaching right now?
- Where and how do you find time to think?
- What does it feel like when you are able to be honest with yourself? Is that something that happens frequently?
- How do you learn complex things?
- How comfortable do you feel with the 'constructive chaos' of creative thinking?
- Do you want coaching to focus on the really big, scary issues or on everyday problems? How do you feel about moving from one to the other in the same conversation?
- How much challenge can you honestly take? What would other people say?

Using 360 degree feedback in coaching and mentoring

The use of 360 degree feedback has become much more common in coaching and mentoring, especially in large organizations, in both the public and the private sector, particularly in the context of executive coaching. While there are significant problems in the way this powerful awareness tool is used (its origins lie in the old Soviet Union, where it was used by the Communist trade union to keep line managers in check and this penal nuance seems to cling on in many applications), it does provide a means of both identifying areas in which coaching is needed, and subsequently of measuring improvements in a relatively accurate way.

There are at least four common, practical situations where 360 degree feedback can be very helpful in coaching and mentoring:

- When the learner needs help in determining where to focus their self-development resources.
- When the learner has potential blind spots, of which they need to be aware.
- When they want a more rounded view of their performance.
- When they need more detailed, more accurate information about their progress towards behavioural change.

Feedback from above is often the least accurate and predictive of long term leadership potential, while feedback from below is usually the most accurate and predictive (Alimo-Metcalfe, 1998). As a coach or mentor, you can help the learner to:

- Determine which areas they would like to obtain feedback on and why.
- Decide whose feedback they would respect/listen to; and explore the value of feedback from people to whose opinion they might give less weight.
- Select appropriate questionnaires or create questions, which will allow for both open and closed responses.
- Prepare for and subsequently manage their reactions to unpalatable messages.
- Think through how they will encourage others to give honest feedback; and how they will follow through, so that feedback-givers feel they have been listened to.
- Develop and implement plans to address the issues raised by the feedback.

A recent case study from colleagues in Turkey used 360 degree feedback to measure manager competences before and after a 12 month coaching relationship. The results showed that bosses by and large didn't notice improvements that were obvious to direct reports. We have named this phenomenon 'reputation drag'. As so often happens, having identified it, we encounter increasing anecdotal evidence to support the view that this is a common problem.

Smither et al. (2003) found that setting goals in a coaching relationship led to improvements in 360 degree rating in a before and after evaluation study. This emphasized the need for coach and client to plan action after reviewing 360 degree feedback data.

One conclusion, therefore, is that the coach and the client need to be careful how much credence they give different groups of 360 degree respondents. That doesn't mean that they should ignore feedback from bosses; rather that they should pay a lot more attention to how they are going to make bosses more aware of changes that occur. Here are some suggested actions from David Clutterbuck and Carol Whittaker, based upon an article in the journal *Coaching at Work* (Clutterbuck and Whittaker, 2008).

Some of the basic actions the coach can take include:

- Contracting with the boss about how they will identify/recognize changes and improvements. If they are not looking for change, they are likely to miss it, especially if it is incremental. Useful questions may be:
  - What specifically would positive change look like?
  - What hard and soft measures would apply? (If you are honest with yourself, which will you give greatest credit to?)
  - What specific impacts would it have on:
    - Relationships within the boss's team?
    - Relationships within the coachee's team?
    - Your ability to relax and feel confident that key tasks will be carried out well, without need for your intervention?
    - What other people say about the coachee?
  - How will you make sure that you obtain a balanced picture?
  - How frequently do you need to discuss this aspect of performance with the coachee, to understand the efforts he or she is making?
- Engaging the whole system. To what extent is the performance issue one that depends on behaviour by the coachee's team, the coachee's peers and the coachee's boss? What specifically are they going to do to support the changes? With the coach's help, the coachee may need to contract with each of these stakeholders to agree when and how they will make him or her aware of positive and negative observations with respect to the area of change, as they happen. This immediacy is important, because it is very easy to forget to give positive feedback once the moment has passed. If they seize the opportunity, however, the incident is more likely to be remembered and to influence their overall perception of the coachee's performance. The more the coachee opts to 'go it alone', the less likely it is that improvements will be noted. By contrast, there is evidence from research into team effectiveness that, while telling your boss about your achievements can boost your reputation in the short term, in the medium to long term, it is what he or she hears from other teams and their managers that moulds the boss's perception (Ancona, 1990; Ancona & Caldwell, 1988).

- Encouraging a deeper than normal level of openness about the learning goals and how the coachee plans to achieve them. Many managers and executives struggle with exposing their weaknesses to their own direct reports and/or peers. Yet these people can provide a remarkable level of support. One manager, finally persuaded to go through his performance appraisal in detail with his team, found that they offered a number of ways in which they could compensate for his areas of weakness, allowing him to concentrate on his strengths. Although he did improve in the skills in question, the primary factor in his improved reputation derived from the tasks for which his team took responsibility.

- Help the coachee to manage his/her reputation by encouraging peers/subordinates to feedback to the bosses improvements or changes they perceived as this feedback seems to have more positive impact with bosses and they are more likely to change their opinions when faced with evidence from others.

- Reviewing with the client how they will manage their personal and team reputations. (It's often hard to separate the two.) Many executives have never learned the skills of reputation management. Some even dismiss it as 'playing politics'. Yet reputation management is just as important for an individual as it is for a company. Some useful tactics include:

  - Inviting observers from other teams to sit in on the coachee's team meetings. This helps to spread the word about both what the team is doing and why, along with the obstacles they face and are trying to overcome.
  - Establishing a team communication plan – who needs to know about our activities?
  - Building into the team business plan a strategy for supporting the key objectives of each of the coachee's peer departments
  - Generate positive stories and anecdote. Although leaders may think they are influenced most by hard facts, the reality is that they are more often influenced by powerful stories. Sharing such stories – or better still, enabling others to share them – is a rapid and long-lasting means of building the coachee's personal brand. The coach can help capture such stories and demonstrate the power of story with statements and questions, such as: 'I found that really emotional. How did you think your boss would react, if she heard that same story?'

Another perspective on 360 degree feedback is to consider how to minimize resistance, denial and second guessing about who said what. A short 'How to …' article in *People Management* (Goodge and Watts, 2000) recommended that the conversation starts with an exploration of what the issue is that the coachee wants to use the 360 data to illuminate. Coach and client then interrogate the data from that point of view. Our experience is that this process enhances ownership and minimizes denial.

Referring on

Knowing when to refer a client on can be a difficult decision. The simplest guideline is that you should consider referring on when you are aware that the issues under discussion or the depth of the discussion are outside of your competence, or require a re-contracting of the relationship.

The process of referring on should involve:

- Explaining to the client why you feel that you have a boundary issue.
- Exploring their feelings and preferences about the order issues should be tackled in (e.g. should you leave discussing a career decision until they have dealt with a bereavement issue, which may be clouding their judgement?).
- Exploring, if appropriate, the benefits and disadvantages of referring on or working on the issues within the current relationship.
- Advising on who to refer on to (should you offer a choice?) – this may require you to take advice in turn from a coaching/mentoring supervisor or from the HR department.
- Ensuring that the handover is managed efficiently and empathetically. (The professional you refer on to will need to have some basic information about *why* you felt this was appropriate, but may not require your thoughts on a diagnosis, if you have made any.)
- Ensuring there is an efficient process for liaising between the professional therapist (or other specialist) and the coach/mentor, either while the two relationships continue in parallel, or when the client is 'handed back'.

If you decide to continue in the relationship, at the same time as referring on, it is important to recontract with the client and to form a clear contract with the therapist. The decision whether to re-contract should depend on:

- How confident you feel in your ability to work in the new area (and what evidence/relevant experience you have to justify that confidence).
- Whether the issue *can* be isolated from the initial or overarching purpose of the relationship; or whether it replaces that purpose.
- Whether it will be in the client's best interests to deal with these issues together or separately.

Contracting with the therapist should cover at a minimum:

- What understandings and communication should there be between the therapist and myself? (In particular, what are the boundaries of confidentiality in this circumstance?)
- What conversations do we need to have to ensure that the boundaries are maintained?
- What process will we have to ensure that we can raise concerns with each other?

It goes without saying (but we'll say it anyway) that any situation where the coach considers referring on is a potential issue to discuss with a supervisor.

Case study   Meena

During supervision Meena brought the case of a young man, who was in remission from cancer. His firm, a large multinational company, had supported him through this difficult period. The client was a complex person. The youngest sibling in a high achieving, emotionally and geographically distant family, he defined himself very much in terms of how much he earned and how successful he was in his high-intensity job. He had few close friends, but was beginning to 'get a life' with the help of his coach – developing social networks and rethinking his career ambitions. Then disaster struck. Not only did his cancer return, but his company retrenched and he was suddenly out of a job.

Although Meena was qualified as a counsellor to help deal with the emotional trauma, this situation was way outside the contract of the original coaching agreement. The client was calling her frequently, in a state of increasing panic and, in spite of her professional approach, she was herself panicking and even projecting that panic onto the supervisor.

Working the issue through with the supervisor, it became clear that she did not want to take on the additional role of therapist – she was already too close to the client and needed to give herself permission to draw a boundary on her involvement. Having done so, she could begin to sketch the separate roles and responsibilities of herself and a therapist, with her focusing heavily on practical issues, such as how the client could maintain his social networks and use the career break (until he was in remission again, there was little potential to return to a similar high-intensity job) to develop new working skills; and the therapist focusing on helping him develop emotional resilience. With this role clarity, she was sufficiently re-energized to have a firm discussion with the client about seeking therapeutic help through the hospital (it had been offered, but he had not yet taken it up) and supporting him in making the request.

The thinking/feeling matrix

In the companion volume we introduced the technique 'Stepping in, stepping out' to help the coach or mentor shift the learning dialogue between questions that explore the rational and the emotional, and between questions that explore the client's own perspective and other people's perspectives. The matrix below provides a different way of structuring where the client and hence the conversation is positioned in terms of emotional and rational thinking.

Thinking about thinking	Feeling about thinking
Thinking about feeling	Feeling about feelings

Thinking about thinking relates to how the client structures information. Is there a logical, step-by-step process to move from one conclusion to the next? Woolly thinking is one of the most common issues coaches encounter in their clients. Helping them develop more structured, disciplined approaches can be a valuable legacy of the coaching intervention.

Thinking about feeling relates to the degree of conscious awareness the client has about how their emotions (their values, beliefs, fears and so on) are influencing how they draw conclusions. The illusion of rationality behind decision making is just that – most decisions are made emotionally and rationalized later. Building awareness in the client of how this process happens for them gives them opportunities to be more critical of their thinking, leading to more effective decision making. Given time, the coach can help the client recognize patterns of emotional–rational interaction.

Feeling about thinking relates to the way in which emotions may block or permit us to bring issues into conscious reflection. From a psychodynamic perspective, they are exhibiting resistance. When clients say 'It's too painful to think about' or seem to be avoiding an issue, this is essentially an admission that their emotions are preventing them from making progress on it. Here, the coach can help by creating a safe space in which to begin addressing the issue. Emotional release may be an important part of this process and coaches need to be sufficiently emotionally mature in themselves to accept and work with it.

Feeling about feelings concerns the client's ability to give expression to their emotions and to bring unconscious emotions to the surface, through language, posture or other means. So often, clients attempt to avoid the expression of emotion, seeing it as a weakness. Again, the coach or mentor can create a safe space in which these barriers can be lowered. In time, the client may learn to become comfortable with greater emotional openness with other people as well. In Chapter 8 of this volume Vivien Whitaker offers a range of creative methods for accessing feelings.

The matrix is more than an academic curiosity. Coaches and mentors need to take stock from time to time of the client's mental state and how it is affecting the quality and outcomes of the learning conversation. Identifying which of the four perspectives the client needs help with – and which they are ready to be helped with – can result in radically different, more helpful dialogue.

The three stage process

Contributed by professor Bob Garvey, Sheffield Hallam University

The three-stage process is a useful process model in coaching and mentoring conversations. It was adapted from Egan's (1994) 'Skilled helper' framework and developed by Alred et al. (1999). In essence it is a map and as such helps us to:

- Think about our route.
- Find where we are when we get lost.
- Choose another route.
- Make choices about direction and destination.

It is therefore of great practical use. Some users suggested that they like its fluidity and flexibility. Others suggested that it works well with the GROW model in that it can help with the emergence of goals. So, the three-stage process may be a preliminary to GROW. It is also a process in its own right. It can be a plan for the individual meeting as well as for the longer term relationship. It is important to share the process with the learner so that he or she can use it to progress the conversation as well.

> The process is – Stage 1, Exploration; Stage 2, New understanding; Stage 3, Action.

Many managers acting as coaches or mentors are very tempted to move straight to Stage 3 but it is important to remember that the quality of the Action is dependent on the quality of Stages 1 and 2. The ultimate aim of the process is for the learner to develop ownership and autonomy, so, as the coach or mentor, it is important to suspend one's own desire to problem-solve on the client's behalf.

In practice, the three-stage process rarely moves in an orderly manner. More often the conversation moves in cycles between the different stages, each cycle deepening the dialogue.

Summary is a key skill at any stage. This can take many different forms and the coach mentor may invite the learner to summarize or may do it on the learner's behalf. Both approaches often yield insights and understanding.

Perhaps the most interesting thing about the three-stage process is that, with practice, it becomes very natural and does not seem like an intrusive technique.

Stage 1 strategies
- Take the lead to open the discussion
- Pay attention to the relationship and develop it
- Clarify aims, objectives and discuss groundrules
- Support and counsel.

Stage 1 methods
- Open questions
- Listening, listening and listening
- Developing an agenda
- Summary.

Stage 2 strategies
- Support and counsel
- Offer feedback
- Coach and demonstrate skills.

Stage 2 methods
- Listening and challenging
- Using both open and closed questions
- Helping to establish priorities
- Summary, paraphrasing, restating, reframing
- Helping identify learning and development needs
- Giving information and advice
- Sharing experience and story telling.

Stage 3 strategies
- Examine options and consequences
- Attend to the relationship
- Negotiate and develop an action plan.

Stage 3 methods
- Encouraging new ideas and creativity

- Helping in decisions and problem solving
- Summary
- Agree action plans
- Monitoring and reviewing
- Giving and receiving feedback about the relationship and the meeting.

'Relationship droop'

A common occurrence in coaching and mentoring is that, after the first flush of enthusiasm, the relationship begins to run out of steam. Both parties are reluctant to take each other's time when there appear to be no urgent or significant things to talk about. The initial sense of purpose becomes dulled.

Managed effectively, this apparent set-back can be an excellent opportunity to revitalize the relationship and set it upon a much deeper and useful track. Key steps here include:

- Openly recognize and discuss what you feel.
- Review and celebrate what you have achieved so far.
- Be honest in considering what issues, if any, you have avoided discussing – these are often fruitful areas for more substantial personal development.
- List the mentee/coachee's medium- and long-term personal goals (both career and personal competence): what learning conversations would help make these easier to achieve and/or achievable in a shorter time period?

Insight provoking questions (MDQs – see Chapter 10) have an important role to play here, stimulating the mentee/coachee to think more deeply and from different perspectives about the challenges they face. In many cases, they may be unaware or only partially aware of these challenges.

If the mentee/coachee still feels they now have everything they need to get on with their original goal(s) and wants to focus exclusively on this for a period, using their own resources, it's best to accept the situation gracefully. The mentee/coachee should never feel you are struggling to find reasons to keep the relationship going! However, you can legitimately:

- Make it clear that you are available to them when they do have an issue to discuss or if they run into difficulties.
- Offer occasional – regular or ad hoc – goal-free meetings, where they can simply use you as a sounding board on current issues.

- Drop them a short monthly or bi-monthly e-mail to pass on some relevant information or contacts you have found, or to pose them a new question to think about.

It is very common in these circumstances for the learning relationship to renew itself in a more powerful form, after a period of reflection.

Moments of disconnect

Most coaching and mentoring textbooks make the assumption that effective conversations are relatively seamless, semi-structured events without major hiccups. Yet even the most experienced coaches encounter occasional *moments of disconnect* – points in the learning conversation when they begin to doubt their ability, are unsure how to move the dialogue forward, or feel that they simply aren't helping the client as well as they might. When you do have such feelings, don't feel guilty; feel grateful, because they are valuable for reflective practice and the continuous improvement of your coaching competence.

Some of the most common moments of disconnect occur:

- When you begin to lose rapport with the client.
- When you feel the learning conversation has lost its energy.
- When the learning conversation doesn't seem to be going anywhere.
- When the client's problem seems insoluble.

Effective coaches learn to live with and savour these moments as opportunities for their own learning – and for breaking new ground for and with the client. One coach explained in a supervision session: 'I got to a point in a coaching session, where I hadn't a clue what to say next. I started to panic as the silence deepened. Then, in desperation, I said: "We've met three times now, so you should have a good idea of how I go about trying to stimulate your thinking. What's the question you've been hoping I wouldn't ask you at this point?" It was as if I'd suddenly turned the tap on. A whole flood of concerns and new information emerged, which put the issue into a very different perspective.'

Some of the lessons that have emerged from our conversations with groups of coaches include:

- *Believe in your intuition*. If it tells you that you are heading for a moment of disconnect, you probably are. Recent physiological studies have explored eye micro-movements, which are so fast and small that they are undetectable at a conscious level. Although the science behind NLP claims about gross eye movements is dubious, at the micro-level the movement of the pupil is now demonstrated to be a window on where a person's unconscious attention is focused. These and other postural and tonal clues may stimulate the coach's intuitive awareness of signals, which the conscious brain may not become aware of until much later, if at all.

Listening to your intuition provides time to reflect upon what is happening and decide whether a change of tack is necessary, or whether there may be benefits from allowing the disconnect to develop and observe what comes from it. For further ideas in this book about the use of intuition, see Chapter 5 by Megan Reitz.

- *Don't feel you have to fill the silence.* If the disconnect causes a pause in the dialogue, use it as reflective space for both of you. You might even say, 'I think this might be a good opportunity to reflect upon where we've reached and how we want to go on in this conversation.' Or even, 'What do you think might be a useful question for us to reflect upon now we've come to a natural pause?' One of the observed characteristics that distinguishes effective and ineffective coaches is how comfortable they feel with silence. Ineffective coaches tend to become more anxious and are more inclined to ask questions before the client has completed the reflective process. In extremis, several minutes may be needed. (The most we've experienced is 15 minutes, which was *hard*, but critical for the client to work through her feelings and the implications of insights gained.)
- *Consider and discuss the disconnect openly.* Has it occurred because:
  - You are making assumptions about the issue, which led you into questions, which the client does not feel are helpful?
  - The client is avoiding the issue?
  - The process you are using does not fit the client or the issue (or both) sufficiently well?
  - You are being too mechanistic in using the process?
  - The *pace* of the learning dialogue is inappropriate?
  - You are working on the wrong issue entirely?

  The fact that a disconnect has occurred should stimulate the curiosity of the coach. What have we missed in the conversation so far? At what point did the disconnect begin to occur?
- *Have a large portfolio of tools and techniques to call upon.* The bigger your kitbag of tools and techniques, the more likely you are to find an alternative approach that will work. The wider the portfolio of approaches that you feel comfortable using, the more confident you are likely to be in proposing another approach. The more confident you are, the more relaxed you will be and the easier it will be to re-establish rapport and the confidence of the client that their issue is resolvable. Some proficient coaches make a practice of acquiring at least one new and practical tool every month.

- *Be prepared to experiment.* Although it's usually better to use an approach with which you are familiar, sometimes even an extensive toolkit doesn't contain anything quite right. That is the time to consider combining different techniques; or creating a new approach, simply by following your instinctive perceptions about alternative perspectives that might stimulate an insight in the client. See Chapter 13, 'Building your own techniques', in the companion volume (Megginson and Clutterbuck, 2005).
- *When you use a different technique or tool, ensure that the client is aware you are doing so, and consents.* One of the most common causes of disconnect is that the client feels they are being manipulated – that the technique is being done *to* them rather than *with* them. Explaining how the technique works and perhaps giving examples of where it has helped someone else builds the client's confidence in the process, helping them to relax into it. In general, the more a client understands the process, the better they are likely to work within it.
- *Accept that some problems are insoluble.* If you have both run out of possible solutions, and you have exhausted the creative thinking processes that might have generated acceptable alternatives, then use the disconnect as an opportunity to consider how the client can move on. Key questions here may concern:
  - What is the least worst solution?
  - How will the client manage the process of acceptance?
  - What 'living with it' means for them and other stakeholders.
  - What they can do to alleviate the discomfort of not solving the problem (and any residual guilt about that)?

Managing disconnections

It is easier to prepare for moments of disconnect if the coach/mentor makes a point of reflecting from time to time on the quality of the conversation. Some useful questions include:

- Why are we having *this* conversation?
- To what extent am I reflecting back my experience of the conversation?
- How relevant is this to the broader context?
- Do we both feel comfortable with the conversation, even if we don't know where it is going?
- Is my intuition switched on? Is theirs?
- How aware are we both of what is going on in the present, even if we are dealing with issues relating to the past or future?
- Are we both being truly authentic?

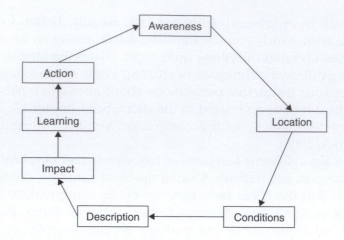

Figure 12.1   Moments of disconnect: a process management model.

We have recently developed a model, to try to bring some structure to the management of disconnection. The model (see Figure 12.1) has seven stages, which seem broadly to describe a logical sequence of reflections.

The process consists of seven key questions:

1. *Who is aware of the disconnection?* Often the coachee/mentee is unaware. Signs might include postural change, a change in the pace of conversation, a shift in mood, mindfulness or even a breakdown of communication altogether.
   Useful questions that a coach might ask of themselves might be:
   (i)   What might prevent me from recognizing a disconnection?
   (ii)   How strong does it have to be for me to become aware?
   (iii) Can I increase my sensitivity to disconnections?
   (iv) How can I most helpfully make myself aware of a disconnection?
2. *Where is the disconnection located?* It could be within the client (e.g. something they are avoiding), within the coach (e.g. a question or comment that has an unexpected effect, interrupting the client's reflection, or a distracting body posture), or in the space between them (e.g. different interpretations of the same word or phrase). It may also be part of a pattern.
3. *Do we have the conditions for sustained connection? Issues to consider include*:
   (i)   Are the conditions for flow present?
   (ii)   Where is the energy?
   (iii) Did we begin with an appropriate mood for reflection?
4. *In what ways can we each describe the disconnection?*
   (i)   What sense do we both have about what happened?
   (ii)   What sense do we each have about the client's role in the disconnection?

(iii) How effectively is the supervisee bringing the client into the conversation?

5. *What is the impact of the disconnection?* The impact may be immediate (e.g. the conversation dies), or potential (recognition of an opportunity for learning and personal growth). Useful questions might include:
   (i) How did it affect the flow of our conversation?
   (ii) What conflicts, if any, did it illuminate?
   (iii) What else has now entered our awareness?

6. *What learning potential does the disconnection contain?* What lessons can we extract about the client's issues and/or about the coaching/mentoring process?

7. *What action, if any, do we want to take as a result?* Can we now take the learning conversation more deeply? Do we want to park and return to the issues that the client raised? Do we want to change the coaching process?

Overall, moments of disconnect, while occasionally scary, are a valuable resource for both the coach and the coachee. If you see them as a resource rather than as the cliff edge of catastrophe, they can and will enrich your coaching practice.

Summary

Coaching and mentoring process is a fertile area for the research and for the development of new ideas and models. The basic models of both coaching and mentoring are beginning to look dated and some appear increasingly to be simplistic and empirically unsupported. We think this is an exciting area for research into the dynamics of what actually happens between coach and coachee, mentor and mentee, and we look forward to continued updating of received wisdom!

References

Alimo-Metcalfe, B. (1998). 360 degree feedback and leadership development. *International Journal of Selection and Assessment*, **6**(1), 35–44.

Alred, G., Garvey, B., Smith, R. (1999). *The Mentoring Pocket Book*. Arlesford, Hants: Management Pocket Books.

Ancona, D. G. (1990). Outward bound: strategies for team survival in an organization. *Academy of Management Journal*, **33**(2), 334–65.

Ancona, D. G. and Caldwell, D. F. (1988). Beyond task and maintenance: defining external functions in groups. *Group and Organizational Studies*, **13**(4), 468–94.

Bullis, C. and Bach, B. W. (1989). Are mentoring relationships helping organizations? An exploration of developing mentee–mentor-organizational identification using turning point analysis. *Communication Quarterly*, **37**(3), 199–213.

Casserley, T. and Megginson, D. (2008). *Learning from Burnout: Developing Sustainable Careers and Avoiding Career Derailment*. Oxford: Butterworth-Heinemann.

Clutterbuck, D. (1992). *Everyone Needs a Mentor*, 2nd edition. London: CIPD.

Clutterbuck, D. (2009). Coaching and mentoring in support of management development. In: Armstrong, S. and Fukami, C. (eds), *Handbook of Managerial Learning, Education, and Development*. London: Sage.

Clutterbuck, D. and Megginson, D. (2004). All good things must come to an end: winding up and winding down a mentoring relationship. In: Clutterbuck, D. and Lane, G. (eds), *The Situational Mentor*. Aldershot: Gower, 178–93.

Clutterbuck, D. and Whittaker, C. (2008). Managing reputation through coaching. *Coaching at Work*, **3**(3), 54–5.

Egan, G. (1994). *The Skilled Helper: A Problem Management Approach to Helping*. Pacific Grove, CA: Brooks and Cole.

Goodge, P. and Watts, P. (2000). How to manage 360-degree feedback. *People Management*, 50–2.

Hale, R. (2000). To match or mismatch? The dynamics of mentoring as a route to personal and organizational learning. *Career Development International*, **5**(4/5), 223–34.

Kram, K. (1985). *Mentoring at Work: Developmental Relationships in Organizational Life*. Glenview, IL: Scott, Foresman.

Megginson, D. and Clutterbuck, D. (2005). *Techniques for Coaching and Mentoring*. Oxford: Butterworth-Heinemann.

Smither, J. W., London, M., Flautt, R., Vargas, Y., Kucine, I. (2003). Can working with an executive coach improve multi-source feedback ratings over time? A quasi-experimental field study. *Personnel Psychology*, **56**(1), 23–44.

Chapter 13

Conclusion: what we have learned about the place of techniques

David Megginson and David Clutterbuck

In this chapter we reflect back on the journey we have taken in writing this book and its predecessor, and seek to draw conclusions about what we have learned in the process about the place of techniques in coaching and mentoring. We look at the different places that coaching and mentoring have started from and their direction of travel over the years that we have been thinking and writing about techniques. We offer some thoughts about where the field of one-to-one helping might go from here and we round off the book with three checklists on whether to use techniques, which technique to use and how to use them.

Conclusions

We have travelled a long way since our travails with the companion volume, *Techniques for Coaching and Mentoring*. In that book (Megginson and Clutterbuck, 2005, 7–9) we agonized a certain amount about whether techniques were a good thing at all. In this volume we have become more matter of fact about the existence of techniques and their utility.

Our personal journeys

We both still see coaching and mentoring primarily as an open ended conversation with a purpose. However, as coach/mentor we find ourselves more frequently than heretofore using technique to focus on achieving the aspiration of the client. We don't see techniques as part of a routine: rather they come after the intent of the client has been clarified. We say, 'If that is what you want to achieve in this conversation, then would you like to try exploring it this way …?'

Assembling this book has been an important stage in our journey. It has helped us to get to the point where not only do we value particular traditions from psychology, but also where we recognize the usefulness of intuition, creativity and mindfulness in the process. Middle class, white men of a certain age need a good amount of shaking up if they are to keep their minds open and to resist what someone described as 'a hardening of the oughteries'. The production of this book and immersion in the arguments and passions of our authors has proved valuable in this process.

The coaching profession

Coaching has – if anything – been too wedded to technique. Too many coaching schools have persuaded far too many coaches that the exercise of their profession is about adherence to a single framework and a narrowly defined curriculum: real coaches are co-active or solutions focused or NLP. We don't see it that way and the evolution towards the managed eclectic approach seems to us to represent a valuable path towards maturity and making the widest possible range of options available to our clients. Indeed, we see a fundamental ethical dilemma in the single-philosophy approach – by narrowing the range of responses to those the coach feels comfortable with using and/or which align with their specific model of helping, the coach is potentially imposing their own agenda and sense of purpose over that of the client. Given that the value of coaching and mentoring often lies in enabling the client to view their issues from other perspectives, is it ethical and appropriate for the coach or mentor to limit those alternative perspectives to those which fit the coach's or mentor's own philosophical approach? Of course, we acknowledge the power of using a well tried approach that enables clients to achieve things that an unspecialized coaching conversation wouldn't, but nonetheless our reservations remain. Process and content are inseparable.

Mentoring as a social movement

Mentoring, by contrast with coaching, has probably not been enough focused on technique. One of us remembers carrying out an evaluation of chief information officer mentoring where one of our respondents said of his 'been there, done it and got the t-shirt' mentor that talking with him – agreeable, affable and experienced though he was – was like a saloon bar conversation. This – it seemed to us – was a sign of too little rather than too much use of technique. Similarly in a large national scheme for small business mentor training with which one of us was involved, many of the volunteer mentors had a vision of helping that was firmly embedded in the giving of advice grounded in the hard-won field of experience. The only trouble was that the experience was the mentors', and often it did not correspond with the circumstances and capability of the mentee. Similarly, with those working with the dispossessed and the disadvantaged, the issues of self-esteem and a feeling of self-efficacy will not be enhanced by having another expert tell you what you are doing wrong and what you don't know about your world. Mentors need ways of going on that will enable them to emancipate the people that they are working with.

This issue is thrown into stark relief by the perceptual gap between baby boomers and millenials (those born after 1980). The latter expect to be mentored, but want equal respect for and acknowledgement of the value of their own experience and intellect.

Checklists

To conclude, we offer three checklists that we have developed from our coaching and mentoring journeys so far, to address the following issues:

- Whether to use a technique.
- Which technique to use.
- How to use a technique.

Whether to use a technique

1. Does the use of a technique offer something that the to and fro of dialogue can't, and/or does it get there quicker than a normal conversation?
2. Does it put 'another party' into the room – a piece of paper, a flip chart, or some other object that helper and client can interrogate?
3. Is it easy to make clear to the coachee/mentee what is involved and how the process will go?
4. Does it leave open the content of the exploration so that it does not represent a 'queggestion'?
5. Is it possible to ensure informed consent from the mentee/coachee?
6. Are our motives for using the technique about supporting the inquiry of the client, or are we being driven towards the technique by a desire to be seen to be clever, or (equally unhelpful!) a desire to be seen to be helpful?

Which technique to use

1. Have you a good range of techniques in your store cupboard so that you are not using a few too often whether they offer a good fit with the client's needs or not?
2. Is it the simplest technique that will do the job?
3. Have you tried it out on yourself or on fellow learners or fellow supervisees?
4. Are you responding to a recognized and acknowledged need or wish of the client?
5. Can you adapt a technique that you have used before so that it more closely matches the needs or wishes of the client?
6. Does the technique maximize the freedom of the client to come to their own conclusion about the issue and to have a say at all stages about whether to continue?

How to use the technique

1. Explain the principles behind the technique. Are these agreeable to the client?
2. Offer a brief, vivid explanation of the purpose, process, benefits and any downside risk of using the technique. Check again for acceptance.
3. Set up and run the technique.
4. Simplify it if that is what the client wants.
5. Review it: was it useful? Did it add anything compared with just talking about it?
6. Write up your learning from the process in a journal.

We wish you every success in your journey of development as a coach or mentor.

Reference

Megginson, D. and Clutterbuck, D. (2005). *Techniques for Coaching and Mentoring*. Oxford: Butterworth-Heinemann.

Bibliography

Agor, W. (1984). *Intuitive Management; Integrating Left and Right Brain Management Skills*. New York: Prentice-Hall.

Agor, W. (1986). The logic of intuition: how top executives make important decisions. *Organizational Dynamics*, Winter, **14**, 5–18.

Alimo-Metcalf, B. (1998). 360 degree feedback and leadership development. *International Journal of Selection and Assessment*, **6**(1), 35–44.

Alred, G., Garvey, B., Smith, R. (1999). *The Mentoring Pocket Book*. Arlesford, Hants: Management Pocket Books.

Ancona, D. G. (1990). Outward bound: strategies for team survival in an organization. *Academy of Management Journal*, **33**(2), 334–65.

Ancona, D. G. and Caldwell, D. F. (1988). Beyond task and maintenance: defining external functions in groups. *Group and Organizational Studies*, **13**(4), 468–94.

Atkinson, T. and Claxton, G. (2000). *The Intuitive Practitioner – and the Value of Not Always Knowing What One is Doing*. Milton Keynes, Buckingham: Open University Press.

Baker, A., Jensen, J., Kolb, D. (2002). *Conversational Learning: An Experiential Approach to Knowledge Creation*. Westport, CN: Quorum/Greenwood.

Beisser, A. R. (1970). The paradoxical theory of change. In: Fagan, J. and Shepherd, I. L. (eds), *Gestalt Therapy Now*. Palo Alto, CA: Science & Behaviour Books. Available via www.gestalt.org/arnie.htm.

Belf, T. E. (2002). *Coaching with Spirit*. San Francisco: Jossey-Bass/Pfeiffer.

Berg, I. K. and Szabó, P. (2005). *Brief Coaching for Lasting Solutions*. New York: Norton.

Blackwell, L., Trzesniewski, K., Dweck, C. (2007). Implicit theories of intelligence predict achievement across an adolescent transition: a longitudinal study and an intervention. *Child Development*, **78**(1), 246–63.

Bohm, D. (1980). *Wholeness and the Implicate Order*. London: Routledge and Kegan Paul.

Bonabeau, E. (2003). Don't trust your gut. *Harvard Business Review*, May, **80**, 116–23.

Boniwell, I. (2008). *Positive Psychology in a Nutshell*. London: PWBC.

Brantley, J. (2003). *Calming your Anxious Mind*. Oakland, CA: New Harbinger.

Bullis, C. and Bach, B. W. (1989). Are mentoring relationships helping organizations? An exploration of developing mentee–mentor-organizational identification using turning point analysis. *Communication Quarterly*, **37**(3), 199–213.

Casserley, T. and Megginson, D. (2008). *Learning from Burnout: Developing Sustainable Leaders and Avoiding Career Derailment*. Oxford: Butterworth-Heinemann.

Clarkson, P. and Mackewn, J. (1993). *Fritz Perls*. London: Sage.

Clutterbuck, D. (1992). *Everyone Needs a Mentor*, 2nd edition. London: CIPD.

Clutterbuck, D. (2007). *Coaching the Team at Work*. London: Nicholas Brealey.

Clutterbuck, D. (2008). Creativity Toolkit. Unpublished paper.

Clutterbuck, D. (2008). A Longitudinal Study of the Effectiveness of Developmental Mentoring, Doctoral thesis submitted to the University of London.

Clutterbuck, D. (2009). Coaching and mentoring in support of management development. In: Armstrong, S. and Fukami, C. (eds), *Handbook of Managerial Learning, Education, and Development*. London: Sage.

Clutterbuck, D. and Lane, G. (2004). *The Situational Mentor: An International Review of Competences and Capabilities*. Aldershot: Gower.

Clutterbuck, D. and Megginson, D. (2004). All good things must come to an end: winding up and winding down a mentoring relationship. In: Clutterbuck, D. and Lane, G. (eds), *The Situational Mentor*. Aldershot: Gower, 178–93.

Clutterbuck, D. and Ragins, B. R. (2002). *Mentoring and Diversity: An International Perspective*. Oxford: Butterworth-Heinemann.

Clutterbuck, D. and Whittaker, C. (2008). Managing reputation through coaching. *Coaching at Work*, **3**(3), 54–5.

Csikszentmihalyi, M. (2002). *Flow*. London: Rider.

Curwen, B., Palmer, S., Ruddell, P. (2000). *Brief Cognitive Behaviour Therapy*. In: Palmer, S. and McMahon, G. (eds), *Brief Therapy Series*. London: Sage.

DiChristina, M. (2008). Let your creativity soar. *Scientific American Mind*, June/July, 24–32.

Drucker, P. F. (1954). *The Practice of Management*. Oxford: Heinemann.

Dryden, W. (1999). *Rational Emotive Behavioural Counselling in Action*. London: Sage.

Dweck, C. (2006). *Mindset: The New Psychology of Success*. New York: Random House.

Early, P. C. and Mosakowski, E. (2000). Creating hybrid cultures: an empirical test of transnational team functioning. *Academy of Management Journal*, **43**(1), 26–49.

Edmondson, A. (1999). Psychological safety and learning behavior in work teams, *Administrative Science Quarterly*, **44**, 350–83.

Egan, G. (1994). *The Skilled Helper: A Problem Management Approach to Helping*. Pacific Grove, CA: Brooks and Cole.

Egan, G. (2002). *The Skilled Helper*. Belmont, CA: Thomson.

Eifert, G. H. and Forsyth, J. P. (2005). *Acceptance and Commitment Therapy for Anxiety Disorders*. Oakland. CA: New Harbinger.

Ellis, C. and Bochner, A. P. (1996). *Composing Ethnography: Alternative Forms of Qualitative Writing*. New York: Sage.

Engstrøm, T. (1997). Personality Factors' Impact on Success in the Mentor–Protégé Relationship. MSc thesis to Norwegian School of Hotel Management, Oslo.

Eppinger, P. (1994). *Restless Mind, Quiet Thoughts: A Personal Journal*. San Francisco: White Clouds Press.

Gersick, C. (1988). Time and transition in work teams: toward a new model of group development. *Academy of Management Journal*, **31**, 9–41.

Gigerenzer, G. (2007). *Gut Feelings: The Intelligence of the Unconscious*. London: Penguin.

Gill, E., quoted in Cameron, J. (1996). *Vein of Gold*. New York: Putnam Press.

Gladwell, M. (2005). *Blink: The Power of Thinking Without Thinking*. London: Penguin.

Goodge, P. and Watts, P. (2000). How to manage 360-degree feedback. *People Management*, 17 February, 50–2.

Groom, J. (2005). Effective listening. *Coaching Psychologist*, **1**, 21–2.

Hackman, J. R. (1990). *Groups that Work (and Those that Don't): Creating Conditions for Effective Teamwork*. San Francisco: Jossey-Bass.

Hackman, J. R. and Wageman, R. (2007). *Senior Teams: What It Takes to Make Them Great*. Boston: Harvard Business School Press.

Hale, R. (2000). To match or mismatch? The dynamics of mentoring as a route to personal and organisational learning. *Career Development International*, **5**(4/5), 223–34.

Hampden-Turner, C. and Trompenaars, F. (1997). *Riding the Waves of Culture: Understanding Diversity in Global Business*. Maidenhead: McGraw-Hill.

Harper, S. (1988). Intuition: what separates executives from managers. *Business Horizons*, **31**(5), 13–9.

Hawkins, P. and Smith, N. (2006). *Coaching, Mentoring and Organizational Consultancy, Supervision and Development*. Maidenhead: McGraw-Hill.

Hay, J. (2007). *Reflective Practice and Supervision for Coaches*. Maidenhead: McGraw-Hill.

Hayashi, A. (2001). When to trust your gut. *HBR at Large*, **79**(2), 59–65.

Hayes, S. C. (2005). *Get Out of Your Mind and Into Your Life*. Oakland, CA: New Harbinger.

Hermann, S. M. and Korenich, M. (1977). *Authentic Management: A Gestalt Orientation to Organizations and their Development*. Reading, MA: Addison-Wesley.

Hodges, W., McCaulay, M., Ryan, V., Stroshal, K. (1979). Coping imagery, systematic desensitization, and self-concept change. *Cognitive Therapy and Research*, **3**(2), June, 181–92.

Ibarra, H. (2003). *Working Identity: Unconventional Strategies for Reinventing Your Career*. Cambridge, MA: Harvard Business Press.

Ibarra, H. and Lineback, K. (2005). What's your story? *Harvard Business Review*, **83**(1), 64–71.

Joseph, S. (2006). Person centred coaching psychology – a meta theoretical perspective. *International Coaching Psychology Review*, **1**(1), 47–54.

Kabat-Zinn, J. (1994). *Wherever you Go, There you Are*. New York: Hyperion.

Karpman, S. (2006). Lost in translation: Neo-Bernean or Neo-Freudian? *Transactional Analysis Journal*, **36**(4), 284–302.

Katzenbach, J. R. and Smith, D. K. (1999). *The Wisdom of Teams: Creating the High-Performance Organization*. London: HarperBusiness.

Kauffman, C. and Boniwell, I. (2009). Positive psychology coaching. In: Clutterbuck, D., Cox, E. and Bachkirova, T. (eds), *Sage Handbook of Coaching*. London: Sage.

Kegan, R. (1982). *The Evolving Self*. Cambridge, MA. Boston: Harvard University Press.

Khatri, N. and Ng, H. A. (2000). The role of intuition in strategic decision-making. *Human Relations*, , **53**, 57–71.

Koffka, K. (1935). *The Principles of Gestalt Psychology*. Princeton, NJ: Brace & World.

Kolb, D. A. (1976). *The Learning Styles Inventory Technical Manual*. Boston: McBer.

Kram, K. (1985). *Mentoring at Work: Developmental Relationships in Organizational Life*. Glenview, IL: Scott, Foresman.

Latner, J. (1986). *The Gestalt Therapy Book*. Highland, NY: The Gestalt Journal Press (first published in 1973).

Lazarus, A. (1981). *The Practice of Multimodal Therapy: Systematic, Comprehensive, and Effective Psychotherapy*. New York: McGraw-Hill.

Lee, G. (2003). *Leadership Coaching: From Personal Insight to Organisational Performance*. London: CIPD.

Leimon, A., Moscovici, F., McMahon, G. (2005). *Essential Business Coaching*. London: Brunner Routledge.

Mathews, A. (1988). *Being Happy – A Handbook to Greater Confidence and Security*. Singapore: Media Masters.

McMahon, G. (2006). *Behavioural Contracting: Coach the Coach*. London: Fenman.

McMahon, G. (2008). *No More Anger: Be your own Anger Management Coach*. London: Karnac.

McMahon, G. and Leimon, A. (2008). *Performance Coaching for Dummies*. London: John Wiley.

Megginson, D. (2004). Planned and emergent learning: consequences for development. In: Grey, C. and Antonacopoulou, E. (eds), *Essential Readings in Management Learning*. London: Sage, 91–106.

Megginson, D. and Clutterbuck, D. (2005). *Techniques for Coaching and Mentoring*. Oxford: Butterworth-Heinemann.

Megginson, D. and Whitaker, V. (2006). *Continuing Professional Development*. London: Chartered Institute of Personnel and Development.

Neenan, M. and Dryden, W. (2002). *Life Coaching: A Cognitive-Behavioural Approach*. London: Brunner-Routledge.

Neenan, M. and Dryden, W. (2004). *Cognitive Therapy: 100 Key Points and Techniques*. London: Brunner-Routledge.

Neenan, M. and Dryden, W. (2006). *Cognitive Therapy in a Nutshell*. London: Sage.

O'Neill, M. B. (2000). *Executive Coaching with Backbone and Heart. A Systems Approach to Engaging Leaders with Their Challenges*. San Francisco: Jossey-Bass.

Pardeck, J. (1998). *Using Books in Clinical Social Work Practice: A Guide to Bibliotherapy*. London: Haworth Press.

Passmore, J. (ed.) (2009). *Diversity-in-coaching*. London: Kogan Page.

Perls, F. S. (1969). *Gestalt Therapy Verbatim*. Utah: Real People Press.

Perls, F. S. (1971). *Gestalt Therapy Verbatim*. New York: Bantam.

Perls, F. S. (1973). *The Gestalt Approach and Eye Witness to Therapy*. Palo Alto: Science & Behavior Books (republished by Bantam Books in 1976).

Perls, F. S. (1978). Finding self through Gestalt therapy. *Gestalt Journal*, **1**(1), 54–73.

Picasso, P. (1956). *Vogue*.

Prietula, M. and Simon, H. (1989). The experts in your midst. *Harvard Business Review*, **89**(1), 120–24.

Reitz, M. (2007). Leading in the moment. *Ashridge*, **360**, Spring, 24–9.

Rhodes, T. and Whitaker, V. (2006). http://www.learnforever.co.uk/articles/ The Masks of Mentoring. Accessed 14.3.08.

Richardson, L. (2005). Writing: a method of inquiry. In: Denzin, N. K. and Lincoln, Y. (eds), *The Sage Handbook of Qualitative Research*. Thousand Oaks, CA: Sage, 959–78.

Rock, D. (2008). Keynote speech. European Mentoring & Coaching Council UK Conference.

Rogers, C. (1961). *A Therapist's View of Psychotherapy: On Becoming a Person*. London: Constable.

Rogers, P. and Blenko, M. (2006). Who has the D? How clear decision roles enhance organizational performance. *Harvard Business Review*, Jan, **84**(1), 53–61.

Rooke, D. and Torbert, W. (2005). Seven transformations of leadership. *Harvard Business Review*, **83**(4), April, 67–76.

Rosinski, P. (2003). *Coaching Across Cultures*. London: Nicholas Brealey.

Roth, G. (1990). *Maps to Ecstasy*. London: Mandala.

Rowan, R. (1987). *The Intuitive Manager*. New York: Berkley Books.

Sadler-Smith, E. (2007). When you just know …. *The Times*, 13 August, 2–4.

Schön, D. (1987). *Developing the Reflective Practitioner*. San Francisco: Jossey Bass.

Schön, D. (1991). *The Reflective Practitioner: How Professionals Think in Action*. Aldershot: Ashgate.

Shaw, S. and Hawes, T. (1998). *Effective Teaching and Learning in the Primary Classroom: A Practical Guide to Brain Compatible Learning*. London: Optimal Learning.

Sheldon, K. M. and Lyubomirsky, S. (2006). Achieving sustainable gains in happiness: change your actions, not just your circumstances. *Journal of Happiness Studies*, **7**(1), 55–86.

Sheldrake, R. (1981). *A New Science of Life: The Hypothesis of Formative Causation*. Los Angeles: Tarcher.

Simon, H. (1987). Making management decisions: the role of intuition and emotion. *Academy of Management Executive*, **1**(1), 57–64.

Simos, G. (2002). *Cognitive Behaviour Therapy*. London: Brunner Routledge.

Skiffington, S. and Zeus, P. (2003). *Behavioural Coaching: How to Build and Sustain Personal and Organisational Strength*. Sydney, Australia: McGraw Hill.

Smither, J. W., London, M., Flautt, R., Vargas, Y., Kucine, I. (2003). Can working with an executive coach improve multi-source feedback ratings over time? A quasi-experimental field study. *Personnel Psychology*, **56**(1), 23–44.

Sparkes, A. (2002). Autoethnography: self-indulgence or something more? In: Bochner, N. A. P. and Ellis, C. (eds), *Ethnographically Speaking*. Lanham, MD: Altamira.

St Claire, B. A. (2005). *Carrying Cultural Baggage: The Contribution of Socio-cultural Anthropology to Cross-cultural Coaching*. Oxford: Oxford Brookes University.

Stevens, D. and Cooper, J. E. (2008). *How to Use Reflective Journals for Effective Teaching and Learning, Professional Insight, and Positive Change*. Vernon, VA: Stylus.

Thompson, L. (2000). *Making the Team: A Guide for Managers*. New Jersey: Prentice Hall.

Vaughan, F. (1979). *Awakening Intuition*. New York: Anchor.

Whitaker, V. (1996). The rhythms of organisational life. *Organisations & People*, **3**(1), 23–5.

Whitaker, V. (1998). The holistic manager. In: Lock, D. (ed.), *The Gower Handbook of Management*. Aldershot: Gower.

Index